GRANADA

granada

A POMEGRANATE

in the

HAND OF GOD

STEVEN NIGHTINGALE

COUNTERPOINT
BERKELEY

Library of Congress Cataloging-in-Publication Data Is Available

ISBN 978-1-61902-460-1

Cover design by Natalya Balnova
Interior Design by Megan Jones Design

Counterpoint Press
2560 Ninth Street, Suite 318
Berkeley, CA 94710
www.counterpointpress.com

Printed in the United States of America
Distributed by Publishers Group West

10 9 8 7 6 5 4 3 2 1

A nuestros vecinos Albayzíneros—
por vuestra inteligencia y gracia, y vuestro espíritu
acogedor y juguetón

A Christyn Marshall-Ramirez—
tan fiable, lúcida, y generosa

y

A Lucia y Gabriella—
por vosotras vivo.

Por qué Cristóbal Colón
No pudo descubrir a España?

Why wasn't Christopher Columbus
Able to discover Spain?

<small>PABLO NERUDA, LIBRO DE LAS PREGUNTAS</small>

Contents

One Afternoon in Granada

*t*HE JUICE OF the pomegranate sweetens our hands. All afternoon, we have picked from the fruit the crimson pods of juice. Within each pod, a seed. On our table, the bowl fills with the luscious harvest. The roughly handled seedpods shine in the clear hot light of Granada.

I sit close together with Lucy, my wife, and Gabriella, our 3-year-old daughter. We live here, in the medieval neighborhood of the Albayzín, in a house with a garden. The Albayzín gathers its white houses on this south-facing hillside; gardens and houses here fill with light all morning, and then, warm and fragrant, settle into the languorous afternoon.

Granada, in Spanish, by a happy chance, means "pomegranate." The fruit is the symbol of the city. It is seen everywhere, on plates, in designs set into the cobblestones, on the faces of buildings. When we pick the seeds from a pomegranate, we hold the history of the city in our hands. As the fruit is swollen with juice, so is it packed with the ideas, the lives, the secrets and stories of the people of Granada, and of the great Mediterranean cultures that have made their home here.

Let's take, for starters, some experiences common to us all, because we are flesh: say, sexual love and death. And some ideas common to us all, because of our spiritual heritage: say, paradise and the sacred. How might all this be mixed up with these bright seeds in our hands?

In the *Song of Songs*, the lover delivers this praise to a woman he loves: "A crimson ribbon your lips—how I listen for your voice! The curve of your cheek a pomegranate in the thicket of your hair." It is the voice of a man in love, who wants to taste the woman of his longing. He would find his way into her hidden sweetness. He says, "An enclosed garden is my sister, my bride, a hidden well, a sealed spring. Your branches are an orchard of pomegranate trees heavy with fruit." As the temperature of this already-molten book of the Old Testament rises further, she gives him her promise: "Let us go early to the vineyards to see if the vine has budded, if the blossoms have opened and the pomegranates are in flower. There I will give you my love." The cultivation of the pomegranate, we note, spread in the ensuing centuries all through the lands of the Mediterranean.

Yet we know that images of this erotic fruit adorned a holy place— Solomon's temple itself. The design of the temple is described in the Old Testament. The materials were stone, sheets of gold, cedar, precious gems; and set prominently on the capitals of the pillars astride the entrance, carved images of pomegranates, hundreds of them, in rows. In fact, the only artifact we possess known to be of use within Solomon's temple is an inscribed piece of ivory, thought to be the head of a priestly scepter, and unmistakably a pomegranate in flower.

If all this were not enough, if one cuts a pomegranate lengthwise and lays it open, the seedpods show themselves bunched into the six-pointed star we know as the Star of David.

What is it about this fruit that touches the sacred? The tree, native to Persia, shows a dark, straggly silhouette. But in spring, among sudden leaves of reddish green, deep orange flowers appear, which darken to red and fold in as the fruit begins to take shape. As it grows, the skin thickens and roughens until it is the texture of old leather, as though it had lived through seasons of sunlight and had long tales to tell. Then, late in the summer, over a course of days, the rough skin splits, as if it could not contain its sweetness. Crimson seedpods show forth in sensuous bunches. Each pod is full of juice. It is the color of blood. It will darken your hands. It marks your clothes indelibly. It tastes of a strange, direct freshness, both sour and sweet. The harvested seeds heaped in a bowl so ravish the eyes that we stop our labors to watch the glistening.

Living through the seasons with a pomegranate tree, we can guess why the fruit is thought to partake of the sacred. It is incorrigibly beautiful. In the fecund splendor of packed seeds there is a promise of life irrepressible. The fruit swells and opens in the hot months, showing crimson and delicious flesh; it's intensely sexual, putting us in mind of lovemaking and life-making. And the way the skin bursts to show an inner beauty makes us think of a coming forth of soul from the body.

If all this means something, then we are likely to find the pomegranate associated with paradise; and so we do. Some scholars believe that the tree of knowledge in the Garden of Eden was a pomegranate. In the Koran, Allah sketches the gardens of paradise in the Sura of the Merciful, the Gracious One. This hypnotic Sura of high poetry, by tradition revealed early and as a whole in Mecca, speaks of a delicious space in the next world: fresh springs, dark leaves of lush trees, women with ruby and coral skin—and fruit trees, which encompass all varieties, but of which, curiously, only two are mentioned: the date and the pomegranate. In the Hadith, which are the statements of Muhammad noted down while he lived, we hear him say: "There is not a pomegranate on earth that does not have a pip from one of the pomegranates in the Garden of Paradise." This useful idea we find frequently in the Koran: that we have here present on earth pieces of heaven, signs that we learn to recognize. Such signs are called, in Arabic, *ayat*. By understanding them, it is said, we may discover a way to move intuitively and irresistibly toward the divine.

Five centuries later, we have Jalalludin Rumi's great book, the *Mathnawi*. Rumi was born in Afghanistan, lived in Konia, in Asia Minor (present-day Turkey), and was a contemporary of Saint Francis. Many consider the *Mathnawi*—a hive of stories, injunctions, metaphorical adventures, songs, and parables—to be the most powerful mystical poem ever written. In one section, Rumi writes about companionship with saints, and about the signs that mark a teacher of real knowledge. He likens our encounter with such a man or woman to the buying of a pomegranate: "buy it laughing and open-mouthed, that its laughing may give information about the state of its seeds. How blessed is its laughter, that shows the heart in its mouth." Such is Rumi's portrayal of one whose knowledge is so uncommonly advanced that it has come forth in joy. In Rumi's teaching, a real teacher shows himself directly and usefully to anyone who, with suitable preparation, seeks just such knowledge.

Jewish worship, the Old Testament, the Koran, Rumi's mystical poem: these are but some of the adventures of the pomegranate, symbol of Granada. As the seeds mount up on our table, do we find the fruit has a place in Christian devotion?

It is the symbol of the Resurrection. With the famous Christian ability to confiscate the stories of other faiths, Christians took over the pomegranate from the Greek myth of Persephone, the goddess who returns each year from the domain of death to bear us springtime, to be a "wonder to gods and mortal men." Hades had tricked Persephone by putting pomegranate seeds in her mouth, obliging her to live with him beneath the earth part of every year. But as the earth warms and trees flower, she returns from the place of death. So the pomegranate of the goddess of spring became the symbol of the ascendant Jesus, bringing us not the springtime of earth, but by his sacrifice, a springtime of the soul. The infant Jesus will be seen with pomegranate in hand, in drawings by Botticelli, Leonardo, and Raphael.

But the Christian imagination was not done. In astonishment we find the fruit pressed into action to signal, of all things, the virginity of Mary. This is traveling rather far afield, given that throughout the Mediterranean, for millennia, the fruit had shone with forces of fertility and sexuality. Many drawings have the virginal Mary sitting beatifically beneath a pomegranate tree. For defense and support, she often has nearby that icon of chastity and purity, the unicorn. This mythical beast is, no doubt, ready to lower his horn and charge all those centuries of erotic associations.

So have we three faiths of the Mediterranean, here on our table. And we have, as well, the emblem of a man who lived not far from this garden, just below our house, in fact. His residence, a hospital for the poor which he founded, still stands. His name was John of God, and his story is unforgettable.

Born in 1495 in Portugal to a Jewish family, John was at the age of eight taken forcibly from his parents, as part of the ethnic cleansing of those times. He was placed in a Christian family in Spain and later worked as a shepherd. In his twenties, he went off as part of the army of Charles V to attack France. Failing in his sentinel duty, he ended up with a noose around his neck, only to be saved (like Dostoevsky) from execution by a pardon at the last possible moment. He went to war a second time, lived violent, debauched years, and finally revisited Portugal to learn of the death of his parents. His mother had died a few days after he was torn away from her, and his father, alone, had lived until his death as a Franciscan monk.

He found work again as a shepherd, observing that people take much better care of their animals than of one other. His life lurched in poverty from place to place. He worked as an overseer of slaves; as a builder of walls to fortify Ceuta, in North Africa; as a vendor of firewood; as an itinerant bookseller.

One summer day as he walked with his books along the dusty roads of Andalusia, John came upon a boy in rags, and barefoot. He offered the boy his shoes, but they were too large. With the boy still barefoot, John was too ashamed to don the shoes again. So he took the boy onto his shoulders and bore him thorough the scorching heat of southern Spain to a cool stream. He put him down so that he could fetch water for them both, and when he returned, he recognized the boy as the Divine Child, who showed him a lush, open pomegranate surmounted by a cross, and said, "John of God, Granada shall be thy cross."

Soon John was in Granada, and insane. He was locked in a mental hospital and given the standard treatment: repeated whipping with double-knotted leather and drenching with freezing water. Rescued after many months by another converted Jew, the Christian preacher John of Ávila, he traveled with him for counsel and succor.

Later, he returned to Granada, once more to sell firewood in the streets. He was without a place to sleep. He moved among the poor. John of Ávila intervened once again to arrange shelter at night in the vestibule of a house of a wealthy man who lived in the Albayzín. Into his shelter, the future John of God invited the most needy of his companions to sleep by his side. Soon the vestibule was filled with the destitute, and all of them were expelled.

So began the hospital of John of God. At first, he cared for his companions in a hovel near the fish market. The idea, from the beginning, was straightforward: give care to anyone in need. He took in everyone he could: the sick, the abandoned, the persecuted; the poor, starving, and despised; cripples, paralytics, lepers, mutes, the old and dying, prostitutes, madmen and pilgrims. All day, every day, he begged for them. In the morning and at night he cared for them. He cleaned their beds, fed them, fetched water. Slowly he began to receive donations of blankets, beds, firewood. Then later, bread and bowls and milk. Finally, a building for his hospital, then another, larger, for there was never enough room to help all the desperate in Granada.

He was beloved by men and women of all faiths. At his death in 1550, the city convulsed in sorrow. Today, the Hospitaller Order of St. John of God provides healthcare worldwide. Its emblem, five hundred and fifty years later, is still the pomegranate and cross.

We have a hill of seeds on our table now. In the room above the garden where we sit, windows of green and azure glass show a Star of David. Inside that room, above those windows, tiles with Arabic script give a Muslim profession of faith: "There is no conqueror but God." On the windows of another room next to the garden are portraits of conquistadors, the legendary, brutal knights of Christ.

We have lived in Granada almost four years. Our house, and this city, ride the religious crosscurrents of more than two millennia of devotion. It is a history of genius, strange perfections, of beauty and poetry; of imbecility, hatred, and murder.

There is a singular power here. The city has had an uncanny influence in the history of Europe and the world. It is a hive of stories, of sweetness, and of secrets. We might call it a pomegranate in the hand of God.

We love the Albayzín. And so this writing, out of the obligation to try to understand how one place could hold, as a pomegranate holds its seeds, so many gifts.

The Carmen *of Our Serendipity*

*t*O LEAVE YOUR place of birth, to be roughed up by another country, to seek understanding in a new language, to labor in hopes to make a home in the place you land—these are American dreams. I had wanted always to move away from the United States, and my wife, Lucy, had grown up in North Africa, in the Congo, in Paris, and in Mali. She was ready for a sojourn abroad. So it was that in the spring of 2002, we traveled with our 11-month-old daughter, Gabriella, through southern Spain, in search of a city to live. After visiting Córdoba and Seville, we wandered into Granada. Across a narrow gorge from the finest Moorish palace in the world—the Alhambra, egregiously famous—we found the Albayzín. It's medieval, full of balconies and walls like spillways for flowers; and labyrinthine, with zany angles, mysterious stairways, hidden courtyards, and streets just wide enough for two walking abreast. Within an hour of our arrival, we dined in a small plaza. The buildings around us showed white plaster and stone. Old women dressed in black sat on benches talking, their voices like a stream of swift water from the mountains. Bricklayers and gypsies walked by, and couples with babies, dreaming young women, and guitarists with

hair halfway down their backs. The warm, late light of the early evening flowed across cobbles, the trees were leafing out, the food was
hot and delicious. Our little girl chortled at the waiter, who cooed
at her from nearby and winked at her from afar. Less than a minute into the meal, Lucy and I decided irrevocably to move into the
neighborhood.

THE NEXT DAY, we asked a local realtor about houses for rent,
for two years, to a family with a baby and a dog. "*Es absurdo*," he
replied immediately. Now, neither of us wanted to confess to being
absurd, at least not right away. So we stepped off to see some rentals
available to our pushy inquiries. After two useless visits to houses
that had been treated with scorn by their owners, we felt even more
absurd than previously. So we went to a bar to bewail our predicament and muse upon our fate. There, by dint of literal back-of-the-
envelope calculations, checked with a pen that would not work until
dipped in red wine, we seized upon a new plan: to buy a house.

Back we went to the realtor, who now was convinced of our
whimsy; he looked askance at us. We hoped fervently for a garden
where our daughter could play, some privacy, a room for friends to
visit, and a place to work. Shaking his head at our pleas, the realtor
did the obvious thing and turned us over to his mother, one Trinidad,
a savvy woman who led us ably into the labyrinth of the Albayzín.
Only one kind of house had what we sought, a house that, unbe-
knownst to us, was part of the legacy of the city and the legend of the
Albayzín: the *carmen*. A *carmen* is a house with a hidden garden; we
would learn later of its rapturous history.

In the sure, maternal hands of Trinidad, we began to walk about
and look at *carmenes*. After three days, we found one that answered

our taste for idiosyncrasy. All *carmenes* in the Albayzín have names, and this one was named *Carmen de Nuestra Señora de la Purificación*. This, to me, was so melodious that, for the name alone, I was ready to fork over the sales price and close a deal. Who could not use some purification? Would I have to convert to Catholicism? Did a program of austerity and fixed hours for prayer go along with the deed to the house? As I was standing in the street, mulling these important questions, Lucy walked in the door, looked around, and announced immediately: "This is it!" I was of course then gripped by the insane male spirit of due diligence and wanted to see rooms, analyze figures, order inspections; in a word, to meddle idiotically in what was, already, destiny. My foolery would lead us later to an introduction to a pair of contractors, one tall and stern, the other short and jolly. They had looked at the house, and Lucy and I would stand in the garden with them as I asked carefully prepared questions about water quality, the structural integrity of the tower, the condition of the roofs, and so on. The contractors looked at me in silence, until suddenly I heard a buzzing in the air that I could not identify. I looked skyward. Was it a distant airplane? An invasion of insects from Africa? Had someone in the countryside started up a chainsaw? But no, it was the tall contractor, replying to my questions in the speed-of-light Spanish of Andalusia. Once I was able to discern a word or two of the opinions of our advisor, I asked more questions and received more long, mellifluous responses. In fact, their answers, a swirl of winds around a still center, turned on the one word they never really used: fate. You buy a house in the Albayzín, then fate will take you away, and good luck to you as you go. It was the first time I encountered such easygoing fatalism. It turned out to be part of life here.

But that futile shenanigan came later. That first day with Trinidad, we learned the house had been in the same family for most of a century. We went slowly around. Up the stairs, we found a room of Arabic design, with windows of colored glass, soft green with stars of cobalt, that filled the space at morning with blue and verdant light. Nearby was a tiny room that had small, beautiful wall paintings of children playing with toys from early in the 1900s. One story above, we found a tower with a tilting outdoor terrace, looking straight at the Alhambra. We gazed from there down into the garden. Curious barbed-wire designs swathed the garden walls, and a wooden dovecote hunkered down in a corner of the garden near a room where some brother, decades ago, had been locked up for insanity, with the murmuring doves for comfort.

Fate, in a good mood, was by now holding us in a muscular embrace. The price, in euros, seemed fair to us, since at the time the dollar was worth more than a gnat's eye. So the negotiation began, with the help of a magisterial notary who had, from sheer generosity, befriended us. Notaries have, in Spain, a distinguished position, and part of their traditional work is to join in with negotiations to help both sides understand the issues and the law. I was used to American lawyers, whose job is often to snarl, at great expense, and hurl thick documents at their adversaries, or even at their clients. Now I was confronted by a new, disorienting Spanish custom of helpful and honest lawyers who bring goodwill and clarity to business. I felt we had been transported to some odd and distant planet. But I liked the planet, and soon we were signing papers—all four pages of them—to buy the house from the family who had owned it for generations. Closing would be in three months. Since we were headed back to the United States, we proposed in the spirit of efficiency to conclude the transaction through the mail. This innocent idea appalled the family, for it lacked in ceremony, offended tradition, failed in courtesy, and marked us as brutish foreigners. The way you buy a house, we learned, was to hand over a cashier's check, receive the keys into your hand directly, and then go out for a sherry together. Not wanting to give mortal offense, and hoping to earn a glance of affection from *Nuestra Señora de la Purificación*, we of course caved in and agreed straightaway to return to Spain in a few months with money, and thirsty for sherry.

In the meantime, we learned more about the Albayzín, with a view to having some renovation done before we arrived in the next year. We discovered that the whole barrio, from the church of San Cristobal at the top of the hill to the River Darro at the foot of the hill, had since 1570 been crumbling away, an abused and, in some centuries, a despised ruin. No one loved it, unless they lived there. It was too poor and dusty, strange and ancient, even to bother with flattening it. Then in 1994, after much work on the part of its brilliant Spanish advocates, UNESCO declared the whole neighborhood a World Heritage Site, part of what they call the Patrimony of Humankind. This rotund phrase, now affixed to the Albayzín, came with Spain having thrown off just two decades earlier the fascist dictatorship of Francisco Franco. The country had written a constitution, begun a democracy with an independent judiciary, joined the European Union and NATO, and in general, with genius, worked a national miracle. Suddenly, visitors turned up in the forgotten Albayzín, the European Union sent money to help with repairs of the streets and houses, histories of the neighborhood were written, traditions of painting and poetry rediscovered, and Granada recognized publicly what some citizens had said for decades: that it had a jewel in its hand.

We began to feel a wee bit less absurd. And when in June Lucy and I returned with our cashier's check, we came with a coffee pot and some ideas. We camped out like teenagers on a single mattress on the floor of our bedroom, rose with the sun, scratched our heads and looked around. What had we done? There were modern tiles to remove, the garden cement sported fissures, the kitchen held a darkness a tomb would envy. And the property came wrapped in metal: because the selling family had not lived here, the house had been empty except for holidays, and it had been robbed. The young burglars, finding the house to their taste, had after the robbery decided to stay on. They frolicked by candlelight through the warm nights, in all the rooms, with invited and consensual friends. Guitars sounded. Aromatic smoke swirled. These high times lasted for days. When their revels were finally discovered, they unanimously wanted their derring-do to be admired, and their stay extended; but alas, even in courteous Spain, uninvited thieves must eventually go.

This bizarre incident made the owners swoon from distress. They trussed the house in barbed wire, locked up the windows in iron bars, installed bolts, fixed metal doors in place. The keys that we were handed with great courtesy came in a weighty bundle that, put in a pocket, would break a femur.

What to do? We did what we would do so often in our time in Spain: we counted on our Spanish friends. The wonderful notary and his wife, who had been of inestimable help during our house-hunting, now named a contractor who came to see us. José Antonio de la Torre was his name, and he spoke a Spanish so clear that a rock would understand it. We walked about, dreamed, pondered, declared that the barbed wire must all go, marveled at the azure radiance in the Arab bedroom. We sought a way for the house to exhale, for dark rooms to open to the light and the garden. We thought it would be nice to have heat in the winter. We gathered ideas from books on the houses of southern Spain and Morocco, from our visits to *carmenes* in the Albayzín, and our look into the Moorish traditions of design in Granada that have fascinated so many for centuries. All in all, our idea was simple: we wanted a house and garden respectful of the traditions of Andalusia, and we wanted a place where our daughter could rumpus safely with other children.

The *Carmen de Nuestra Señora de la Purificación* had an older section with beautiful old tiles in the entryway—blue and gold and bone-white. Stairs led above to the child's room with the lovely paintings, the Arab room, and then up to the tower. Downstairs, off the garden, there were the two storage rooms we would make into bedrooms, with orange and lemon trees outside their windows.

Soon, we had a plan and a contract. We left on the idea that the work would start in the fall. The main house, except for the kitchen, would be finished in January, when we would arrive in Granada to begin a life here. We'd move in, get settled, take stock; then we'd do the garden rooms and whatever else made sense, on the ground, as we looked around and learned more.

The months whirled by, our little girl learned to walk, we wrapped up sundry labors, and soon autumn was upon us. We sold our cars. Off went our boxes of books on a slow boat from San Francisco. We went on a last camping trip in Nevada, in our wild, beloved Great Basin, where we were challenged in the middle of the night by a big, snorting, white mustang stallion. We saw bighorn sheep, walked among the aspen going gold, rubbed our hands and faces with sage-brush, and knew what a sorrow it would be not to have this blessed country to explore. The light in the Great Basin is more than light.

It's a kind of intelligence and will lead anyone in that desert wilderness over ridges and into hidden canyons, where coyotes will come to your side and propose curious theological speculations. And these are the ordinary things of the wilderness of the Basin.

Winter wheeled round. We had a last Christmas stateside, said our goodbyes, put our golden lab in her crate for the long flight, kissed and murmured to the now 18-month-old Gabriella about our daft adventure, and we were off.

We arrived in Granada late at night, in a thick, freezing rain. Of course, this being the Albayzín, there was no way to get anywhere near our house in the rented car. In addition, both Lucy and I were wondering, given the tangle of the streets, if we could even find our house. This doubt made us laugh, and so we parked at the side of a cobblestone street and sat there musing and joking, with little thought that, in such a fix, we would see our Spanish cohorts of months before. Of course, the notary and his wife just then drove by and leapt from their car to shelter us with their friendship. They promised to fetch umbrellas and meet us down by our house. We set off through the narrow streets of the Albayzín, hauling our belongings through the tempestuous night, with a soaked dog by our side and tired infant in our arms. The rain was merciless, the sky was black. "Gabriella!" we exclaimed to our dubious baby, "we're moving into our house in Granada!"

Anyone could have predicted what happened next. We threw open the door to the house, and it was dark as a grave, dusty, frozen, and full of rubble. We were wet, exhausted, and cold. I think, but could not swear, that Gabriella winked at us.

The rain, of course, did not notice a thing. We advanced a foot into the house, enough to see that going further meant a fall over bricks and a tumble face forward into a mound of plaster. Not wanting to add fractured skulls to the curiosities of the night, we backed into the street, where we found our notary, by now a candidate for sainthood, standing with open umbrellas and ready to help. Together we toted our bags to a nearby *carmen* that had been made into a little hotel, and we burst into the lobby like a late-night edition of the grapes of wrath. The desk clerk looked us over. We dripped upon the carpet. Our bags were blotched and askew. Our dog shivered and mewed. I asked, rather hysterically I think, for rooms for all of us, regaled him about our wrecked house, and threw ourselves on his mercy. I expected very little, since, standing there and panting from our exertions, we were so bedraggled a spectacle.

"We have rooms for you," he said immediately. "And your dog. We love dogs."

Maggie the Labrador, to show her gratitude, shook herself with vigor, casting a fine mist of rainwater to the far reaches of the lobby.

THAT NIGHT, IT snowed—a rare event in Granada. The Alhambra, the Albayzín, and all the city came whitened and startled to morning. It seemed that half the neighborhood ventured onto the streets, marveling at the stuff, as though the heavens had visited upon them some rare alchemical mixture. We ventured out to join them, homeless but game, with our tiny, happy daughter and the baffled Maggie.

So began, with mishaps and amusement, our years in Granada. Those first weeks held a pattern that would come round again in our time living here. First, the sainted notary and his equally blessed wife put us up in a house they owned in the upper Albayzín: the kindness of neighbors. Next, we went in search of cafés where we could sweep in and stay awhile, eating and musing over our next moves. As soon as we walked in anywhere, we enjoyed courteous and gentle service, for a reason we did not anticipate—the helpless love of the people of Granada for children. They love them unreservedly. They know that children have been recently formed in heaven, and so on earth need special devotions. And so the blond 1-year-old Gabriella was praised, whispered to, winked at, teased; she was given ripe oranges, warm bread and honey, fresh juice and gentle encouragement. We began going to the same café every morning for breakfast, and our daughter developed a small fan club among the other regulars, who greeted her in the morning with a sweetness I found astounding. It made one think the world has a goodness at the heart of it. Sometimes one even thought that humankind might have a future, after all. Such is the naïveté that rose in our thoughts, our first mornings in Granada, wholly dependent on strangers.

One morning, a man passing by in the street saw Gabriella through the window, entered the café, came straight to our table, took our little girl's hand, and kissed it gently. Then he turned and walked back onto the street and went his way, all without a word.

Meanwhile, we awaited our chance to learn about our newly ruined house. The story took shape charmingly, with many shoulder shrugs, arched eyebrows of surprise at plain bad luck, sweeping gestures toward the inscrutable sky, pained references to the hardships of working in a rainy winter, not to mention the many and solemn ceremonies of Christmas and New Year's, the Day of the Magi, etc., all of which came with vacation days. What was more, everybody had been busy working on another job—it could not be helped!—until really rather late in the autumn. And in any case, all was well. Our house had a heart, liver, stomach, blood, all in place and working. It merely lacked a few cosmetic details.

We looked around skeptically. The dust over everything was impenetrable. The pile of rubble in the patio rivaled Annapurna. Half-rolled and still-twanging rolls of barbed wire sat in the garden. Boards lay over the floor for the passage of wheelbarrows. Everywhere we found cans of paint, tools, cigarette butts, electric saws, and the occasional jackhammer. We were intrigued with the idea of cosmetic touches applied with a jackhammer. This was a new country. We were here to learn. All the same, we did live in Spain now, and it would have been helpful if we could have lived in our own house. And to set aside for a moment the cosmetics, what about the vital organs? Heat, hot water, electricity? And could we, in this historical epoch, look forward to a kitchen? We saw how our many years of experience camping in the backcountry might come in handy right here in Granada.

Brows were furrowed, lickety-split conversations ensued, chins were stroked. Perhaps in three weeks we would be able to begin camping out on the second floor. A room for us, a room for Gabriella, a bathroom with occasional hot water. And then of course construction would continue right under our noses. How did that sound?

It sounded better than living in the streets.

To make the three weeks, of course, some labor was required on our part. With bandannas on our faces, we cleaned and swept, and finished the day looking like coal miners. We went on hands and knees to scrape paint, wax, and odd deposits off the floors. We ruined socks and pants with the acid used to rid the floor tile of detritus. We wearied of seeing, indoors at noon, our breath frost in the winter air, and grew intensely curious about the startup date for the heat. The heaters were installed, but to fire them up we needed a technician to hook up cables that carried a special current, and

only one man in all Granada could do it, and then with a muttering
of incantations. It could not be known when he would come. But
he would come. Periodically, we gazed into the heavens, thinking
he might float down, tools in hand, with our electrical deliverance.
Finally, our suave contractor turned up, in the nick of time, with
small portable heaters that worked on standard current.

So at the appointed three weeks, we trouped down through the
Albayzín, spilling jokes as we went, and moved into our house.
Gabriella was delighted, which proves that kids, with enough snug-
gles and kisses, will put up with anything. We slept with the portable
heaters roaring and lamented not bringing our sleeping bags and
camping stove. But we were in residence, as a family, with company:
Pedro, Mario, and Rafael, the three workers—called *albañiles*—who
carried on the labor on the house. An *albañil*, in southern Spain, can
do anything except electrical work and finish carpentry. They combine various and exotic work experience with common sense close to
genius. Now we got to know them better.

They taught us the rhythm of life. Our first afternoon, when we
returned to the house, an otherworldly silence reigned. No sound
was heard, neither of voice nor of electric saw, nor of cement mixer
nor hammer. Then, finally: their coordinated snores. It was siesta
time. Every afternoon it was the same: at two o'clock, they stoked up
a fire in the living room, heated up lunch—they *did* have stoves—and
then leaned back in their chairs and fell thunderously asleep. At three
o'clock they rose, rubbed their eyes, lit cigarettes, murmured, spat,
pondered, then set to work with goodwill.

So it was for five months. At eight every morning—you could set
an atomic clock by it—they came to the door to begin. At ten in the
morning, sandwiches and coffee. At two, lunch and siesta. At five,

out the door. All day, they got things done, made things work, put up with our ideas and bewilderment, offered their smart suggestions—the three of them were aestheticians—and all of this, mind you, while smoking continuously. Pedro and Mario were brothers and sent thoughts telepathically to one another. Rafael was a young apprentice with the bearing of an Arab prince; Gabriella, though still an infant, was smitten with him. Lucy and I were very fond of them all.

These men regarded brick as a plastic material. They could take down one wall, put up another one, and seal it and plaster it before the birds of first light were done singing. Their wonderful phrase was "*se puede quitar*," which means "it can be removed." Their jack-hammers were at the ready. If, looking at some wall or pavement you might want to remove, you nodded (or even if you twitched involuntarily), then it would vanish in a trice. One had to be careful, lest an innocent wall was jackhammered to bits in their enthusiasm and derring-do. I think the three of them should be sent up to the International Space Station to do an upgrade; the place would be more roomy, and everything would work up there.

The winter continued cold. At five minutes after eight every morning, the cement mixer would start. Soon we would hear the electric saws and hammering, the clattering of the wheelbarrow, and the engine of the minute tractor used to deliver sand and bricks and appliances in the Albayzín. With shaking hands we'd make a bottle of milk for our daughter, huddle in bed, tell stories, then rise and head out though the narrow streets to our café, with our little girl toddling between us. Hand in hand, we found a way through the rainy, cold months. In the days, we figured out what to do with our new house, helped as we could, and then went out to study the streets of our adopted city. Needing to prospect for food, we went about

to see who would have us. Nearby, a Moroccan family with a res-
taurant—the Mancha Chica in the heart of the Albayzín—virtually
adopted us, and we ate their delicious food nights on end. Gabriella
soon had friends all over town, from Maria José de la Miel to Adbul-
Fatah the baker, from Dominique the French chef, our neighbor, to
Miguel the vendor of *jamon serrano*. Once, buying a bottle of wine, I
saw with delight that the storeowner had noted down our address in
her little book under "G," for "*los padres de Gabriella*"—the parents
of Gabriella.

The months passed, and the mountains of rubble slowly eroded.
We could even see a bit of our future garden, and a good thing, too,
since an amorous visitor now embraced the Albayzín: springtime in
Granada. Leaves bolted from the trees, roses bloomed everywhere
you looked, jasmine flowers on vines flung themselves over walls, the
redbud raised up blossoms the color of skin in a blush of pleasure.
Flocks of swifts turned through the air, big magpies strode along
rooflines. And as the days heated up, the sheltering trees brought to
the plazas of the Albayzín a cool and fragrant shade.

One day, we had a workroom—with reliable broadband access,
which is considerably easier to get, than, say, a kitchen cabinet. The
next month, the cabinets, and even—*mirabile dictu*—a stove, found
their places. Three and a half months after our arrival in Spain, we
made coffee in our own house. Another month and, suddenly, everything was done. We sat in the light of early evening, at dinner outside, just as we did our first night in the Albayzín. It felt as if a gust of
good luck had borne us from the one evening to the next.

Perhaps the exhaustion of the months had levered open our ideas
and made us candidates for enchantment. But looking around, after
the months of dust and noise and improvisation, we felt as if we

lived in the midst of something conjured. Just outside the blue-tiled entry, on a patio of cross-laid brick, we sat at a table under cover of grape leaves spread from two gnarled, thick vines. We looked out straight toward the stone fortress of the Alhambra. On one side of our garden, to our left, a small shed with dark-green door, and in front of it, a hundred-year-old olive tree. In the center, next to us, a fountain of white marble, whose water ran along a brick channel to a rectangular pool called an *alberca*. Alongside the *alberca*, a fan palm, slender and graceful, newly planted. To our right, the main garden with four mature, flourishing trees: persimmon, pomegranate, lemon, and orange. Beneath these mature trees grew mock orange and rosemary. We had room where Lucy would add a fig, a mandarin, another orange, and an almond. At the far end of the garden, a rough stone fountain, called a *pilar*, set into the wall. We had found the *pilar* on the outskirts of town, at a yard that sold *olvidos*— forgotten things. The water fell into a heavy, seamless basin made by hollowing out a single stone. Above the *pilar*, we had started a vine of fragrant white jasmine. Behind us, a rose vine had begun its spin around a drainpipe.

Now it was time to learn where we had landed, beginning here, in the garden.

The Time Travels of a Garden

SOON AFTER WE swept away the last construction dust, we invited into our house our neighbors, who had been so kind to us during our move into the Albayzín. In fact, they were more than kind—they offered us late dinners and rambling conversation, they cuddled our daughter, they gave us mysterious recipes for curing olives. Their hospitality seemed to this American like something out of *The Arabian Nights*: if, for instance, any weekend evening, we knocked upon the door of any family among them, soon we would be at table, our daughter would be playing with their children, and we would be talking late into the night over superb bottles of *vino tinto*. They were so good to us that with shame I admit that at first I thought they might be pulling our legs. But no, they were not; it was their nature and our privilege.

In the Albayzín, to invite someone into a *carmen* is to invite them into your garden, the hidden center of life. Our whole house gave on to the garden: the blue-tiled entryway and the dining room both had double doors that we could open upon the fruit trees and flowers. The bedrooms had small idiosyncratic terraces, and the *torreón* above, where we had our bookshelves and computers, had its own tilting terrace that looked over the grapevine and roses, honeysuckle and jasmine. In the warm air of twilight and evenings, we dined outside with our new friends, in sight of the Alhambra, to the felicitous music of the fountain, the air full of the fragrance of orange and lemon blossoms. As the sky darkened, we lit candles as the children played under the trees, splashed in the fountain, costumed themselves in any clothes they could find, and dashed through all the rooms of the house. Later, as they tired, they would one by one wander sleepily until they found a couch, a bed, or a cushion, until the house was full of snoozing children. In whatever room you entered, there might be one or two dreaming little ones.

These nights were so peaceful, I sometimes thought I was dreaming. To what rare world had we been transported?

As our first summer ripened, I grew more curious about the design of the garden, for it seemed to inspirit us all. A loved garden, with the right design, brings to most of us a rare pleasure; it seems like a blessing of centuries, enveloping, protective, suggestive.

I would like, reader, to have you at this table, just now, with us, so that we might talk of the time travels of this one garden, in the middle of this ancient neighborhood. It is a small garden, but its presence had in our lives an uncommon influence and gentleness. As we set ourselves to read our way into the history of our barrio, we began with our curiosity about our garden, and how so modest a space could offer such welcome and provoke such musings. It seemed to have a power beyond itself.

The original part of the garden, with the big trees, comprised four rectangular beds created by pathways crossing at right angles in the center. As we looked into the history of gardens, we found that this four-part symmetry had ancient Middle Eastern roots. The first recognizable such garden is pictured on a bowl from the ancient city of Samarra—a sketch which, astonishingly, is four millennia old. And an existing archeological site, the garden of the Persian Cyrus the Great from 550 BC, shows clearly the same four-part design. A long road, full of delights, leads from those early centuries to our little plot in the *Carmen de Nuestra Señora de la Purificación*.

The form is common and classic. It combines a restricted set of elements: symmetrical beds, moving water, a peaceful blaze of flowers, a rich assortment of fruit trees, slanting light, and aromatic plants, all in a protective surround of walls. Though this kind of garden is often called an "Islamic Paradise Garden," the design is pre-Islamic; more than pre-Islamic, it is pre-Biblical. I think of it as something at the root of the mind. We find it in site after excavated site in the Middle East, and in the writings of classical antiquity, beginning with accounts of Persian gardens by the bellicose Greek adventurer Xenophon. He translated the Persian word *pairidaeza*, which meant "a wall around," into the Greek *paradeisos*. This word held on to its meaning of pleasure-ground, or enclosed garden and orchard. Centuries later, when the Hebrew of the Old Testament was translated into Greek to produce the legendary Septuagint, the translators, needing a word for the Garden of Eden, were delighted to have one at the ready.

Any musing about gardens leads straight to the Book of Genesis, which held to the blessed association of paradise and gardens, an association that runs all the way back to the wedge writing of Sumer. That is, as far as a written reference can go. As happens so often when I read through texts I know, I found that I had never read Genesis carefully enough. I had thought that Eden was a garden. I was wrong. Eden itself is not a garden at all; rather, it *includes* a garden, planted especially and personally by God, whom we should call the first gardener. He put it, smartly enough, on the east side of Eden in the morning light. It is there, and not elsewhere in Eden, that Adam and Eve are given life. And it is there that the water of paradise, after passing through this singular garden within Eden, splits into four rivers which descend to favor the earth below with the fresh water of life. Eden was then not just the place where human life began and beauty took form; it was the source of the water which gave life to the world around.

We came to see the way the garden worked in favor of life, and to see what the garden walls were good for: they were not for keeping people out, but for concentrating beauty within. As we sat outside and talked with our neighbors in the candlelit evenings, sometimes with children asleep in our laps, we would settle into a rambling and branching conversation unlike anything I had ever known. Near us the fountain made its feathery music, the pomegranate and persimmon trees stood in a full flourishing, and the rose wound up a pipe beside us. Even the shadows seemed fragrant. It looked to me as if our friends, without their knowing, had come to shine with their natural patience and generosity; by some millennia-old theurgy, the garden around us had made their good natures visible.

Conversation and gardens belong together. Both are forms that, rightly used, bring into view what otherwise is hidden. Each has its own rhythms and requirements, but with the same power as other art forms to provoke the emergence of some idea, some hope, some joy, into the light of understanding. Somehow, living in another language brings a person into meditation upon conversational art and its hidden rules, which are as liberating as the rules which govern the sonnet, or haiku, or geometric tile work of the Alhambra, even the paintings of the Annunciation; or the rules that govern the art of gardening. All these rules, however differently they are applied, set a demanding order, necessary so that a clear liberty might rise within us.

The garden being an ancient form, there are myriad ancient stories meant to give meaning to the form. Genesis led me on into this tradition of stories. And although Genesis is finally, of course, a story of disobedience and expulsion, it is not, despite its almost-crazed influence upon our ideas, among the most beautiful or playful of its genre.

So many stories ran through our conversations that we should tell one of them. We will throw off the sour narrative of Genesis and go instead to one of complex whimsy and pagan energies: the story of the Garden of the Hesperides. This divine garden grew, like the garden within Eden, on the side of a mountain. Flourishing there was a tree with golden apples that bountiful Mother Earth had given to the delighted goddess Hera, the wife of Zeus, as a wedding present. Anyone who ate an apple would become immortal; and once immortal, if she then had some ambrosia, she would be granted godly powers. This, of course, looks forward to Genesis, when an alarmed God is trying to prevent Eve and Adam from becoming "as gods." Yet rather than Adam and Eve, in the Garden of the Hesperides lived three nymphs known for their melodious singing. Curiously, their garden, as though the mythmakers had Persia in mind, grew within a wall. In that place of protected pleasures, the lovely nymphs were in full possession of the apples, and guarded them in company of, you guessed it, a serpent—there he is again, this time one with a hundred heads. Enter Hercules, who had already cleaned the Augean stables and wrestled the Minotaur to the ground. Hercules first, and comically, has to *find* the garden, and on his search he is always being challenged to combat by swaggering young men, scatterbrained as usual, all the more so because most of them are sons of gods. Hercules dispatches them all and finds his way to Prometheus, who once stole fire from the gods and gave it to all of us. In punishment, Prometheus is chained to a rock, where an eagle comes and stays all day, eating his liver; then overnight, his liver grows back, and so arrives the eagle the next morning to dine again. Hercules, who has learned a thing or two, is having none of it. He kills the eagle, Prometheus tells him where the garden is, and Hercules goes straight on to kill the serpent and take possession of the apples, which are eventually returned to Athena. Athena then passes them on—straight back to the nymphs in the garden, to whom, she decided, they rightfully belonged. Even the slain serpent found his place among the stars, in the constellation we know today as Draco.

This is just one garden story, but it is wonderful, full of suggestive detail and drama. We wish that Eve had been able to have some nymphs for company, so as to be able to make use of all she learned at the Tree of Knowledge. But Eve had the dull Adam, rather than the valiant Hercules, and she had the Old Testament God, in a foul mood, rather than the helpful, wise Athena. Such men have given her trouble ever since.

But however much the two stories of Genesis and the Garden of the Hesperides mark two poles of our experience of the sacred, there is a telling, deep theme the two stories share: gardens are where fate is decided; gardens mark decisive turns of events in the story of our life on earth; gardens safeguard wisdom; gardens hold beauties that help us learn how the order of nature offers the secrets of life. The special garden in Eden, the nymphs' garden of the Hesperides, and various other mythic plantings would all take form and have a place on earth as the iridescent gardens that mark history throughout the Middle East. These same gardens, bearing their fragrance and coolness, came to be cherished across northern Africa, coming finally to the Iberian peninsula. Warm Andalusia holds some of the finest of these gardens. Granada held some of the finest in Andalusia. In all these travels, such gardens have held fast to their association with the origin and future of beauty.

As the summer began to loosen with heat, this history came home to us as we watched Gabriella and her friends ride tricycles along the garden paths, lay out like leopards on the thick branches of the fig, eat persimmons and pomegranates, and cry out at the world they made as they romped together in the green shade. If all that hard work by God, Cyrus the Great, Hercules and Athena, nymphs and snakes, and centuries of gardeners across countries and continents can lead to the making of a place that gives such various joys, then it stands to reason that it may be a place of learning.

In the hot months in the Albayzín, we saw the way the plants, with water and care, leapt from the soil. Such was the vigor of the grapevine and the honeysuckle that they began to grow straight into the bedrooms. The garden and house embraced one another, took up an amorous life together, so that every room came to include air and flowers, trees and starlight, rustling water and ripening fruit. How had this unity, so easy and preternatural, come to be here in Granada?

As our neighbors shared their lives with us, so all of us shared in the lives of those before us who loved this sunny hillside and loved southern Spain. As we learned of our compatriots over the past centuries, we found that we were participants in Mediterranean history in ways we could not have foreseen. It was our first hint that Granada, somehow, offers a clear window for looking into our whole past; it offers a chance to see how singular events took form, and why.

Let me give you, in one short paragraph, as the children play, the ebullient history here: it begins in 7 BC, with early settlements of a people known only as Iberians. They lived just up the hill from our house, and throughout Andalusia. In the ensuing centuries, an array of cultures, both distinguished and ragtag—Greeks and Phoenicians and Carthaginians—settled along the eastern and southern coasts of Andalusia, which in those days had more pristine beaches but fewer tapas. Then, beginning early in the second century BC, sonorous and imperial Rome put the region under its military grinding stone, marched all over Iberia, built roads and aqueducts, and moved in for three centuries of sun and red wine and occasional mosaics. Then in the fifth century AD, a rough medley of Germanic tribes invaded, with the Visigoths prevailing after confused decades of spasmodic military action. For two hundred years, Iberia meant Christian Visigothic Iberia. The brawling culture of the Visigoths was followed by the nearly eight centuries of Islamic Spain, a period which is referred to today as Al-Andalus. And then the fateful year, for Spain and for the world, of 1492.

There you have a one-paragraph children's sketch of Spanish history. We will, in this conversation with you, see our way into that span of centuries, in more of their dark, rambunctious detail, as they played out in our experience living in the barrio we would come so wholeheartedly to love.

What did this history mean for gardens? Consider together the myths of the early Mediterranean, Cyrus's careful four-part garden, the paradise in the Bible and the Koran, and the enclosed gardens of the Middle East, which are studies in botany, beauty, and peace:

all this delectation of design and association is concentrated in the Persian garden, a gift of the Middle East to Europe. But before these gardens arrived in Iberia, they made a bizarre detour to Italy, entering Imperial Rome when general Lucullus brought back his own account of Persian horticulture. And not just his account. He brought his own rootstock—peach trees, cherries, apricots—all for his garden in the hills of Rome. The descendants of these gardens, in present-day Rome, are a joy. But they seem distinct from Roman gardens from the classical period—which we know about to some extent from the writings of Pliny and Cicero, among others—mostly because of the fixative qualities of lava. When Vesuvius blew off in 79 AD, it buried Pompeii and Stabiae and neatly preserved their houses and gardens for all of us to study. What we find are not just incinerated gardens, but florid wall paintings of gardens. Many of the scenes are, to my eye, ridiculous; I am heartily glad to have the paintings, in place of the actual plantings. There are ornate fountains, frilly and scalloped flower beds, fishy pools, heaping ivy and myrtle, fussy pergolas, and statues, ad nauseam, of gods and goddesses, to say nothing of the portrayals of large estates imitating the Persian hunting preserve, in which boar and bull, lion and deer, and other magnificent animals sport around, killing each other, or being killed themselves in virile sport. As to the grander horticultural projects of Rome, let us leave aside the bushes trimmed into the owner's initials, the grottoes, and, eventually, the grotesque projects of topiary, in which pliant hedges metamorphosed into ranks of centurions and preening warships. This was a society that wanted to remake even the hedges in its own image.

Roman Italy had the luxury of water, the wealth of empire, and a robust taste for excess. With unrestrained appetite it fed on nature, until in the fourth century the Germanic tribes fed on it.

As they fed on Iberia. When after decades of military scrimmag-
ing the Visigoths took power in Iberia, they fell heir to the villas
of the Roman province, sited in the river valleys or near springs in
the mountains. What they made of these sites of luxury and plenty
is anybody's guess. But we may be sure they did not take trowel
in hand and begin working the soil, nor begin trimming the hedges
into escutcheons, nor adopt botany as a central study. In fact, nothing known about them leads us to think they enriched the verdant
Iberian estates with Teutonic flower beds. Rather, they carried on
in their tempestuous ways. They specialized in theological fisticuffs
with the holy Catholic church, submitting to orthodoxy and winning
the wealth and power that come to losers in such bouts. Battening
down to make their historical mark, they gave us squabbling aristocrats, a furious enforcement of feudal rights, the periodic robbery
of the populace by taxation, cantankerous secession struggles, and
a randomly murderous anti-Semitism. After a couple of centuries of
such devotions, the people of the Iberian peninsula, numbering five
to six million, rightfully began wondering about deliverance. We like
to think that some of them even longed for an experience of gardens
that seemed to live only in scripture and in stories. Their hopes on all
fronts were about to be addressed.

In the year 711, a Muslim leader named Tariq ibn Ziyad set off
from North Africa and showed up in Iberia with seven thousand
soldiers—a tiny force, mostly Berbers. He set up a fort and command
post at Gibraltar, which takes its name from him—the Arabic *jabal
tariq* means "mountain of Tariq." He proceeded inland, encountering almost no resistance. The Visigothic King Roderic, hearing of
the visit, cobbled together his army and attacked Tariq's force, and
here the historical accounts head off into absurdity. For Roderic's

force is variously numbered, all the way up to 100,000 men, enough to crush Tariq and his Berbers like so many little beans. Whatever their numbers, the two armies fought for seven days, the Visigoths lost, Roderic was killed in a ditch, and city after city surrendered to Tariq. Later, with modest Arab reinforcements from Yemen and Syria, the newcomers took over and, swiftly, occupied nearly the entire Iberian peninsula. As conquests go, it was an absolute cake-walk. The ease had little to do with the ferocity of the invaders and much to do with the traditional corruption and rampant idiocy of Visigothic rule. So began a new chapter in Iberian, and European, history. For Al-Andalus would be, for nearly eight hundred years, a mixed Christian, Jewish, and Muslim culture, celebrated in its own time, and now, finally, in ours.

Why do we just now recall this history? Because 711 was not just a promising moment for people. It was a sensational moment for gardens. After 711, in the Iberian peninsula, gardens took on a luster and variety unknown elsewhere in Europe. They became places of longing and thankfulness, meant, in remarkable concord with the classic stories we have visited, to bring together the sensual and divine. A poet in the eleventh century, Ibn Jafaya, who lived not far from Granada, would write:

> O *citizens of Al-Andalus, how happy you must be to have*
> *water, shadows, rivers, and trees! The Garden of Eternal*
> *Felicity is not beyond your world, but is part of your*
> *earth . . . Do not believe that you might enter into hell. No*
> *one enters into hell after being in the gardens of paradise.*

How did these extraordinary gardens get here? By means of coin-cidence, uncanny chance, a strange, fateful chain of cause and effect;

as a result of events so improbable that they seem to belong more properly in a novel of adventure than on the pages of history. The whole story turns on the travels of one desperate, brilliant, hunted man, and to understand our garden we need to know his strange and perilous life.

Let us open another bottle of *vino tinto* and follow this strange history a bit farther. Perhaps two bottles, since this story is of such unlikelihood, and such far-reaching, country-making consequence.

In Damascus, in 750, ruled the Umayyads, the first Islamic dynasty after the death of Muhammad. Just over one hundred years after the death of the prophet, the forces of Islam—first military, then administrative—had settled an area the size of the Roman Empire, having within their dominion the land from present-day Morocco to the Indus River in India. These early years of expansion, even today, we read about with incredulity. The movement of peoples upended the medieval world and brought to power a third great monotheism.

Meanwhile, on the ground in Damascus, the capital of this new empire, political differences festered. The Umayyads, originally from Mecca, had rivals: the Abbasids, named after Abbas, the uncle of the Prophet. In a spirit of reconciliation, the Abbasids invited the extended family of the Umayyads to an opulent dinner in a palace in the capital. As a prelude to the feasting and merriment, the Abbasids suddenly and with gusto slaughtered their guests, one and all. This breach of hospitality formed merely one part of their evening plans, however. Immediately after their strenuous dinner, the new rulers sent horsemen to kill those Umayyad family members who had been unable to attend the macabre dinner in Damascus. One of the Umayyads, a prince of nineteen years, grandson of an earlier caliph, lived with his brother in the village of Rusafa, on the banks of the

Euphrates. The murderous soldiers besieged their house, and the two young men sprinted to the river. The prince swam across and looked back as the soldiers filleted his brother. Assuming, no doubt, that appeals to mercy and witty rhetorical gambits would not save him, he fled. So began five years of traveling in disguise, on the run, hunted and alone, moving cagily and nimbly across northern Africa, relying on friends, passing coded messages, taking refuge, hiding and waiting and watching with the alertness of a man who knows that swords are being sharpened with him in mind.

The perilous journey of this one man transfigured history. For at last he arrived at the northwest of Africa, across from the Iberian peninsula. Looking across the Strait of Gibraltar, what did the prince see? A warm and sweet land only recently taken possession of by the followers of Tariq ibn Ziyad; a land apart, separated by water from the region ruled by the blood-soaked, victorious Abbasids; a peninsula in play, whose political and military chieftains happened to include friends of his family. Just the place, he thought, that could use a Umayyad prince, ready after his adventures to match wits and strategy with anyone in the world. He passed messages to his compatriots, planned his political way forward, crossed the strait, and began his search for allies and power. Enough Syrians, Yemenis, and Berbers sided with the young prince, now all of 25, to give him the throne of Al-Andalus. In July of 756, he entered the city of Córdoba as emir. And all of Europe set off in another direction.

Not long after assuming the emirate, as he consolidated power, managed a vast new dominion, fought local wars, made peace, and fended off assassins sent by the Abbasids, his mind turned to— gardening. For in Rusafa, the Syrian estate he had fled, he remembered the palace of his grandfather, the Umayyad Caliph Hisham.

Through that palace passed a stream that irrigated a symmetrical, four-part garden, the first known such garden in the Islamic world. The young prince, known as Abd al-Rahman I (the name means "The Servant of the Merciful"), soon began to construct for himself his own country palace, just north of Córdoba. He sited it by a stream and designed new gardens, sending abroad for a whole exotic mix of plants and seeds, assembling them carefully, and making a legend from leaf and petal. When the palace was complete, in unity with its extraordinary garden, various in form and fragrance, it was celebrated by the Arab historians of the day and proved so beautiful it was used for the next two hundred and fifty years. Thus began in Iberia, in the eighth century, a tradition of horticultural collection and experiment more devoted than any in medieval Europe, which would wait centuries for comparable botanical devotions. Rahman planted palm trees, he imported the pomegranate, he saw to the cultivation of the fig, the apple, and the pear. The people of Al-Andulus, following his example in ensuing centuries, would cultivate widely in Iberia most of the crops and plants we find today in Spain, thirteen hundred years later. The orange, for example, as well as the lemon, quince, and apricot, the date palm and peach, asparagus and jasmine, rice and sugar cane. Even the artichoke.

Historians have even looked at the pollens of the Iberian peninsula and written up a whole list of the plants grown there in the Middle Ages. It stuns in its scope: carob and acacia and mulberry, lilac and hydrangea and a dozen distinct roses, lavender, wisteria, and acanthus, water-lily, chrysanthemum, and sweet violet. Some were imported, others not. But all were used, for food, or for medicine, for their fragrance, or for the unabashed joys their company provoked.

Abd al-Rahman I was the emir who loved growing things, whether countries or plants. And he loved gardens so much that, during his rule, he left the royal residence in the heart of Córdoba and went to live among the gardens he had created. He named his country palace Rusafa, and so united his lost family house in Syria with his new, cherished home in Iberia. So was the dynasty of the Umayyad boisterously reborn, this time in Europe.

Power and gardens came into a close bond in Al-Andalus. Our young prince would rule for thirty-two years. During his life, country houses with gardens and light-loving water and flowering fruit trees would curl around Córdoba like arms full of stars. These estates, called *munyas*, held all manner of delectations but also were deliciously productive, part of an agricultural revolution that took hold in Al-Andalus.

These are the time travels of our little garden in the Albayzín, full of children. It held a meaning and a design that had come into our lives from the green havens of early myth and Holy Scripture, and from the legendary gardens of early Persia, across North Africa with Islam, and then, borne in the mind of a runaway and hunted prince, to Iberia. In the centuries that followed the creation of Rusafa, near cities throughout Andalusia, people built gardens modeled on the original *munyas* encircling Córdoba. And throughout Al-Andalus, in the histories of the day, we read of the families of the time bringing to their gardens all the beauties they could gather. Poets wrote there, in new, brilliant forms with melodious names like the *muwashaha*, or the *zajal*, and recited their lines among friends in the fragrant shade. When the practical men of Al-Andalus perfected distillation, intoxicating drinks were shared alongside the lemon and flowering almond, the pomegranate and basil, grape and olive and blue lily.

Musicians invented new forms of song and used instruments like the
'ud, which became the lute used in the Renaissance, and the *rabab*,
which gave birth to the viol family. So were gardens used for the
gathering of talent; and into such places of peace and refuge and
music, for centuries men of power invited scholars and mystics for
conversation and counsel.

I have wondered whether the course of politics and power in
Al-Andalus was determined in large part by clear, improvisatory conversations in one or another garden in Toledo or Granada, in Seville
or Córdoba, and I wish for all of us an assured method of time travel
to visit those gardens and those gatherings. In any case, more than
any European epoch I know, the history of Iberia in the Middle Ages
is inseparable from a history of horticulture. It is a good omen in a
culture and should be encouraged in our present day. Heads of state
would work more justly and humbly, I think, if they had to attend
to the flowerbeds and prune the fig and pear trees, and so came to
play a role in the mindful, observant, responsible life of a society that
understands and cultivates the land. A quote from an agricultural
manual of the time will give us a sense of life in the country houses
that were the model for our *carmen*. This is a description of the work
in August:

> . . . *juice is extracted from two different kinds of pomegran-*
> *ate and mixed with fennel water to make a thick ointment*
> *for the treatment and prevention of cataracts and other*
> *diseases of the eye. The first dates and jujubes begin to ripen,*
> *the smooth-skinned peaches are ready for plucking, the*
> *acorns take shape, the water melons, known as "al-hindi,"*
> *are now ripe. The late-ripening sweet pears are picked and*

jam is made from them. The gray mullets leave for the sea in the rivers and are caught in large numbers. Pilchards are also in abundance. The following medicinal herbs are ready for gathering: sumac, the seeds of the white poppy, from which syrup is made, rue seeds and "badaward," stavesacre seed and abrotanum. Instructions are given for the requisitioning of silk and indigo . . . The gardens are planted with autumn beans, sky-blue stock, turnips, carrots, chards.

Two centuries after the first Umayyad prince arrived in Iberia, a descendant of his, Abd al-Rahman III, would bring to apotheosis all this planting and botanical study. In 936, he began construction of the Madinat Al-Zahra, named, it is said, after a beautiful concubine who had transfixed the caliph. The breathy word *Zahra* means Venus; so did she and that bright planet gave their name to a garden palace that is, to this day, one of most famous missing buildings in the world. In fact, it is better known than many buildings we actually have.

Built about six miles from Córdoba, in the oak woodlands in the hills west of the city, Madinat Al-Zahra comprised three levels, stepping down toward the river valley. Its site was precisely like that of the Albayzín: it fell away to the south, so as to give full light to the flowers and bring slanting, searching light into all the rooms. At Madinat Al-Zahra, the whole site was illuminated throughout the day. The lower levels held houses and mosques, but the level above was full of orchards, with pavilions set among the flowering trees. The upper buildings held sumptuous reception halls: arches made of ebony and gold, walls inlaid with gems and mosaic, and everywhere a filigree and tracery of plaster showed sinuous forms of vines and leaves. The walls glittered, and as the hours of the day passed, the changing light made the incised plant life seem to move slowly, to weave and bloom; it was as if the plasterwork was meant to become a whole garden that gave back light. As if this were not enough, in the ceiling of a ceremonial room hung an enormous pearl, a gift for the caliph from the emperor of Byzantium. Below, in the center, shone a pool filled to the brim with mercury. When the sun struck the pool, the mercury threw light in thick beams into the room; when a servant made ripples in the mercury, the beams narrowed into streaks of lightning. They had brought the very weather inside.

But all this sumptuous intricacy was nothing without the real gardens. Throughout the complex, aqueducts brought water to fountains, which overflowed into channels and filled big quiet pools that extended toward the south. The pavilions rose among pome-granate, fig, and almond trees. Roses and lilies and myriad flowers from throughout the Mediterranean bloomed in the rich soil, and the builders placed miradors with arched entranceways to over-look the shining water and blossoming trees. The water in the pools reflected the miradors, pavilions, and palatial façades, as well as the trees and sky, so that the colors of the garden, the water lilies, the musically beautiful archways and movement of clouds and light all presented themselves again in lustrous reflections. It was an ecstati-cally calculated unfolding of beauties. Reading about it, one thinks of Venice, city of reflections, a splendor so intense that our perception, as though on a hinge, swings open onto another reality.

MADINAT AL-ZAHRA TOOK forty years to build. On November 10, 1010, it took a day to burn it to the ground. An internecine fight between political factions loosed a brutality that destroyed the caliphate, and a contemporary said, "the carpet of the world was folded up and the beauty that was an earthly paradise was disfigured."

It is a fate that the Albayzín, as we will see, came near to sharing. But that was centuries later. Buildings can be burned, and cities razed, but traditions of real beauty have resilient life; and so the love of gardens endured, bearing the form throughout southern Iberia. And in Granada that tradition would be, by a constellation of lucky chances, made part of the daily life of the city. As we sit under our grape arbor, by the side of the pomegranate tree, we look upon the hill where such knowledge took wondrous form. On that hill, a family made a home that would influence crucially the history of Granada and begin the path that leads eventually to our little garden in this ancient neighborhood.

Shortly after the torching of Al-Zahra, the gentleman and scholar Ismail Ibn Naghrela fled Córdoba and ended up in Granada. Naghrela headed a Jewish family of wit and experience, and for some years, he served as vizier to the king of Granada. After his death, this powerful position passed to his son Yusuf. The family built a palace on the Sabika hill, where the Alhambra now stands. The usual poets lurked around, and, rhyming suspiciously, talked up the grape arbor, rose, myrtle beds, and date palms; there were filigreed walls and paving of alabaster and marble, towers and intimate meeting places with walls of arabesques. Lion fountains, by now, could not be avoided, and Yusuf's palace had a phalanx of lions, on the rim of a fountain, once again devoting themselves to the arts of irrigation. Never have so many big predatory cats been pressed into action in the company of orange blossoms and flowering jasmine.

Such luxury held sway among the wealthy, the powerful, the favored. But in Granada, in the eleventh century, we find witnesses to the creation of a simpler house, with a smaller garden. Rather than serving as a base of power, these gardens gave their bounty for the delectation of family, close friends, and loved ones. Such houses ringed the Albayzín and extended into the country. They had a mix of crops grown for the family and for the rambunctious markets of the city center; they had water wheels, corrals, aviaries, and canals.

From the Sabika hill, in the center of Granada, where sits the Alhambra, these small farms could be seen all around, so that chroniclers described their city as adorned in bright, lovely necklaces. In the fourteenth century, the poet Ibn al-Khatib cut loose with this encomium:

> *Farms and gardens were in such number that Granada resembled a mother surrounded by children . . . Villas and royal properties encompassed the city like bracelets . . . vines waved like billows . . . the nightingale of the trees preached a sermon . . . the winds exhaled perfumes . . . Like the sky of the world beautified with stars so lay the plain with towers of intricate construction . . .*

> *There is no space not taken up with gardens, vineyards, and orchards.*

One looked upon a fecund countryside, the like of which can today hardly be imagined surrounding Granada or any other Andalusian city. Listen to this description, by the Italian Andrea Navagiero, classical scholar, aficionado of poetry, and Venetian ambassador to Granada in the early sixteenth century. He writes:

> *As much as on the plain as on the hills, there are to be found, albeit invisible on account of the trees, so many little*

Moorish houses scattered here and there, that if they were
brought together they would form a city equal in extent [to
Granada]. And even though the majority are so small, they
all have their waters, their roses, musk rose and myrtles, and
a complete refinement . . .

All this, from a sophisticated Italian accustomed to the splendor of Venice, the poetry of Pindar, the prose of Cicero, and the
countryside of Northern Italy. It is just these beautiful houses,
descendants of the *munyas* that ringed Córdoba, that are the first
in Granada to carry the name of *carmen*. Our *carmen*, and all the
carmenes in the Albayzín, have as their ancestors these refuges of
knowledgeable beauty.

Navagiero's account is confirmed from more than one source,
including that of Hieronymous Munzer, a German who traveled
through Granada about the same time:

Outside the city, in the Vega, there are large orchards and
plantations irrigated with the water of canals led off the two
rivers [the Darro and the Genil], which also operate many
flour mills; so that everywhere Granada abounds in water
from rivers or from springs. From the houses the view is a
happy and delightful one at all seasons of the year. If one
looks toward the Vega, one sees so many plantations in cool
spots and so many settlements . . .

The adventures of the *carmen* were not over. During the time
of real prosperity and power in Granada, from 1002 to 1492, the
Albayzín came to hold so many houses that its population was over
three times what it is today. The wealthy reserved for themselves the

few spaces large enough to permit a garden to grow as part of the life of a house. How did the *carmen*, a house in the country with an enclosed garden and enough space for food crops, come to be imported into the Albayzín itself?

To understand this simple house with a garden, we had to study our own neighborhood. This we ardently wanted to do, as we settled into the pleasures of living in the Albayzín. Our garden, with fresh mountain water and hot summers, gave us a soft extended fireworks of flowering trees, and the children tracked the petals through the house. We began to cook with everything we grew. We had white figs in summer, which we ate off the tree for dessert, or baked in little galettes with brown sugar and cream. In the fall, we picked the pomegranates as they ripened and made pomegranate juice, or added the seeds to salads, or used them in a pomegranate tagine. The persimmons, which left to themselves fell like neon bombs to coat the unwary in persimmon jam, we harvested gingerly. We used them for luscious breakfasts or dessert, or baked them into moist cakes for Gabriella's school. The blossoms of the lemon tree gave everyone an uplift of pleasure, and we cured the lemons with salt and cinnamon, cloves and coriander, and then used them promiscuously in our cooking of Moroccan dishes. The grapes we left as an offering to the birds.

In November, we harvested and cured the hundreds of olives from our lone tree; and even in January, we were harvesting oranges and drinking their juice, preserved in the cold, in midwinter.

Beneath the fruit trees, Lucy planted more roses, and borders of lavender and santolina, myrtle and sage, thyme and rosemary, violets and iris. The jasmine and passion flower flourished near the *pilar*. On the other side of the garden, a honeysuckle rose up the side of the house headed for the railing of the *torreón*. And in so small a space, there was still room for tomatoes, arugula, and mint. The fountains ran through the hot days and warm nights. In any room of the house, we could hear the sound of water. At night, the down-canyon breeze brought the fragrance of the flowers and the blessing of cool mountain air into the bedrooms.

Every morning, when little Gabriella would awaken, she would come on hands and knees up the narrow, curving stairs into the *torreón*. I would gather her in my arms, and we would go down to the trees to stand in the light together and greet each vine and tree by name, and wish them their fine day in the sun. She would point and chortle and look around wide-eyed. Among so many memories of our first months there, this comes back to me often, this standing in the morning light of the garden with my daughter in my arms.

We wanted to understand the Albayzín, just because we wanted to know whom we had to thank for all this.

Where Walking Is Like Flying

O NE SUMMER MORNING, we walked out our dark thick door into the slanting sunlight. On our narrow street, along the base of the high white wall of our neighbor's *carmen*, we found five soft pink mounds. It took us a moment to see that each one was composed entirely of rose petals.

All night, in the warm breeze, the rose hedges of our neighbor had showered the street with petals. And in the morning, the famously handsome street-sweeper, Salvador, had gathered and arrayed the petals with his nicety of judgment into symmetrical mounds. They glowed against the white walls of our street.

As we walked through the neighborhood, hardly a day would pass without some such event. Call them blooms of another sort— the flowers of idiosyncrasy.

GABRIELLA'S SCHOOL WAS at the top of the Albayzín, so we had the chance to amble together through the barrio, hand in hand, day after day. Come with us.

As Gabriella had her school, the joyful Arlequin, the barrio itself became our school. We, too, looked forward to leaving the house to explore the whole neighborhood, passing from sunlight to shadow and back again, as we walked along the narrow streets full of flowers.

Our *carmen* was not far from the Darro River, which runs along the southerly edge of the neighborhood. Walking north from the Darro, that is, going uphill through the Albayzín, if you would climb with us, you will rise about two hundred twenty feet and cover just over a half-mile to the top and northernmost point of the barrio, marked by the church of Saint Christopher. Going from west to east, that is, from Calle Elvira to the beginnings of the gypsy barrio, the Sacromonte, the distance is just three-quarters of a mile. In this small space, ten thousand people live.

As we go together through these streets, one thing is certain: we will get lost, and we will be glad.

The street pattern shows its medieval origin: narrow cobbled lanes, perfect for two people walking together. These pathways come together in whimsy, branching here into a stairway, swooping there round a corner, darting off sideways in shadow, only to open into a plaza with trees and fountains and benches. Walking around, at first you muse, then you are amused. To make sense of it, you must surrender wholly to the playful design. Rather than straight lines in a grid, we have here a puzzle, a subtlety, a crazy quilt and playground of streets, formed by a labor of centuries of the people of the Albayzín. Not only are the streets narrow and eccentric, but the walls reject the plumb line. It's as if the whole barrio is on tilt—straight lines and right angles have been banished. Crookedness is the rule. Long garden walls lean into the streets or proceed in meandering waves along a lane. Inside the houses, everything is equally cattywampus. When we installed bookshelves in our house, the carpenter had to cut a subtle set of curves into the wood to fit the undulating plaster of the wall behind. Furniture we set down along a wall in a bedroom leaned comically forward, as though about to leap onto the mattress. And one of Gabriella's soccer balls, placed anywhere on a floor, rolled off by itself, as though booted by a phantom.

We came to love this swerve and tilt of things. Rather than clear lines of conceptual order, this was a neighborhood full of buildings that showed by their worn and worked surfaces their centuries of usefulness to life.

Most of the houses are white, often two stories with an occasional tower rising to a third story, for a lookout, a workroom, a trysting place. In some houses, windows open onto the street, and on the second story the house walls are studded with black iron balconies whose high doors can be thrown open to the sun and air. If the house is a *carmen*, then walls without windows enclose a secret garden, which shows above the wall some of the thriving within: palm trees, junipers, persimmon trees, a grape arbor, sunflowers, orange and lemon trees. From these gardens, vines and flowers clamber over the walls and arc down toward the street: roses, pink trumpet flowers, ivy, plumbago, white and gold-leaved jasmine, bougainvillea. At any time walking in the Albayzín, you may turn a corner and find a full current of flowers spilling toward you. Sometimes, with the bougainvillea, more than a current—an avalanche of flowers.

Our street, at its widest point, is about seven feet—just wide enough for Lucy and me to walk with our little daughter toddling between us. Many streets are more narrow, with bizarre angles, zigzags, and high, haggard walls that shadow the street even in midsummer. And some streets, known by a Spanish word—*adarve*—lead nowhere. You walk down one such lane, and it may end abruptly in a wooden door so worn you begin to think in geological time. The neighbors will say they believe it is used, but no one has ever been seen going in or out. My theory is that the doors at the end of *adarves* open into the tunnels in space and time that physicists tell us about, and so lead us to the past or future, or even to other interesting and habitable planets. Advancing this theory over brandy in nearby cafés, I received knowing looks.

Be that as it may, on the streets of the Albayzín, we have been lost, and early in our wanderings we noted the key principle: the barrio was not made for automobiles to live well. It was made for people to live well. There are only two roads that pass east to west through the Albayzín; they are used principally for public transport, and on one of them is located the single large garage for private cars. Going north to south, the only roads run at the far edges of the barrio. What difference does all this make in life?

It's a godsend. Gabriella and her legion of friends (and their parents with them) could rumpus in the little streets, invent stories, play soccer, sing to the trees, and in general dash around unforgettably, yet every parent is easy in the flesh. No truck is going to crush the children. Not only are kids safe, but the neighborhood is quiet, with no spewing and hacking of internal combustion engines. But even more than all that, something obvious and splendid: none of your neighbors are walking out to find their cars and go off to their lives. They are all walking out, straight *into* their lives. So all of us who live here run into one another, often. What begins with salutations turns easily to stories, to curiosities and exclamations, all of it leading to a friendship that has our children playing at each other's houses. This happened again and again in the Albayzín. It happens because our neighbors have sweet natures, and it happens because the barrio itself, the very design of it, has a genius, an irrepressible, gift-giving life.

Take, for example, Plaza Larga, in the upper Albayzín. We passed through it on the way to school and always paused to take in the spirits of the place. You walk into the plaza through an arched gate in a fortress wall at least a thousand years old, built on the foundations of another wall made a thousand years earlier. It is where Lucy and Gabriella and I dined our first night in the Albayzín. On weekdays, the plaza is filled with fruit and vegetable stands on one side, and at the other, a rack and tables of clothes for sale. Nearby is a legendary café, Bar Aixa, with coffee so intoxicating it should qualify as international contraband. Along the two mains streets that lead from the plaza—Calle Panaderos and Calle Agua (the street of the bakers and the street of water)—you'll find a hardware store, a ceramics store, fish markets, restaurants, a pharmacy, remnants of Arab baths, a big church that preserves the courtyard of a medieval mosque, small grocery stores, a newsstand, a flower shop, the butcher, the baker, and, I am sure, the candlestick maker. It's roistering and buoyant, with babies in strollers, kids hiding behind piles of artichokes, nuns gliding to and fro like swans, shouts of recognition or outrage, a garrulous humming of conversation, a blind gypsy selling raffle tickets, and black-garbed old women sitting on benches and talking, no doubt, about Aquinas. And of the side streets, you'll find work that asks more solitude and intensity—the guitar maker, and a world-class blacksmith.

Action and repose, idiosyncrasy and purity, flowers and surprises: the Albayzín offers daily some strange art of cumulative beauty. As the days and months pass, wherever you go, a host of details quicken the senses. Because everyone is living so close to one another, yet privately, life is in your face with rough edges, past tragedies, and a daily sense of promise. What came round to us, as we walked here, is a certainty that each day, we have our chance.

One might think that a neighborhood composed of small buildings, close together, and using so few elements—gardens, stone,
brick, wood, plaster—would be monotonous. All the more so since,
constrained by the rules that govern historic neighborhoods, no one
may construct, say, a three-story aluminum house with a front lawn
and a big garage. But the severity of the constraints invites beauty
to move in and stay awhile. An analogy is the sonnet: with its strict
fourteen lines, rhyme, and metrics, the form does not limit our labors,
but offers a place where meaning may flourish.

So in the Albayzín, the restricted space, history, simple building materials, and municipal regulation have created a place where
daily life may flourish. In fact, all the rules have ignited the most
promiscuous variety of ideas for making a space to live. One day,
walking around, we chose one element in the barrio, the terrace,
and we made it our study. The first terraces we see are tiny balconies, looking like aeries, which can be reached only by spiral
staircase. Others have cane roofs and resplendent tiles; they are
outfitted with chairs and a table for sherry and open toward the
Darro and the Alhambra. Larger terraces have canvas awnings and
iron railings woven with honeysuckle, within which a bed may be
hidden, for an outdoor tryst. Some terraces at the top of a house
have four-sided tile roofs of shallow pitch, open to the air on all
sides and holding a white hammock strung between posts; others are without any roof and open to the stars and to the mystery of the city. The largest terraces you enter through arches of
plaster carved in arabesques and painted in soft azure, and walk
onto an esplanade whose swirling pebblework floors hold pools
of cool water for blessed relief from the summer heat. One could
take a summer, walk around, go to the heights of the Alhambra,

look over the whole of the Albayzín, and write the definitive treatise on terraces. Or chimneys. Or garden pathways, rooflines, the
shapely columns that support balconies around a courtyard full of
flowers—for in the Albayzin, these common elements come into the
most bemused variety. With a few rules and a handful of elements,
we have a feast of forms. And all of them within one small barrio,
fifteen minutes to walk, from the river to the church at the top of
the hill.

If you and I walked through the Albayzín, to school or to market,
to see friends or just to have a ramble; if we took a whole day, what
would we find? Among white walls, flamenco guitarists practice.
And flamenco singing—at once fierce and melodious—comes from
doorways and terraces. Wafting from windows is the sound and
smell of the simmering in olive oil of lamb or onions and tomato. We
hear jokes being made, the susurrus of conversation, rambunctious
toasts, a clink of dishes being washed. Around the next corner, a
dozen orange trees in full blossom in a big *carmen*. Around the next,
a little plaza with a bench, and a brouhaha of bird songs—because
of all the gardens and plazas, the barrio is full of swifts and magpies.
Sitting in a plaza, you may see through a gate to a wall of tiles that
makes up a fountain—white stars set in large squares of baked clay.
By your side, through another gate, another fountain, this one faced
with blue and green Moorish tiles, and beyond it a kitchen garden in
a surround of fruit trees, all meticulously kept. Moving on, we watch
the light of the afternoon slant across one lane, fill another to the
brim with soft heat, and fill the next with a filigree of shadow as light
passes through the leaves of a grape arbor. As the afternoon carries
on, we rise though the lanes of the barrio to see junipers straight
as geysers and windows covered and adorned by wood jalousies,

whose openings are six-pointed stars, so that when the sun flows through, the walls within are bright with their own constellations. Some houses have a *torreón*, a high, open room whose ceiling has fine wood carvings called *alfarjes*, with their own mystical geometry. Walking higher up the narrow streets of the barrio, we come to a door set in a horseshoe arch, that arch itself set into a classic pattern of tiles, this time of ten-pointed stars that move, grow, and unfold before you. If we carry on until the sky darkens around, the lights of the Alhambra come on, and we turn around to sudden views of a pale stone tower rising out of a dark green hillside. Another few minutes, rising higher on the hill, we see the whole palace, curiously graceful—as though stone could float.

At night, iron and glass streetlights come on throughout the Albayzín, amber lights glow in the bell towers of the churches, white lights stream from the doors of little bars whose hubbub falls on the street like bright paint. In quiet stretches of meandering streets, and in tiny, isolated plazas called *placetas*, there is peace, and occasionally, thieves. Shadows patch the white walls, so they look like the robe of harlequin. Young people gather in plazas to drum and kiss and swig hard liquor.

How does any place become so eccentric, exultant, and hardscrabble, all at once? By sheer unlikelihood, and as a result of twenty-seven hundred years of luck and work and anguish. It's a story that begins early, in the seventh century BC, so long ago it's the century of the Old Testament Jeremiah.

The Albayzín holds a history of pagans, wacky church councils, classical civilization, genocidal outbursts, amorous shenanigans, incomparable works of genius, terrible religious fevers, and ethnic cleansing—all these, set into a story of Visigothic, Roman, Islamic, and Christian conquests. It's as if the great currents of Mediterranean history all coursed through this one neighborhood. If this were not enough, it's a history that holds as well the discovery of Holy Scripture from the first century bearing the magical Seal of Solomon. It was a find that rocked the Christian world.

Into that history we now gave ourselves, in hopes of understanding where we now lived. The story of the Albayzín led us into so zigzag and labyrinthine a maze, it was as if, in our reading, we walked in the barrio itself.

THE LAND, IBERIAN MYSTERIES, PLEASURES OF THE ROMANS

Let's start with the geography, which could hardly have conferred more blessings upon a townsite. To the southeast, the Sierra Nevada arcs into view, the highest range on the Iberian peninsula, with peaks rising beyond eleven thousand feet. To the east, another range, the Sierra de Huetor, full of springs, forming the headwaters of the Darro River running at the base of the Albayzín. South, just across the Darro canyon, is the Sabika hill where the Alhambra was built. On the far side of the Sabika runs the boisterous Genil, coursing with snowmelt from the Sierra Nevada.

It has extraordinary sweetness: big mountains, broad foothills, a promontory aloft between two rivers, the warm high hill of the Albayzín looking toward that promontory, all complemented by a plain—the vega—of rich soil, superbly watered with torrents of fresh snowmelt, and stretching out under hot summer days. Circling the vega, more mountain ranges, leaving only narrow passes for entry. Formidable security, then, for the city, and for its agricultural lands. Early communities on the lookout for a place to settle must have counted the advantages and gone off straightaway to thank their gods.

It is the seventh century BC. In the eastern Mediterranean, the Assyrian empire shoulders its way into Egypt. In Greece, Athens is already a politically complex city governing most of Attica. In the west, Etruscan civilization is flourishing on the Italian peninsula. Celtic tribes, with their iron weapons, settle in Gaul. And right here on the hill of our Albayzín, the early peoples of Spain built a compact, fortified city. They are called *los Iberos*—the Iberians—and they still fascinate Spain, since they have whimsically withheld so many of their secrets. But they chose the site so intelligently that future settlers—Roman, Visigoth, and Arab—would build their walls on the foundations of Iberic walls.

They constructed their city at the high point of the hill, with good vantage up the Darro canyon and out toward the vega. Every day, on the way home from Gabriella's school, we walked by an excavation that seemed to go on endlessly. Finally, we stopped and talked to the workers, who of course threw down their tools, lit cigarettes, and explained everything to us as Gabriella ate her ice cream.

It turned out that in the area near the site, closer to the stone gate that gives entry to Plaza Larga, near the bars and schools and bakeries, archaeologists have dug up the foundations of houses and sanctuaries twenty-seven hundred years old. They've found ceramics, money, inscriptions, and urns; even a whole necropolis. And slowly, in combination with other finds throughout Spain, the culture of *los Iberos* has come into view. They left us lovely small bronze horses and little soldiers with tiny shields and swords, who go into battle very warily indeed, since both sword and phallus are erect. They left famous sacred statuary of women in elaborate robes, tightly wound hairdos, and clunky necklaces; their female gaze is fixed so intently on some faraway world that we want to turn our heads and look carefully, just in case it swims into view.

They left us coins and tablets with their written notes and declarations in a language that has stumped the scholars who have studied it. So we await their poetry and their praises of the strange goddess. Best of all, they gave us what has to be my favorite sphinx, a muscular bull with the head of a man, mustachioed and irresistibly jolly. Even to look at the thing makes you laugh.

In their redoubt at the top of the hill, the Iberians lived for five centuries, until Rome began to march its legionnaires all over Europe. The date given for the beginning of decisive Roman influence on our hillside is 193 BC. Iberian culture makes a slow marriage with Roman law and custom. By 1 BC, Latin, which at least we can read, was the language stamped on money. Being no fools, the Romans took one look at the Iberian fortified city on the hill overlooking a river and a fertile vega and moved right in. They built stronger and higher walls, extending the footprint of the settlement to the west and south, that is, toward the vega and down the hill toward the river. We could walk with you from our *carmen*, going north up the gentle hill, and in two minutes arrive just where the Roman wall ran east to west along the present street of Aljibe de Trillo. From their freshly fortified vantage point, the Romans set to work, bringing to the art of ceramics what have to be the dullest pots in the history of the region—the pieces are covered with red varnish, making them look even more like mud than they would otherwise. But at least they had dishes.

Farther afield, the Romans did their Roman things: found gold in the Darro and Genil and created quarries in the foothills so they could carry on building. Above all, they grew satisfied and prosperous from that root and font of wealth, agriculture. With the vega under their military vigilance and production organized into large estates, their tables were laden with grapes and cereals and olives. With the heat of the summer, the swollen and luscious grapes of the region made their way, suitably stored and aged, to wine-bibbing citizens who partied in seigniorial mansions whose foundations have been excavated in the Albayzín. Those mansions, of worked stone, sometimes built up ingeniously without mortar—called in Spanish *mampostería*—were so well put together that their walls, in the open air after twenty centuries, stand intact and strong. In our wanderings around the barrio, we have seen them; they look as if they were held together by some undiscovered cosmic force. Some houses even had the mosaic floor found elsewhere in the empire—an oddly direct precursor of some of the streets in the present-day Albayzín, which have pebbles inlaid laboriously in the form of flowers, or pomegranates, or arabesques sinuous as wind.

The Ibero-Roman city held the usual Roman accoutrement—a forum, basilica, courtyards with columns, marble statues, and the lot—so that the soil of the Albayzín has proved to be a lumpy staging ground for the discovery of cornices, fountains, republican and imperial coins, fluted columns, and affectionate inscriptions in praise of slave boys. And we find also one detail that was to mark the Albayzín forever: reading of it now, we have the sense of something coming to be born. In the upper reaches of the Albayzín hill, a Roman house was excavated with a fine small pool, lined with bricks, which must have looked out over the countryside. And why not, since the ingenious use of water would transform the Albayzín—the clear, fresh water from the mountains, in its full sensuality, that has flowed into the neighborhood over centuries like some benediction of history.

When on a mercilessly hot day in the summer we throw ourselves into the cool water of the *alberca* in our garden, I think of our Roman antecedents, who doubtless did the same, with the same joy and relief. There were springs on the hill of the Albayzín, and on the hill above, and Roman roofs were designed to drain water into underground cisterns, just as hundreds of years later, cisterns would be built throughout the neighborhood, even within houses. We have an ancient one in our own *carmen*. We have thought to make a cellar, or fill it with garden vegetables on shelves, or set down racks for wine. But it seems somehow to want to persist in its historic form.

In this Roman period of the Albayzín, the region steps out onto the stage of the world. In the first century of the Christian era, Pliny the Elder wrote his *Natural History*, wildly subtitled "An Account of Countries, Nations, Seas, Towns, Havens, Mountains, Rivers, Distances, and Peoples Who Exist Now or Who Formerly Existed." He tells us, wonderfully, that the region "excels all the other provinces in the richness of its cultivation and the peculiar fertility and beauty of its vegetation." Two Roman emperors—Trajan, who broke the monopoly of Italians in that august position, and Hadrian, the orphan turned lover and warrior—were born in Andalusia. And the future Albayzín turns up in Pliny's summary of the towns in the region, under the name of Iliberri or Ilupula. My guess is that these names were chosen because they feel ripe in the mouth.

And we begin to see others come forth from the hillside of the future Albayzín to historical notice. Let us name one of them: Publio Cornelio Anulino, who was, if we may be permitted a deep breath, quaestor, tribune, legate, commander of the Seventh Legion, sometime governor of the Roman provinces of his home territory Baetica, as well as Africa, and Germania Superior (which is present-day eastern France), and eventually a prefect in Rome—that is, a key player in the administration of the empire. The compatriots of this gentleman, over the centuries, were variously soldiers and consuls and priestesses, giving us a sense of the high energy of the locals. Perhaps it was the trustworthy sunlight and delicious red wine of their hillside neighborhood.

It is at the close of Roman domination that we witness the Albayzín begin to consider how to mix pagan devotion with Christian and

Jewish practice, since all three ways of worship existed here. With foreboding and fascination, we may watch how, very early on, men of faith in the Albayzín tried to turn the centuries in their direction.

THE CLERGY GATHER IN THE ALBAYZÍN TO TAKE A CRACK AT HISTORY

In the first centuries of our era, Christian communities, fledgling and persecuted, spread though the Mediterranean and had a beach-head, literally and figuratively, on the Iberian peninsula. Official tolerance throughout the empire was not, of course, granted until February of 313, with the Edict of Milan, which gave Christians legal rights, restored their confiscated property, and permitted the founding of churches. So it is with astonishment that we read of a council of the church held in southern Spain that *predates* the Edict of Milan. Called the Council of Elvira, it took place around 306 AD. A mighty weight of church officials—nineteen bishops with assorted presbyters, deacons, and legates—gathered on this hillside overlooking the Darro and the vega and cogitated piously about orthodoxy, sin, punishment, women, pagans, and Jews. We wonder if they knew what they were doing, especially how their musings would reverberate down the centuries. For the Council of Elvira was not just the first church council in Spain. It was the first council anywhere from which written canons survived. It is a fascinating episode, for we see in its daft propositions a young church besieged with events and confusions, and trying to figure out what on earth to do. Some of these early canons have the feel of grumpy social judgments, such as:

62. Chariot racers and pantomimes must first renounce their profession and promise not to resume it before they may become Christians.

So were those rakish charioteers and suspicious entertainers cast off by this stern group. And the church wanted to tidy up the churches, even venturing this bold proclamation:

36. Pictures are not to be placed in churches, so that they do not become objects of worship and adoration.

Iconoclasts before their time, this attitude would destroy, in the centuries to come, uncounted mosaics and paintings. For the sake of Fra Angelico, Raphael, Bellini, and the countless other luminaries of Christian art of the ensuing centuries, we may be permitted a prayer of thanksgiving that this canon did not prevail.

But beyond the housekeeping, the reach of the canons is extraordinary. They are seeds, set down in the Albayzín, that grew into history. An extraordinary number of them—a full quarter of the total—assert control over women's conduct, especially of woman's sexuality. As to conduct, some canons are so persnickety that we want to know the story behind them. There is, for example,

67. A woman who is baptized or is a catechumen must not associate with hairdressers or men with long hair. If she does this, she is to be denied communion.

This particular canon has the smell of a grudge: a hopeful deacon, say, mad at a lovely Christian girl cavorting near the Darro, her hands in the long hair of her suitor. A long-haired charioteer, perhaps? There is another of this same stamp:

81. A woman may not write to other lay Christians without her husband's consent. A woman may not receive letters of friendship addressed to her only and not to her husband as well.

No doubt such letters had been discovered, who knows with what promising innuendos.

But beyond such curiosities, the struggling church exerted itself to name and regulate the sexual antics of Christians. To judge from the canons, the council must have spent long days on the subject. Perhaps the sensual climate of Andalusia had heated the theological reasoning of our clerics. Witness the following canons. Some are crisp and forgiving. Such as:

44. A former prostitute who has married and who seeks admission to the Christian faith shall be received without delay.

A host of canons then go on to study adultery with what we might call algebraic exactitude, and try to cook up different punishments, depending on gender, faith, and the sexual facts at hand. The permutations are endless, as though the august assembly of clerics felt compelled to list all the couplings ever confessed. Some of these are wonderfully phrased, with a lot of ferocious prohibitions which give way to a wonder of hedging, backtracking, and exception-making. The results are bizarre, even for a church:

9. A baptized woman who leaves an adulterous husband who has been baptized, for another man, may not marry him. If she does, she may not receive communion until her former husband dies, unless she is seriously ill.

Then, of course, what about sexual variety? And certainly they had to consider the case of a cleric who adores his adulterous wife—

72. If a widow has intercourse and then marries the man, she may only commune after five year's penance. If she marries another man instead, she is excluded from communion even at time of death . . .

65. If a cleric knows of his wife's adultery and continues to live with her, he shall not receive communion even before death in order not to let it appear that one who is to exemplify the good life has condoned sin.

We note that it seems to have been common for a priest to have a wife.

Having begun to tidy up the lascivious behavior of the married clergy and laypeople, they forged bravely ahead in the hopes of assuring that virgins remained virgins; unless, of course, they didn't, in which case the ex-virgin could make amends. This was tougher for so-called consecrated virgins, the forerunners of nuns. For a laywoman, all depended on the number of her lovers. The more sexually active the woman, the more amends would be required. What's interesting is that even though such amorous conduct got a big frown in the canons, such women still had a way to enter the community of Christians.

13. Virgins who have been consecrated to God shall not commune even as death approaches, if they have broken the vow of virginity and do not repent. If, however, they repent and do not engage in intercourse again, they may commune when death approaches.

14. If a virgin does not preserve her virginity, but then
marries the man, she may commune after one year, without
doing penance, for she only broke the laws of marriage.
If she has been sexually active with other men, she must
complete a penance of five years before being readmitted to
communion.

Having reviewed in such detail the sexual frolics of the community, it probably was inevitable that the clergy address their own conduct. And so fate had its way when the council, having cast so critical an eye on the embraces of laypeople, now turned with severity on each other.

27. A bishop or other cleric may have only a sister or daughter who is a virgin consecrated to God living with him. No other women who is unrelated to him may remain.

Note the daughter! And the sizable begged question, crying out to be answered: What about a woman who *is* related to him, who *does* remain? And the council dropped its bombshell:

33. Bishops, presbyters, deacons, and others with a position
in the ministry are to abstain completely from sexual inter-
course with their wives and from the procreation of children.
If anyone disobeys, he shall be removed from clerical office.

It is a calm, stunning, momentous prohibition, the first such canon of the Catholic church. It does not forbid the marriage of clerics; rather, it reaches into the heart of such marriages, to forbid the physical celebration of a man and woman promised to one another. To cherish the pleasures of a wife is to abandon the work of the church. And implicit in this reasoning is the idea that such cherishing cannot lead a couple in love close to life, or closer to the divine.

It is the declaration of one small church council, in a small settlement on a hillside in southern Spain, far from Rome and Constantinople, early in the history of Christianity. Yet we should not discount its power and influence. Later canon law tended to build upon the cracked foundation of Elvira. Not only that, but of the nineteen bishops in attendance, some of them would go on to play crucial roles in later councils. To mention only one: Hosius of Córdoba, a key player in the Council of Elvira, went on to participate in the authoritative Council of Nicaea in 325, perhaps in the name of the pope himself. Hosius even managed to totter, at age 99, all the way to the Council of Milan in 355. Such councils, with the promulgation of the Nicene Creed and its confirmation thereafter, set down a fierce and final theology that has remained in place to our day. If the Council of Elvira had understood the world differently, today our world would be different. And whatever one thinks of the blizzard of prohibitions of the Council of Elvira, some of their canons we must read today as a planting of evil seeds:

> *49. Landlords are not to allow Jews to bless the crops they have received from God . . . Such an action would make our blessing invalid and meaningless. Anyone who continues this practice is to be expelled completely from the church.*

> *78. If a Christian confesses adultery with a Jewish or Pagan woman, he is denied communion for some time. If his sin is exposed by someone else, he must complete five year's penance before receiving the Sunday communion.*

So Jewish blessing is condemned, and as to sex, a Jew is no better than a pagan. But the council was not done.

50. If any cleric or layperson eats with Jews, he or she shall be kept from communion as a way of correction.

A mere three centuries after the death of Jesus, a Jewish teacher in Palestine, it is an early, clear expression of contempt.

The Christian community in the Albayzín, entrenched and literate, continued to be influential. In the fourth century, a bellicose and orthodox bishop, Gregory, lived in the Albayzín. In addition to penning five volumes on the *Song of Songs*, he took the time in another book on the Old Testament to detest Jewish religious observance. And we must not forget the hysterically ambitious Juvencus, also of the early fourth century, born into the neighborhood, a presbyter and budding epic poet. Juvencus wanted to get rid of those ancient pesky storytellers, Homer and Virgil. To replace their unholy paganism and messy digressions, he left us a tidy Latin commentary on the New Testament—no fewer than 3,211 verses in dactylic hexameter. No old-fashioned muses are to be found; he happily substitutes, in their stead, the freshly minted Holy Spirit.

THE VISIGOTHS LOSE THE
NEIGHBORHOOD TO AL-ANDALUS

In the fifth century, into the Iberian peninsula and eventually to the Albayzín, came the Germanic invasion that extinguished the Roman Empire. The skirmishing tribes that ransacked the Iberian peninsula have names that stick in the mouth like clay—the Siling Vandals, the Alans, the Suevi, the Asdings, the Visigoths. Our neighborhood saw

these newcomers hacking away at Romans and one another, as it was
dominated first by Visigoths, then by Suevi, then again by Visigoths,
until by the sixth century the Visigothic aristocracy supplanted the
dominant Roman families, and Roman villas sported Visigothic decoration. Even Granadan bishops took on Visigothic names, which
is fascinating, because the Visigoths were not what we have come
to call Orthodox Catholics. This being early in the struggles of the
young, sprawling church, fundamental ideas were still in play. The
Visigoths were Arian Christians. Now, library shelves have been broken by weighty books written about Arianism, and rightfully so. Let
us boldly summarize: the Arians believed that Jesus, though a divinely
inspired prophet, was not himself divine; and so Jesus is the "Son of
God" not in a literal sense, but in an emblematic sense. Think of him
as being adopted by God, because of his loving, his goodness, and his
understanding. The Christianity of the Arians, then, stood in contra-
diction to the orthodoxy of the Council of Nicaea, which held Jesus
to be divine, literally the Son of God.

The Albayzín, then, was full of Arians, which goes to show some
things never change. The neighborhood is freewheeling and rebellious
now, and so it was then. It's something about all the sunlight and music,
we think. In any case, throughout the Mediterranean, Christians of
the early Middle Ages fought about the nature of Jesus. They battled it
out in Iberia, as well, and the story is full of rousing political intrigues,
conspiracies, exiles, excommunications, and miraculous reversals of
fortune. In Iberia, in 580, Leovigild, the Visigothic king, gathered the
Arian bishops of Spain in a synod to set forth a new Arian Christian
orthodoxy. Unfortunately for his initiative, Leovigild's son converted
to the Nicene Creed, which held Jesus to be divine. He went to war
against his father, only to be captured, imprisoned, and, then, rather

conveniently, murdered by his jailer. After all that, Leovigild's other son, Reccared, assumed the kingship—and then himself converted to the Nicene Creed. Arian bishops revolted. The monarchy threw itself into the arms of Orthodox Catholic Christianity, and the hubbub continued. Reccared's son was assassinated, and his murderer, Witeric, tried to bring back Arianism; but alas, Witeric was decapitated at a banquet. So went the pacific exchange of ideas that formed Christian theology in Spain.

So our Albayzín, after centuries with the Iberians, Romans, pagans, Jews, early Christians, then pagan Germanic invaders turned Arians, finally cruised into the seventh century full of Catholics who kneeled down and swore to the Nicene Creed in their churches. Their Visigothic rulers went on to distinguish themselves by a habit of internecine slaughter and, just to round things out, a doctrinal hatred of the peninsula's substantial Jewish population.

When, in 711, Tariq Ibn Ziyad turned up with his seven thousand soldiers, everything changed for the Albayzín, for most of the Iberian peninsula, and for Europe. It was the beginning of Al-Andalus, and we still live with the forms and in the light of those eight hundred years. The Albayzín, in particular, takes from that period the layout of its streets, its architecture, its monuments, its gardens, and myriad elements of its way to life.

The Arabs and Berbers, both bearing Islam to the peninsula, came first as soldiers. But the swift collapse of the Visigoths delivered the entirety of Iberia into their hands, and they stayed on as settlers. Our hillside, with its customs and churches and history of agreeable habitation, yielded itself easily to the newcomers, not least because of the help of the Jewish population of the city. In the years following, we hear of the future Albayzín now and then in the historical record.

In 743, a group of Syrians received permission to set up house in the neighborhood. We have excavations of some of their houses from the period, with cannily constructed walls of stone, private baths, and interior patios. In 755, the first emir of Spain, the gardening Abd al-Rahman I we have met, gave his permission to fortify the building on the Sabika hill, on the site that would one day hold the Alcazaba, fortress of the Alhambra. We have a picture, then, of a small community now spread over the hillside of the Albayzín and the Sabika hill, with a small, politically dominant Muslim cohort, a vigorous Christian presence, and a well-established Jewish quarter.

For the first three centuries of Al-Andalus, much of the action moved to another hillside to the west, farther from the Sierra Nevada, but still with good access to rich agricultural lands. The settlement there, called Medina Elvira, flourished until the beginning of the eleventh century, when the momentous decision was made to move everyone to the better-fortified and tantalizing hill of the future Albayzín. So began the reign of the Zirids, a Berber tribe whose kings, in seventy years, made the fine judgments that formed the neighborhood where we live. They brought power and big plans, but most of all a thoroughgoing practicality. They built the walls we see today, and some of their gates we still have, like the Arco de las Pesas, that gives access to Plaza Larga. They built a mosque, the Almorabitin, whose minaret (now a belltower) still stands, with rough, admirable beauty. Most of all, and best of all, they brought water. It came from a miraculous spring called Aynadamar, across the foothills to the top of the Albayzín, and flowed through the neighborhood, to be collected in twenty-eight cisterns called *aljibes*. You can still see them in the Albayzín, like stone keys to the heritage of life here. It is worth quoting a description of the water:

*The water is most healthful, and a natural medicine against
fevers and so helpful to the digestion, that no matter how
abundant the food, it passes easily through the stomach; its
temperature is that of natural springs, warm in winter and
cool in summer, and so clear and delightful to see, for its
bounteous quantity and its effervescence, that for it alone
Granada would be superb, even if the city did not have so
many other excellent qualities.*

Even to read about it makes one thirsty. The engineering was
so sound, it lasted a thousand years. There are still residents in the
Albayzín who remember drinking this water. Such are the virtues of
thoughtful engineering—a millennium of daily benefits.

In that same eleventh century, a king by the name of Badis built
his palace somewhere around San Miguel Bajo, a plaza today full of
restaurants and rollicking children. The settlement expanded, and
the walls with it, and neighborhoods radiated out from the central,
fortified zone, which remained where it had been for the previous
seventeen hundred years. The new barrios took on their wonderful
names: there was a Barrio of the Caves, of the Cliffs, of the Potters.
There was a Barrio of Delights, of the Solitary Worshippers, and
finally, just on the other side of the Arco de las Pesas, the Barrio
of the Falconers. It is this last barrio—*ar-rabad al-bayyzin*—whose
name gives us Albayzín. Though men with falcons on their wrists are
rarely sighted, at least for now.

Throughout the Iberian peninsula, political power knotted
and unknotted whole regions, as armies led by Christian sovereigns advanced from the north, won and lost battles, and the leaders of Al-Andalus, whether Christian or Muslim, made and remade

alliances with one other. But Al-Andalus, whatever the governance
of its cities and regions, continued to be the same fecund mix of
language, faith, and art, with strong Christian, Jewish, and Muslim
communities. And the Albayzín—the core and origin of Granada,
was to be for two and a half centuries a place for kings.

After the arrival of the community of Elvira, the Albayzín remade
itself into an energetic, well-fortified city. To the provision of sparkling water, successive kings and their talented subjects added a large
hospital, new mosques for the increased population, and a bridge
across the Darro to permit easy access to the Jewish quarter of the
city and to the fortress atop the Sabika hill. Today, one may walk
in a matter of minutes from our house to all these sites. The twenty-
eight *aljibes* have been recovered. The footings of the bridge across
the Darro still stand; in the nineteenth century, they were to give a
Romantic *frisson* to visitors from France and England.

The population grew and changed and strengthened as new skills
were demanded, and new prosperity incited a new way of life. The
number of people in the Albayzín began a steady climb that would
culminate, after four centuries, in a population of around forty thousand people, a nice medieval contrast to the ten thousand who live
here today.

During this time, the neighborhood took on the quality that, as
we read about it today, impresses us: rambunctious diversity. Already
diverse in religious faith, with the agricultural bounty to support
them, the community came into its own. Who were these people,
what did they know, how did they live?

There were farmers, laborers, muleteers; millers, bakers, basket-
makers. There were tile-makers who were to carry further the rich
traditions of arabesque and ingenious geometry; there were potters

who adorned vases and plates with lovely blue and green designs. So lovely that when we bought a set of plates for daily use in our new kitchen, the paintings upon them turned out to be copied from a fourteenth-century original. There were wood-carvers who translated the octagons and whirling dodecagons of the tile-makers into ceiling panels of wonderful, sidereal variety. There were the famous orchardkeepers, who produced for the city a promiscuous variety of fruit—peaches, grapes, pomegranates, figs, apples, oranges, dates, lemons, along with pistachios and cashews. Through the Albayzín, and down in the marketplace that developed in the level area just west of the neighborhood, there thrived the specialists—blacksmiths, rope-makers, shoemakers, book-binders, stonecutters, pharmacists, midwives. In the Albayzín itself, the spinners of silk made the silk merchants and sultans of Granada rich with their shimmering production, which was exported all over Europe and the Mediterranean. And all this is a mere sample of the work undertaken in the city. Studies of old records show over five hundred established occupations. It gives the picture of a bounteous, secure, diverse city, blessed with sun, water, and wit.

Where did they live? Along with the floral *carmenes* built throughout the countryside around Granada, their houses in the Albayzín were small, their rooms set around a courtyard, with a fountain in the center, flowers, or a grapevine. Off the courtyard on the ground floor were closets, a kitchen, and a storehouse with bins for cereals, beans, and fruit, and large jars, sometimes buried in the earth, for water or oil. Above, small bedrooms. It is a simple, beautiful order that asks light and air into the house all year, yet in the hot months holds enough shade to make for cool refuge. Here and there in the Albayzín, such medieval houses are preserved. A door opens, centuries fall away, and we enter a patio flanked by columns, with a small fountain in the center giving water into a channel that leads to a rectangular pool holding water for household use. Such a small space, proportioned sweetly, feels private, and yet at liberty, open to the sky. They are places of singular peace.

Houses had no place to bathe. But each part of the Albayzín offered public bathhouses, with steaming hot water, essential to public health and social concord. The ceilings of these bathhouses had star-shaped openings that brought slanting beams of light across the steamy air within. They were gathering places, places of refuge and tranquility, places to rest, swap tales, reflect. Especially among the Muslims of Granada, they were a cherished part of daily life.

What did they eat? It was, by the standards then and now, an unusually healthy diet. They ate oranges, wheat, dates, artichokes—in fact, the whole suite of fresh fruits and vegetables grown in the vega and on the hillsides around Granada. All this fresh produce, as well as lamb, and animals killed in the hunt, was sold in the humming markets of the city. As to their cooking, we read of simmered vegetable soup with toasted wheat, spiced lamb with onion and coriander, hot pies filled with two kinds of cheeses and coated with cinnamon sugar, chicken with pepper and ginger, and the use of mint, saffron, sesame, anise, mace, citron. The citizenry of all faiths, including Islam, drank wine; sanctions applied only to drunken and disorderly escapades. And for the love of heaven let us not neglect the desserts of the day: sugary quince tarts, pastries of blackberries and elderberries with honey, pomegranate syrups, almond cookies, cakes with rosewater and hazelnuts, cinnamon bread with honey and pistachios.

They dressed in loose clothes that visitors found fantastical and whose mellifluous names still hold their place in Spanish—*almalafa* (a full-length robe of wool or silk), *zaraguelles* (wide pleated breeches), *pantufla* (a soft, colored slipper), *marlota* (a loose, ornamented gown buttoned down the back). Many of the longer garments were hemmed in cloth of vivid color or, among the affluent, with gold thread to complement a showing of precious gems.

This period, from around 1000 to 1492—an extraordinary span of years—is of legendary accomplishment. For the Iberians, and for the later Roman and Visigothic inhabitants, this settlement had offered a pleasance, a place of safety, a place to work and invent and dream. Now the Albayzín made itself into one the best places in the world to live. It had fine fresh water and sunshine, newly fortified walls, the blessing of religious tolerance, flourishing gardens and fields, a rapturous tradition of poetry and music, and hard-working, exploratory citizens.

There were setbacks. One of them was so terrible, we must give it notice. In 1091, the city suffered the conquest of the Almoravids, a powerful tribe of new converts to Islam who originated in the area where we now find Mali and Mauretania. The Almoravids had risen to power in North Africa by astute, fanatic military aggression and had gone on to make their capital the city of Marrakesh. The rulers of the cities of Al-Andalus, militarily weak and threatened by the invasions of Christian kings from Northern Spain, appealed to the Almoravids for help. And help they did, doing battle with the invaders from the north, and even invading territory where Christians ruled over citizens of the three faiths. After their success, they turned viciously on their supplicants. Worst of all, in Granada, their persecution of Christians in the name of Islamic fundamentalism reached such an extreme that several thousand of them emigrated, under protection of a Christian army, to northern Spain. Such was the severity

of the Almoravids that they even turned on the popular mystics of the
day, the Sufis, and suppressed their schools and burned their books.

The population revolted at these oppressions, and a rival power,
more tolerant and constructive, was invited in from North Africa.
Called the Almohads, they possessed a formidable military prowess
and were builders in their own right. Welcomed by the populace,
they put an end to the depredations of the Almoravids, whose rule in
Al-Andalus lasted only fifty-six years.

Here in the Albayzín, just below our house, rises a strong, lovely
Almohad minaret, the bell tower of the church of Saint John of the
Kings, even now being restored as the Albayzín, building by building,
reclaims its heritage.

In 1238, the Almohads gave way to the first of the Nasrid kings,
one Yusuf Nasr, of Granada. His quarters were in the Albayzín, and
he and his descendants, through their political suppleness, improvi-
sational diplomacy, and the sheer talent of their subjects, would keep
Al-Andalus alive in the south of Spain for another two hundred and
fifty years—longer than the United States of America has existed. The
same year Nasr took power in the Albayzín, he began the last phase
of building in Granada, the one known worldwide today. For across
the way stood the Sabika hill, and upon that hill, Nasr determined
he would build an entirely new barrio of the city. It would be full of
gardens, and in the center would rise a new palace, the Alhambra.

It was an opportune time for the construction of a palace. During
these centuries, as Christian armies slowly dismembered the reign
of Islamic emirs and reconstituted Al-Andalus under Christian rule,
gifted craftsman and scholars sought their place in society in one or
another city. Some were welcomed and valued in Christian Spain;
others were persecuted. And some traveled to southern Spain, to

Granada or to its surrounding territories, to begin new lives. After five hundred years of progressive development in gardening, agronomy, architecture, poetry, philosophy, the natural sciences, and design, Al-Andalus had a preponderance of talent, whomever ruled the city in which they lived.

With its population and prosperity increasing, the city had grown. The Albayzín for many centuries *was* Granada. Over decades and centuries, from the early 1200s, the city spilled down the slope to fill the area between the Albayzín and the Genil River. And as the Alhambra and its environs rose on the Sabika hill, Granada and its surrounding countryside, full of *carmenes*, took on an iridescent beauty. We have travelers' accounts, from a German traveler, Jacobo Munzer, in 1494, and from the Italian Andrea Navagiero, in 1526. It is worth the while listening to their voices.

First, Munzer:

> *At the foot of the mountains, on the good plain, Granada has, for almost a mile, many orchards and leafy spots irrigable by water channels; orchards, I repeat, full of houses and towers, occupied during the summer, which, seen together and from afar, you would take to be a populous and fantastic city . . . there is nothing more wonderful. The Saracens like orchards very much, and are very ingenious in planting and irrigating them to a degree that nothing surpasses.*

And Navagiero:

> *All the slope . . . and equally the area on the opposite side, is most beautiful, filled with numerous houses and gardens, all with their fountains, myrtles, and trees, and in some there are*

*large and very beautiful fountains. And even though this part
surpasses the rest in beauty the other environs of Granada are
the same, as much the hills as the plain they call the Vega. All
of it is lovely, extraordinarily pleasant to behold, all abound-
ing in water, water that could not be more abundant; all full
of fruit trees, like plums of every variety, peaches, figs, quinces
. . . apricots, sour cherries and so many other fruits that one
can barely glimpse the sky for the density of the trees . . .
There are also pomegranate trees, so attractive and of such
good quality that they could not be more so, and incomparable grapes, of many kinds, and seedless grapes for raisins. Nor
are wanting olive trees so dense they resemble forests of oaks.*

Another writer, Bermudez de Pedraza, commented directly upon
the Albayzín:

*[The houses] were delightful, embellished with damascened
work, with courtyards and orchards, beautified with pools
and fountain basins with running water . . .*

The Albayzín had reached some apotheosis it would never enjoy
again. The mosque offered a courtyard full of lemon trees, and flowering trees found their way into the names of things. There was
a "Mosque of the Walnut Tree," a "Street of the Fountain of the
Cherry Tree," a "Promontory of the Almond Trees." Up on the hill,
in the area of the original settlements of *los Iberos* and the Romans,
were public squares, a hospital, markets, hotels, warehouses, and the
ateliers of silk spinners. In the lower part of the Albayzín was the
legendary Maristan, a sumptuous building dedicated exclusively to
the care of the mentally ill. The barrio as a whole was a hive, with

labyrinthine streets so narrow you could reach across to a window on the other side. The minuscule branching lanes seemed infinite to travelers. Arches of stone stood over tiny streets, and tunnels linked some houses to one another. Balconies, sheds, rooftop gardens, and latticed windows set above cul-de-sacs all complicated further the layout of the barrio. Some quarters had their own gates, for closing off the neighborhood at night. The overall complexity of the place was such that Munzer thought it looked like a hillside covered entirely with swallow's nests; though he found the houses clean, almost all with their own cisterns and plumbing.

The last competent Nasrid king, Muhammad V, died in 1391. He completed, following on the work of his father, Yusuf I, the construction of the Alhambra. The two hundred eighty-eight years from the arrival of the Zirids, in 1013, to the last of the Nasrids in 1391, offered a beauty of complex power. That beauty would suffer the torments history brings often to such a comely target. Yet the life force in the work done could not be extinguished. And we can learn from the story of the fall of Granada, its aftermath and dark detail.

INTO THE SLOW INFERNO

Late in the fifteenth century, in 1469, Ferdinand of Aragon and Isabel of Castile made their famous marriage. It was not a century in which Granada had enjoyed prescient leadership. In fact, the most powerful families in Granada marked the century with treachery, the extermination of rivals, the revolt of sons against fathers, and other episodes of imbecility. All this destructive governance culminated in the sultanate of the ludicrous Boabdil, a onetime captive of Ferdinand who was freed to return to Granada. Ferdinand knew his man. For it was

Boabdil who would bear down on Granada with the full weight of his fear and vulgarity and hasten the end of the city by his useless quarreling and confusion.

In 1491, Ferdinand and Isabel's armies besieged the city and denied it the bounty of the vega's agricultural lands. Granada was starved into submission. With famine increasing, a surrender was negotiated, on terms set down in what is known as the Articles of Capitulation, signed by the king and queen. They make splendid reading today for the express goodwill that shines there. Let us treat ourselves to four brief passages, from a document that is dead center in the history of Spain and of Europe:

> 3. Isabel, Ferdinand, and Prince Juan [their son] would after the surrender accept all Granadans . . . "great and small, men and women," as their vassals and natural subjects. [They are] guaranteed to remain in their "houses, estates, and hereditaments, now and for all time and for ever . . . nor would they have their estates and property taken from them . . . rather they would be honored and respected."

> 4. Their highnesses and their successors will ever afterwards allow the King, [civilian] and military leaders, and good men and all the common people, great or small, to live in their own religion, and not permit that their mosques be taken from them, not their minarets nor their muezzins . . . nor will they disturb the uses and customs which they observe.

> 21. Law suits which arise between Moors will be judged by their law . . . as they customarily have . . . but if the suit should arise between a Christian and a Moor, then it will be

judged by a Christian judge and Moorish qadi, in order that neither side may have any grounds for complaint.

29. No Moor will be forced to become a Christian against his or her will . . .

These passages illustrate the tenor of the document as a whole, which reconfirms and extends the promises of protection for religion, property, and custom. It is a document wholly in the spirit of Al-Andalus. The Muslims were to be treated with tolerance and respect, in the present and for all time—such was the commitment of the sovereigns of Spain. It was as if Ferdinand and Isabel had looked carefully into the eight hundred years of Al-Andalus, under the administration of Muslim caliphs or Christian kings, both with the active and brilliant help of the Jewish community of Spain. It was as if they had studied the achievements of the past centuries in the arts, in poetry, music, science, and technology, and wanted just such energies in their own kingdom. It was as if they wanted to honor the accomplishments of the period and the wisdom of their own Christian forebears. In reading the Capitulations, one wants to salute the genius of two intelligent rulers, who at their moment of triumph looked into the past, so as to provision their nation for the future.

Even today, one can walk around the Albayzín and imagine the hope that must have arisen in these streets. A document full of justice, noteworthy for its fairness and decency, issued directly and personally by the monarchs, now guaranteed for all time the continuance and thriving of Al-Andalus, medieval Europe's culture of genius.

Ferdinand and Isabel lied. It was a lie of such horrific grandeur that we live today with the consequences. An important clue to the lie was in the one discordant note in the Capitulations:

48. The Jews native to Granada, Albayzín . . . and all other
places contained in these Capitulations, will benefit from
them, on condition that those who do not become Christians
cross to North Africa within three years counting from
December 8 of this year.

Isabel and Ferdinand formally took possession of the Alhambra
on January 2, 1492. In their new palace, they set to work immediately and in secret to draft an Edict of Expulsion for the entire Jewish
community of Spain. It was completed swiftly and signed on March
31, 1492. The edict was withheld for a month, then was proclaimed
publicly in Granada and throughout the country. The Jewish quarter
in Granada was to be demolished immediately. The Jews, all of them,
had three months to leave. All of their assets that could not be carried
had to be sold. Family houses were bartered for an ass; vineyards for
a piece of cloth. Even in the case of a sale, the Jews were forbidden to
take into exile any gold, silver, or coined money. What is more, the
Edict of Expulsion went on to say that, after the three months, if any
Christian "shall dare to receive, protect, defend, and hold publicly or
secretly any Jew or Jewess," then he would forfeit the entirety of his
wealth, possessions, royal grants, and inheritance. These absurd conditions effectively transferred the preponderance of Jewish wealth to
Christian hands. If they had wealth remaining, they were systematically robbed of it, by means of extortion rackets, embarkation fees,
looting of concealed assets, or cancellation of debts owed them. At
sea, pirates awaited them, and in North Africa, they were attacked
and sometimes enslaved.

To avoid such confiscation, there were, of course, numerous conversions, as there had been in the decades previously. But the edict

achieved its goal: Isabel and Ferdinand wiped out the oldest and most talented Jewish community in Europe, and one of the foremost in world history. And they did not rest content with such destruction. The Muslims were next, and the action was in the Albayzín.

The respect for Islam and the protection of property granted the Muslims was for ". . . now and for all time and forever." All time and forever turned out to be seven years. But for the Muslims, those seven years gave them hope. Hernando Talavera, the archbishop of Granada, and the count of Tendilla, the mayor of the city, worked with tact and dedication to see the Capitulations honored. Talavera, though a vitriolic anti-Semitic propagandist, thought that the visible grace of Christian practice would lead, in the long term, to the voluntary conversion of Muslims. He even counseled his priests to learn Arabic. There were disquieting signs, though. Especially the policy to isolate Muslims in their own neighborhood. If they lived in other parts of Granada, they were forcibly moved to the historic Albayzín, and the Christians there moved elsewhere with royal assistance. Ominously, this separation of non-Christians into their own ghettos had been the policy, slowly enforced, of Ferdinand and Isabel for over two decades.

Replacing Talavera in 1499, Cardenal Ximenes de Cisneros, confessor to Queen Isabel, had other ideas. Cisneros had been a key negotiator, in 1497, for Ferdinand and Isabel in the marriage contract between their daughter and the king of Portugal, Manuel. Portugal, like the rest of the Iberian peninsula, had at the time a well-established Muslim population. It also had the only remaining Jewish population in the Iberian peninsula. But the king and queen of Spain, with Cisneros as one of their key counselors, had a plan. As a condition of the marriage, they forced Manuel to promise not only

to expel the Jewish population, but—and this was unprecedented—
the Muslims as well. The terms of the expulsions we may recognize.
The Jews had to leave by a set date, they could depart only from
Lisbon, and those who did not meet the deadline were enslaved. Yet
there was a further condition: the authorities forbade the children of
Jewish families to depart with their parents; the children were to be
seized and taken away to be raised as Christians. As to the Muslims,
they were forced, in an astonishing and diabolical turn, to move to
. . . Spain! An exit fee was required, of course. We shall see the
fate prepared for them, to which preparation Cisneros now devoted
himself.

Ensconced in the Albayzín, Cisneros first distributed rich gifts to
Muslim leaders, to encourage conversion. When the results did not sat-
isfy him, he made it known that Muslims who did not convert would
risk imprisonment and torture. The reaction was what we would
expect: despair, disbelief, an incendiary atmosphere in the barrio.

Cisneros meant what he said. For he was not in Granada simply
to help in the spiritual administration of the city. He was there as part
of a powerful religious institution, invested with rampant new power
by Ferdinand and Isabel: the Supreme Council of the Inquisition.
Archbishop Ximenes Cisneros was Inquisitor General.

Cisneros was to go on to play a most prominent role in the government of Spain. He was a man of cunning, martial zeal, torrid
Christian conviction, and dark political genius. His central tenet was
simple: the Catholic church, bearing the teachings of a divine Jesus,
must save the souls of Muslims and Jews by forcing their conversion
and exterminating their culture. He rejected Talavera's interest in
Arabic and the printing of prayer books and hymnals in that language; "pearls before swine," he called it.

Because the Articles of Capitulation were so clear, Cisneros needed room to maneuver; that is, he needed to work as a provocateur. He proved to have a demonic gift for such initiatives. The Capitulations, for example, provided that women with ancestors who at any time were Christian could be questioned in the presence of witnesses. The idea was to induce them to return to Christianity. Cisneros, accordingly, sent agents, including a man fatefully named Barrionuevo, into the Albayzín to seek out the daughters and wives of Muslim families, on the pretext of advancing such questions. The families of the Albayzín viewed such actions as a violation of their honor and a transparent attempt to seize women for forced conversion. In one such incursion, Barrionuevo seized a young woman in the plaza (now called the Plaza de Abad) between the mosque and the hospital. She called out for help to those around her; a crowd gathered, freed her, and then turned on Barrionuevo. He was known to be an agent of the hated Cisneros, and he was seized and killed. Cisneros, when he got wind of the uprising, hid himself in another part of the Albayzín (in a place now called the Hospital de la Tiña), within the most fortified section of the barrio. When the fierce archbishop made his escape, he had what he wanted: a pretext for ethnic cleansing.

He commenced with that centerpiece of hatred, the book-burning. Cisneros ordered the confiscation of all copies of the Koran, including private copies looted by priests and soldiers from residents of the Albayzín. To this haul he added most of the contents of the Madrasa, which served as a kind of university library in the center of Granada. Cisnero's associates went on, in addition, to seize any religious tract, including the exquisite stories and poetry of the Sufis. Many precious manuscripts with beautiful borders and classic calligraphy, plated with gold and silver, were added to the pile in the lovely Plaza Bib-Rambla, near the central marketplace and by the side of the most famous school in the city. There, Cisneros had all the books incinerated. It amounted to more than five thousand volumes, though some estimates are astronomically higher. It was the first major book-burning after the surrender of Granada, that is, in newly Catholic Spain. But far from the last.

Some anguished residents of the Albayzín emigrated immediately. Some joined a revolt in a beautiful valley, the Alpujarras, high in the mountains above Granada. Ferdinand himself commanded the Christian troops, and one of his companions in arms, one Luis de Beaumont, in a battle near Andarax, in the eastern Alpujarra, took three thousand prisoners. He slaughtered them all and went on to blow up a nearby mosque with six hundred refugees, children and women, inside. These massacres soon were known throughout the Mediterranean. The revolt in the Alpujarras was put down in two bloody years.

The Muslims of the Albayzín, under constant pressure, with some of their numbers threatened, imprisoned, or tortured, began to convert in large numbers. By early 1501, there was hardly a Muslim left. The culture, eight hundred years old, of course remained, with its public baths, distinctive dress, culinary specialties, and its gift for music and love of dance. And because the conversions were forced, many Muslims were only nominal Christians. In the Albayzín, many families carried on their traditional way of life.

In the same year as these forced conversions, Ferdinand and Isabel issued another edict that required the Muslims of most of the rest of Spain, specifically in Castile and Leon, to become Christians or go into exile. The rules that applied to exiles had the usual malignant absurdity: they had a year to leave. They could take their possessions, but no gold or silver. The exiles could not go elsewhere in Spain, nor to North Africa, nor to any territories under control of the Ottomans. They could go, then, to Egypt. But they could only sail to Egypt from the Bay of Biscay, in the north of Spain. Unfortunately, almost no ships sailed to Egypt from the Bay of Biscay. Why would they?

It was a program to force a final round of conversions. The efforts of Cisneros in the Albayzín had proved to be a deliberate test run for all of Spain. Since the fall of Granada had completed the conquests of the Christian armies, Granada had tremendous symbolic resonance. Accordingly, the Albayzín, historic center of the city, with its concentrated Muslim population, had been dealt with first. Now, in the following years, Ferdinand, Isabel, and their successors issued a further series of proclamations. Let us list a range of them, with a view to seeing the progress of the royal will:

1502: *Edict of Conversion: all Muslims must convert to Christianity, or go into exile; Muslims remaining in Spain are to be enslaved. Muslims are made subject to the Inquisition.*

1511: *Moorish converts forbidden to bear arms or carry knives. All books in Arabic are to be surrendered; those having to do with Islamic law or religion are to be burnt. Tailors were fined for making Moorish clothing; butchers who prepared meat according to Islamic practice (called halal) could have their property confiscated. Property could not be passed to children in accordance with Islamic law, nor could former Muslims sell their property.*

1526: The Edict of Granada: complete prohibition of all customs of Moorish life. All Moorish baths outlawed and closed. The owning of slaves, the wearing of any Moorish clothing (even amulets), the dyeing of hands with henna, and the circumcision of infants is forbidden. In exchange for a payment to the Crown, open abuse of Moors in the street and random sacking of their houses is to stop. Principal Andalusian office of the Inquisition moved from Jaen to Granada.

1565: The Synod of Granada: all previous royal edicts confirmed. All aspects of Moorish life forbidden: baths, Arabic books, social ceremonies linked to Islam, traditional rituals such as fasting, and Moorish music and dancing.

So the expulsion in 1492 of the Jewish community of Spain was a prelude to the extinction of the Muslim community. The goal was to tear out the culture—its religion, customs, traditions, ceremonies—by the roots. The means were royal decrees, close surveillance, harassment, humiliation, confiscation of property, imprisonment, torture, and capital punishment. We read, for instance, of people beaten and jailed for not attending church, of Moriscos (that is, Muslims who had been forced to convert to Christianity) being coerced to drink liquor and eat pork. And the Inquisition was fighting, all this while, for exclusive power to enforce the edicts. It was a power they would use with methodical gusto.

This attempt to eradicate a whole culture proceeded by fits and starts. The Moriscos paid bribes, maneuvered, cultivated powerful friends, and continued to make a crucial contribution to the economy of the city. These men and women, after all, were now all Christians.

So they, in theory, were asking only for respect for their centuries of cultural heritage, since their religious heritage had already been abolished. The partial success of these efforts by the Moriscos explains the need, on occasion, to confirm the royal edicts.

But confirmed they were. In the course of the 1500s, the power of the Inquisition increased. And the doctrine of *limpieza de sangre*—blood purity—took on a central and defining importance. At the same time, the Morisco community's knowledge of horticulture, irrigation, silk-weaving, construction, and commerce seemed less crucial, given the weighty current of gold and silver arriving from the New World. By 1567, in the Albayzín, the newly confirmed edicts began to be enforced without mercy. This time, no payment to a high official, nor any political deal, nor any advocacy could help. Rumors circulated that children of Moriscos would be taken from their families. The Albayzín churned with rumor, terror, bitterness, despair. The Moriscos assembled secretly, seeking a way to resist. Apocalypse was in the air. Such mad foreboding is almost always wrong. But not this time; soon, apocalypse was on the ground.

The Morisco community in the Albayzín, along with Morisco settlements in the Alpujarras, planned a campaign of armed resistance. Cautious souls voiced strong arguments against such a rebellion, but a doomed plan took form. By the end of 1568, the community, as though driven insane by seven decades of broken promises, confiscated property, forced conversions, book-burnings, and secret trials of the Inquisition, finally revolted and began a war that was to last two years. Called the Second Granada War (1568–1570), most of the fighting was in the Alpujarras, where the Christian armies, heavily armed and with pathetic, fractious leaders, fought mobile bands of Moriscos, poor and disorganized, with their own pathetic, fractious leaders. There were repellent massacres on both sides before the might of the Spanish military prevailed.

The Albayzín stood no chance. It was the biggest Morisco neighborhood in Granada. Granada symbolized the final conquest of Spain by Christian armies, and the city served as the center of power and religious authority for the whole region. In March of 1569, the authorities massacred all one hundred and ten Morisco prisoners held in the prison at the base of the neighborhood, near Plaza Nueva. Later that year, soldiers entered the Albayzín and tore it to pieces. There is no other way to say it.

Two companies of soldiers entered Plaza de Abad, in the heart of the barrio; another five hundred soldiers circled the neighborhood. In the attack, the troops entered and looted houses, then wrecked whatever was left of them. They plugged or poisoned the fountains, water troughs, and famous *aljibes*. They pillaged stocks of grain, destroyed the market stalls, stores, workshops. In the autumn of 1570, they seized all boys and men between the ages of 10 and 70 and imprisoned them in the churches, then later in a hospital. In total, the count of prisoners was about 4,000. Contemporary accounts record the scene:

> *It was a miserable show, to see so many men of different ages, with heads bowed, hands crossed, faces washed in tears, their demeanor wretched and sad, since they were leaving their cherished houses, their families, their way of life, their farms, and all the good that they had . . .*
>
> *. . . they had only the most terrible lamentations, having known prosperity, the fine order and pleasure of their*

houses, carmenes, and orchards, where [they] had all their
recreations and amusements, and within a few days they
had seen everything laid waste and destroyed, for matters
had come to such a bad end, that it seemed a good thing to
subject [their] most happy city to just such destruction . . .

The Spanish army marched these men out of Granada and into the winter of 1570. Forcibly exiled, and now scattered around the country, mostly within Castile, we lose sight of most of them. We know that hundreds of them died of exposure on the forced march to their new towns. Of the fate of their wives and children, we know little, except that the youngest passed into the service of the so-called "Old Christians" of Granada.

In 1571, royal agents visited the Albayzín to inventory the houses and goods that remained, so that they might be formally confiscated and given to Christian families. They found, out of the many thousands of houses on this hillside, less than three hundred occupied. The livelihood of the workers lay buried in the rubble. The authorities had tried to keep in the barrio workers with knowledge of silk-weaving, orchards, and the water systems. Of the rich scope of skilled professions that had for so long enriched Granada, little remained. The birth rate, measured by baptisms, plummeted. And whatever the enticement offered by the Crown— the gift of confiscated houses, cheap rents, and the like—there were few takers. The population continued its decline, from its high in the 1400s of around forty-five thousand to twenty-seven thousand in 1561, then, after the sacking of the barrio, falling disastrously. Some observers of the time doubted the survival of the Albayzín.

KING SOLOMON COMES TO THE ALBAYZÍN

But then in 1595, at the edge of the barrio, came an event so improbable that it is small praise to call it a miracle: a discovery that bid fair to make Granada into a worldwide center of Christian pilgrimage and worship, and at the same time bring Christian practice into closer alignment with the worship of Allah.

Just at the eastern edge of the Albayzín, an excavation brought to light a series of strange oval leaden tablets, all with Arabic writing. Many of the tablets bore the Seal of Solomon. Often, the excavators found bones and ashes near the tablets. Over the next four years, there were more discoveries in the same district, until about two dozen tablets in all had been collected. They had magnetic titles like "Book of the Truth of the Gospels," "On the Nature of Angels and Their Power," "The Book of the Ceremonies of Jesus and Mary," "On the Essence of God," and "The Book of the Maxims of Saint Mary." The ecclesiastical authorities in Granada examined the tablets and declared them to be authentic writings from the first century, an inconceivably precious treasure. They held in their hands new books of Holy Scripture and actual accounts of conversations of the Apostles. Most electrifying of all, the tablets held declarations and guidance in the beautiful voice of the Blessed Virgin Mary herself. We hear Mary giving answers to Peter, addressing in detail the subtleties of belief and the secrets of the soul.

The findings transfixed the church in Granada. Here, in their own town, a stunning addition to the New Testament had come to light. The texts supported the Immaculate Conception of Mary, a doctrine held intensely in Granada. They roiled Catholic Europe and aroused lively interest in Protestant Europe. The archbishop of Granada, leading a synod, lent his unqualified support to the texts and the relics that accompanied them. As late as 1609, a royal commission that had the king's confessor, a cardinal, the Inquisitor General, and other august members was found in favor of the relics and did not disavow the text of the lead tablets.

Despite the boisterous support of Granada's Catholics, the lead books had certain oddities that one might think would have made their interpreters dubious. For one thing, the Virgin Mary and Saint Peter spoke in Arabic. For another, the lead books omitted any reference to Jesus as the Son of God; he was, rather, the Spirit of God. Curious statements abound in the text, such as "There is no God but Allah, and the Messiah is the Spirit of Allah. The whole book is the truth of the Messiah Jesus." And there is much else, all of it tending, like lines in a drawing to establish perspective, to a single point. The point was that the theological content of the lead books did away with elements in Catholic doctrine that Muslims could not accept; yet at the same time, the books affirmed the divine knowledge of Jesus and the transcendental importance of Mary. It was, at the last moment, a gambit to bring Islam and Christianity into more concord, so as to revive at least some part of the *convivencia*—the coexistence of Christians and Muslims—now in its death throes in Spain. What bold dreamer could have come up with so game, wild, and sweeping a strategy? Probably a converted Muslim, living in Granada and protected by his value to the realm. Whoever he was, he tried something magnificent: to divert singlehandedly the whole current of history and send it off in a more peaceable direction.

Ironically, the core point is not far from the position of the Arian Christians throughout the Mediterranean and the Arian Visigoths of Spain. Both the lead books and Arian theology hold that Jesus, rather than being divine, was divinely inspired. So we have a bizarre

continuity in Spain, played out in our very own Albayzín, that runs
from the religious devotion of Visigothic kings of the fourth century
to mystical lead tablets found in the sixteenth century, bearing the
words of Mary the mother of Jesus.

The Vatican was having none of it. Just as the Arians had been
destroyed, so the church weighed in with its dissent and control. The
church let the pandemonium die down and finally banned any talk
about the texts in 1682.

In the meantime, the Spanish monarchy had followed up its expulsion in 1492 of the Jews with the formal expulsion, in 1609, of the
remaining Moriscos in Spain. It was the final trump of Christianity
and the last step in the dismantling of Al-Andalus.

THE SEVERAL CENTURIES OF DECOMPOSITION

What did this mean for the Albayzín? The population continued its
eclipse. By 1620, only six thousand people lived in the Albayzín,
less than a sixth of its population in 1492. The Crown had tried to
repopulate the barrio and rescue its economy. Its efforts melted away
into failure, to the point where we read of the nuns of the convent
of Santa Isabel, in the heart of the barrio, writing to Philip II for aid.
They wrote because they were dying of hunger.

One historian writes that the Albayzín had suffered

> . . . a radical depopulation, given the scarcity of Old
> Christians living there, and the total desolation of the urban
> space that had in large measure sustained over centuries the
> wealth and prestige of the city of Granada.

Reports to the King in the seventeenth century conclude that

> *. . . the rents from the property confiscated from the*
> *Moriscos cannot make up for the depopulation caused by*
> *the massive deportation of the Morisco community, given*
> *the current lack of revenue, and the difficulty and the fall*
> *in agricultural yield . . . so that neither the conservation of*
> *the cropland, nor the systems of irrigation, nor the houses*
> *themselves can be guaranteed; on the contrary, they now are*
> *falling into abandon and ruin . . .*

Spain was, during this period, ruling a considerable portion of Europe and the New World. But empire did not translate into prosperity for the people of Spain. The tonnage of gold and silver that arrived from the colonies funded military adventures, the violent defense and promotion of the True Faith, and the payment of vast debt incurred to carry on with such escapades.

In the Albayzín, especially the part nearest the Darro River, Old Christian families received grants of land and constructed seigniorial houses. In the rest of the barrio, the mosques had become churches, and the hospital was converted into a monastery. Convents received important real estate, including part of the old Moorish palace where the mother of Boabdil, the last king of Granada, had lived. Most of these convents were cloistered, that is, closed to all the world, save the priests. Scraggly plants took root in the rubble. So the Albayzín became a barrio of rubble, silence, hidden nuns, fierce churches, tormented memory, and poverty.

THE CENTURIES OF Spanish empire ran forward, with their wealth and power—and the grotesque squandering of that wealth and power. Arriving in the middle of the nineteenth century, what did the Albayzín look like? Here is the report of Lady Louisa Tenison, an English traveler:

> *Many are the curious old houses in the Albaycin, which still bear traces of their Moorish origin. The palaces of the Moorish chieftains are now the wretched habitations of the poorest inhabitants of Granada, and squalid ragged children people the patios . . . The population is gradually diminishing, and within the last few years many of the houses in the quarter have been pulled down, their owners finding the ground more profitable when converted into gardens.*

Or the simple declaration of a Spanish geographer and statistician:

> *. . . almost all of this opulent barrio of the Arabs has been converted into a pile of ruins.*

Some superb buildings from the Middle Ages had survived, notably the Maristan, the hospital in the lower Albayzín, whose site was just below our *carmen*. In the middle 1800s, the city pulled it down. Around the same time, the Darro, where it enters Plaza Nueva at the foot of the Albayzín, was paved over. The river, enclosed in a tunnel, was channeled through the center of the city. This dismal decision was accompanied by massive demolition to drive a grand avenue through the city, cutting between the Albayzín and the city center. Ingeniously, the avenue impoverished the Albayzín even further, which was tough to do. The poor who lived in the demolished buildings were thrown out, and the city built showy apartments befitting such a grand throughway. They made Granada look less Andalusian and more like any other European city of the time.

Moreover, the money, the commerce, and the holy attentions of the Catholic church went downtown, on the other side of the new and noble avenue.

Having nowhere else to go, more of the displaced poor moved to the Albayzín, into ruined houses, abandoned patios, makeshift rooms, caves. They lived among the nuns and a few country houses of the affluent families of Granada. The Albayzín, as its buildings crumbled, was turning back into land for orchards and cropland. What had been the historic beginning and center of Granada became now, improbably, the country. It being the country, some of the well-to-do families began restoring or building houses: the first *carmenes* in the Albayzín. It was a perfect fit, since *carmenes* were the classic country houses of Al-Andalus. And since the revival of romantic interest in the Alhambra was now underway, beautiful geometric tiles were introduced to new *carmenes*, horseshoe arches, or decorative woodwork. In our own house, whose deeds go back to 1862, in the room we call the *cuarto arabe*, we find the Star of David and tiles with Arabic script praising Allah, and, surrounding one window, tiny columns that turned out to be replicas of columns in the famous Patio de los Leones of the Alhambra. Someone had done a lot of homework.

WE ARRIVE IN the 1920s. The Albayzín, heart of Granada, with a heritage of more than two and half millennia, once full of palaces and families, bathhouses and bakeries, silk-weavers and gardeners and potters, cynosure of the beauties of Al-Andalus—this barrio falls, abused and forgotten, into a new century. All its history is present, yet darkly, as a mood of blood and wonder. We are fortunate to have the observations of the poet Frederico García Lorca,

from the 1920s. He is a famously close and lyrical observer, so let
us quote him at length:

> *The streets are narrow, with strange broken-down stairways,*
> *like undulating tentacles that twist wearily, capriciously, and*
> *lead to dead ends whence we see the tremendous snowy peaks*
> *of the Sierras, or the splendid, definitive harmony of the*
> *Vega. In some parts the streets are like strange pathways of*
> *fear and ominous disquiet, bound in by walls blanketed with*
> *jasmine . . . We hear the barking of dogs, and distant voices*
> *calling someone in tones of hopeless sensuality. The streets*
> *are like whirlpools, with stairways impossible to climb, full of*
> *big rough stones, walls eaten by time; on the stairs sit tragic*
> *and dumbstruck women, looking brazenly around . . .*
>
> *. . . Leaving aside the mutilations suffered by the barrio at*
> *the hands of some granadinos (if we may call them that), it*
> *has kept its special mood. To walk through its streets is to*
> *be in a stage set for legend.*
>
> *. . . the people of these parts, so sensitive and fearful, invent*
> *stories about the dead and the ghosts of winter, spirits and*
> *hobgoblins who go out in the middle of moonless nights*
> *. . . Muttering old women and roving prostitutes see them,*
> *and talk about them later, frightened and superstitious. In*
> *this criss-crossing of streets lives an Albayzín timorous and*
> *fantastic, with howling of dogs and sorrowful guitars, dark*
> *nights among white walls; the tragic, superstitious Albayzín,*
> *with its witches casting spells and using black magic, its*
> *strange gypsy ceremonies, its cabalistic signs and amulets;*

with souls in agony, and pregnant women, and old prostitutes who know the evil eye, and bloody curses, and passion and seduction.

Here also are streets with cloistered convents, white, simple, with their blunt bell-towers and high dusty windows, touching the eaves with their swallows and dove's nests . . . streets that hear the silvery melodies of the Darro, and the romances sung by the moving leaves of the forest of the Alhambra. This is the Albayzín romantic, distinguished, lovely, the Albayzín of gateways into carmenes and to the grounds of convents like Santa Isabel; the Albayzín of fountains, arbors, cypresses, decorated ironwork, full moons, ancient music, the Albayzín of abundance, organs playing in convents, of Arab patios, of big pianos, roomy salons thick with the scent of lavender.

Here is a tragedy of contrasts. On one solitary street is heard a convent organ playing sweetly, and the divine salutation of an Ave Maria said in softly feminine voices. Across from the convent, a man in a blue shirt curses shockingly, as he feeds his goats. Further on, some prostitutes with dark circles under jet-black eyes, their bodies awkward and deformed by lust, give vent in harsh voices to obscenities of magnificent vulgarity; next to them a delicate little girl in rags sings a pious song of the nuns.

All of this lets us know an atmosphere of infinite anguish, streets on which an oriental curse has fallen.

. . . There is a strong smell of earth, of moisture, incense, wine, billy goats, urine, dung, honeysuckle . . .

García Lorca spent time, in the next years, in a beautiful *car-men*—called the Carmen de Alonso Cano—just up the hill from where we live. It's a classic, with a big, terraced, south-facing garden, and at the back a tall house with big windows looking out toward the Alhambra. In that *carmen*, he drank the fresh, remarkable sparkling water from the mountain spring called Aynadamar. Near that very spring, a few years later, early one dawn in August, Spanish fascists would murder him. And his books would be banned. But that is another story.

Writing here in the barrio at this juncture in its history, I would dearly like to tell my readers that the rotting Albayzín began to recover its heritage and wake up to the millennium of beauties hidden under the rubble. Instead, things got worse, as though history held some leering, fateful grudge against this place.

The poverty, crime, hunger, and hopelessness of the Albayzín led slowly to rebellion. Groups of anarchists took root in the barrio as early as the 1870s; radical wings of unions found good recruiting grounds there. Taken together, we know them by the mouth-filling name of anarcho-syndicalists. With the founding of the Second Republic in Spain in 1930, with its democracy, civil rights, and commitment to an open society, such groups came out into the open.

In the short life of the Second Republic, from 1930 to 1936, Granada suffered tumultuous years. The government moved swiftly to organize a modern state, with liberty of worship, separation of church and state, the elimination of mandatory religious instruction, and the like; such actions discomfited the church, which showed its contempt of the new democracy. The church was understood to be allied with reactionary military and political forces in Spain, which included the Falangists, a fascist political group; and this alliance deepened the hostility of those loyal to the Republic. In the Albayzín, the church's scornful treatment of the barrio set the stage for a bitter upheaval.

After an attempted military coup in Madrid in August of 1932, the city suffered a slow-motion explosion. Demonstrators marched on the house of a local right-wing count implicated in the coup. Snipers guarding the house of the count shot and killed two demonstrators. In the aftermath of the two murders, the demonstrations turned to street fighting, and the conflict grew in hatred and hopelessness. The anarcho-syndicalists felt themselves, rightfully, under attack from the armed security of conservative families, and from the Falangists, already organized in Granada; the propertied class felt themselves, rightfully, under siege and took refuge in military dreams and the declarations of the ecclesiastical bulletin of the local Catholic church, which declared private property "sacred."

In the Albayzín, the anarchists wanted a soft target, where they could show their rage but not be killed. There were two available: churches and convents, mostly unprotected. The barrio was full of them, since in the years after 1499 Cardinal Cisneros had forcibly converted the mosques into churches, and thereafter the kings of Spain had made large grants of land to found convents and monasteries so as to replace the Nasrid palaces, the Moorish hospital, and ruined houses. The Albayzín was full of monks, priests, and nuns, in part because no one else but the poor could be persuaded to live there.

Over the next four years, through 1936, marauding bands pulled down crosses in plazas, set upon church doors with hatchets, and broke into one church after another. Now and again they gathered the pews, tables, altars, doors, cabinets from the sacristy—anything flammable—all in a heap, soaked them in gasoline, and set the whole on fire. If the flames rose high and hot enough, the roof of the church caught fire and brought down most of the building.

In our rambles around the Albayzín, we sometimes passed the church of San Luis, which was burnt to the ground during those years. The destruction was so complete, it was never rebuilt. Just two walls stand, full of weeds, and the bell tower is full of bats. The present-day Church of the Savior (once the central Mosque of Granada) still has posted within photos of the fire that devastated the building.

The military insurrection against the Spanish democracy began July 17, 1936, with a speech by Francisco Franco from Spanish Morocco. The military garrison in Granada was one of the first to betray the Second Republic, taking over the city just three days later. Soldiers shot the mayor—García Lorca's brother-in-law—and the new government formed death squads.

Nobody likes to see history run the same tape over and over, but here we go: to subdue the Albayzín during the insurrection of 1568–70, the Spanish military bombarded the Albayzín with catapults and cannon placed by the church of San Gregorio Alto and on the terrace of the Alhambra. In 1936, the fascist rebels placed artillery in exactly the same places, to fire on what they called the "red barrio." For good measure, military planes bombed the Albayzín. As in 1570, troops surrounded and invaded the barrio. As in 1570, the military used the churches to imprison the residents. Examined there, the authorities led away those thought to be dangerous agitators, took them up behind the Alhambra, and shot them.

One more parallel: beginning in 1499, Archbishop Cisneros, Ferdinand, and Isabel had turned loose the Catholic Church and its Inquisition, backed with military force, to remake the barrio. And then in the years from 1936 through 1939, the leading newspaper of Granada wrote about how the fascist program of "rechristianisa-tion" of the Albayzín would take up once again the historic efforts of Ferdinand, Isabel, and their noble successors. By the time 1939 rolled around, the archbishop of Granada set forth incisively his under-standing of the task at hand:

> *We must redeem the Albayzín from Godless Marxism and its detestable work, which has laid waste to our spirit and forgotten the most exalted aspirations of the soul. We must detoxify the Albayzín of this venom ingested over so many years, as a result of a preposterous, stupid, destructive communism. We need to raise up the Albayzín culturally, morally, and spiritually.*

Unfortunately for the reasoning of the archbishop, there was little communist influence in the Albayzín, but plentiful poverty, sickness, and despair. But communism was one of the preferred demons featured in the militant dreams and homicidal rhetoric of newly victorious fascist Spain, whose flag, of course, was adorned by the emblems of Ferdinand and Isabel. General Franco himself saw his power and his country directly in relation to the Catholic monarchs:

> *The glory of Spain coincides always with the unity of our faith and our nation; and our decadence with their separation.*

> *In this way, the national unity forged by the Catholic Monarchs was connected directly to the spread of our faith, and our military went forth with their flags held close to the Holy Cross.*

> *Spain is the nation chosen by God . . .*

The dictatorship of Franco, in league with their Catholic allies, rebuilt slowly most of the burnt churches. And over the next decades, brave investors, or families looking for dirt-cheap real estate, took up residence again in the Albayzín. The municipal government proposed valiant plans, wrote long reports, assessed the historical legacy before them. Yet aside from some private investment in the barrio, the reports and plans and studies yielded pathetically little to people trying to make a life in the barrio. The population, which had risen to almost twenty-eight thousand by 1970, again commenced a precipitous fall as new suburbs opened up, offering apartments with running water, plumbing, heat, walls sealed against the weather, and other persuasive advantages. People bolted from the Albayzín. By 1990, we hear this refrain, as though sung in a bizarre echo chamber of the centuries:

In fact, the Albayzín has arrived at the present day nearly at the limit of survival, with a social and physical degradation practically absolute.

THE REAWAKENING

The establishment of the Albayzín as a World Heritage Site in 1994 was not the culmination of a program of care, action, investment, and recognition of a cultural and artistic heritage unique in Europe. It was a last-minute end-run around catastrophe, led by a brave, small group of savvy Spaniards whose judgment was honored by UNESCO. Democratic Spain awoke. The European Union sent tens of millions of investment dollars to help in the recovery of the barrio. Residents got money for renovation; families rediscovered its powerful beauties, moved in, reconstructed gardens, and restored ancient houses. In our few years here, the effort has gathered momentum: no fewer than eight old houses, immediately around us, are being renovated. And there are hundreds more throughout the barrio.

Such is the activity that one afternoon, when I asked my little daughter what she wanted for her third birthday, she replied immediately, "A jackhammer."

WHAT CAN WE make of this tempestuous history, so full of sweetness and anguish? After our reading through the history of the Albayzín, we walked through its streets with a sense of miracle. It's not just that it survived; it's that, after such extremes of exaltation and ruin, it survived with such irrepressible gift-giving power. To do so, it needed, like all of us, a healthy dose of luck. It makes us think of the unlikelihood of every blessing in our lives—the random meeting that reconstructs a life; a poem in a tattered book that rocks the heart.

I have never known a place of such concentrated joy. This is where walking is like flying. It is ordinary and offers a fantastification of daily life. It is simple but holds a spirit decanted over centuries. The pleasures are common but leave us in thankfulness and wonderment.

More and more, walking through the crisscrossing, tilted, banking, serendipitous streets, it felt like something more than being in a neighborhood. It was like being in a mind, where history is musing a secret way forward and, despite everything, offering to everyone whispered and hopeful overtures.

In love with this place, we kept trying to understand. First, our own garden, then, the history of the barrio. Finally, we knew that to see the place in its savory detail, we needed to make a journey into the mystery of Al-Andalus.

Al-Andalus: Notes on a Hidden, Lustrous, Indispensable Era

*I*N THE ALBAYZÍN, we lived face-to-face with the Middle Ages. The Alhambra, soaring on its promontory, had its beginning in the early 1200s. And our whole barrio had kept, through its thriving and catastrophe, the basic street pattern of a medieval village.

Gabriella and I used to go whimsically about the lanes, sure that some of the ancient doors opened into another century. Sometimes we sat together before a wall of white plaster, where, as though watching a movie, we conjured the daily life of another epoch. Such fun gave us many laughs, as we rambled and whispered our way through the afternoon. But all these antics did not undo my wretched ignorance of the period.

Let us define what we mean by Al-Andalus: it is the period of history spanning almost eight hundred years, from 711 to 1492, on the Iberian peninsula, under the administration of either Islamic emirs or caliphs, or Christian kings and queens. Whatever the faith of the powerful in whatever region of Iberia, Al-Andalus is a distinctive cultural space. When we arrived in Spain, I had studied the reign of Ferdinand and Isabel, their triumphant unification of Spain, and the explorations of Columbus. But I knew little about the Islamic, Christian, and Jewish leaders and even less about the scholars of the period.

But the conjured movies and magic doors led me to shelves of books, and to the houses of our neighbors, and to the history of gardens and of our cherished neighborhood. And thence to the history of Al-Andalus.

Just as the Albayzín is a study in unlikelihood, so the history of Al-Andalus is itself improbable; so improbable that, until recently, it hardly existed at all. Most of us learn something about medieval European history, but in general, the material covers in more depth the history of countries other than Spain. There is a simple reason for this: to study Christian Europe of the Middle Ages, you needed, principally, Latin, probably Greek, and the vernacular language of the region you studied. To study Al-Andalus, you needed not only Latin and medieval Spanish, but a mastery of Hebrew and Arabic, plus a willingness to understand the contributions of Arabic and Jewish culture. But scholars with such a sweep of languages and interests were rarely to be found, except in concept, like the saber-toothed tiger.

There was another problem, an old-fashioned one: the venom of propaganda and the energy of hatred. Over hundreds of years, the influential medieval chronicles, in combination with religious prophecy, came potently together with political make-believe, military glamor, and righteous conviction, to ensure the virtual erasure of Al-Andalus. Literacy in Christian Spain was for centuries concentrated among the politically influential, and above all among the clergy, who were central and powerful political players.

A medieval chronicle is just an account of historical events, without any real effort to state the facts. It's a wondrous form, full of ideological gusto and narrative invention, just because of the liberty of interpretation allowed. When we read them, we learn a lot about the writer, and about the power and politics of the time. But usually we learn almost nothing about what actually happened. So it was in Spain, where the chronicles tended to be traditional. That is, they took their origins to be the Chronicles of the Old Testament, and they sought to fit the events of their period into a Christian framework. So we get a lot of prophecy and apocalyptic obsessions, simmered with a desire to see their own faith triumphant in Spain and worldwide.

In Spanish chronicles, this desire heated into craving, and history is cooked up before our eyes. So we have, nine centuries after the death of Jesus, the story of James, his brother, bringing the faith to Spain. Of course, James was martyred in Jerusalem a few decades after Jesus, but no matter. The chroniclers whipped up another version, in which his corpse floated preposterously in a marble boat all the way to northern Iberia, then to be dragged onshore by divinely commanded wild bulls, only to be discovered later by one Pelayo, a peasant who saw the heavenly light streaming from a field. This wild version stood for a while. Then a later chronicle upped the ante by declaring boldly that it was Charlemagne himself (or rather, a comic-book fantasy of Charlemagne, fluent in Arabic) who had found the tomb of James. But that was not the end of it. This new version, penned by a mysterious cleric impersonating a French archbishop named Turpin, was itself modified by another cleric, one with more financial acumen. He added on his own admonitions, in which he was delighted to report that the world's Christians were instructed to visit and to offer some portion of their wealth to the Cathedral of

Santiago, the home of the cult of St. James. Thus the tale makes a neat compound of serial forgery in hot pursuit of power and money.

As if this were not enough, St. James soon metamorphosed into St. James the Moorslayer, who would on occasion gallop wildly down from the heavens on a white horse to fight for the armies of the True Faith.

It all worked marvelously. Based on such fluffy inventions, the town of Santiago de Compostela—heart of the cult of St. James— became then and has remained an important place of pilgrimage.

Yet the chronicles that created Santiago de Compostela made, as it turned out, relatively modest claims. Other, more far-reaching texts took on crucial weight in the centuries that preceded the fall of Granada. Many of these texts have a frothy mix of prophecy and apocalyptic fever, yet they provided a narrative foundation for the royal house of Ferdinand and Isabel, as they came to conquer and dominate Spain.

It was a foundation many hundreds of years in the making. It used chronicles, myths, hagiographic texts, political puff pieces, apocalyptic essays, and collected speculation from all over Europe, yet made a consistent, emotionally potent story all about Spain. Scholars have gotten to the heart of the story by sifting through the whole wilderness of texts and looking for the narrative core, which is extraordinary. We will sketch it in a few paragraphs, and it is my solemn duty to assure the reader that I am not making anything up.

Here we go: certain prophecies originally from a sibyl or from Merlin himself foretold the life of a king of Castile that would be called the Lion King, or the Hidden One, or the Bat. This king would conquer all of Spain, and his son would go on to conquer Africa, Asia, and Jerusalem. So would it be that the Lion King would bring all history home to Spain, because it was Spain, and no other country, that had been chosen by God to carry out His will. It was the Spanish Christians who were God's chosen people, and they must take the leading roles in God's drama on earth as he brought humankind to the end of time, with all its terror and salvation.

Why was a king of Spain right for this task? Because after the fall of Troy, Hercules had come to Spain, conquered the country, and ruled it as a great and just prince. Hercules made his nephew the first king of Spain, and all the royalty of Spain were of his blood. And it was blood of Biblical worth, since Hercules was himself descended from Noah. Not only that, but Isabel herself was of the line of the Old Testament King David, the family line from which, as everyone knew very well indeed, would come the Messiah. As to Ferdinand, he occasionally styled himself "King of Jerusalem."

So there we have it: a Spanish King and Queen identified by God to lead their chosen people in the conquest of Spain, and destined to begin the final triumph of Christian culture with the capture of Jerusalem. These victories would commence a golden age, governed by Spanish royalty of messianic destiny. And so would all of human history come home to its fateful and blessed conclusion.

The Spanish pope of the day endorsed this rapt fantasy, writing after the fall of Granada about being in the eleventh hour, the approach to the last days. And of course this vision had little use for Jews or Muslims, who had both suffered the inevitable defeat of a debased, inferior culture and faith. The Christian church was declared to be the new Israel, and the Jewish Messiah was unmasked: he was the Antichrist. All this phantasmagoria and grandeur came together splendidly in the conquest of Granada: it was the decisive moment in which the future came into view, as Satan, the Jews, the

Muslims, and the Antichrist all suffered a defeat that would lead history to its culmination. Ferdinand and Isabel were not just the saviors of Spain. They were the great-souled rulers, finally in place, who were fit to confront the fabulous days at the end of history.

In coordination with the story, the ignorant and bellicose Visigoths were recast as exalted ancestors, virile and fierce in spirit, who had established a Christian kingdom in Spain and then lost it to the infidel, only to wait eight hundred years for redemption.

It is not easy, so many centuries later, to credit this story that Spain told to itself, for itself, about itself. However feverish and ornate, to them it was more than a story. It was the wisdom of deeply spiritual men who looked into history and wanted to clarify for all the course of God's work on earth and in their own time. In fact it proved to be the story whose power would all but erase from the narrative of Spanish history the accomplishments, the culture, the science, the music, and the literature of Al-Andalus. It was the Big Lie, in a medieval version breathtaking for its scope, ambition, and success. The effort stands, even today, as a classically obnoxious example of how religion and politics, in league together, can with consummate political artistry set out to replace real history with a new, fraudulent version. After the taking of Granada in 1492, the expulsion of the Jews, the punishments of the Inquisition, and the ethnic cleansing and final expulsion of the Moriscos, the history of the Middle Ages in Spain was reconceived as a vulgar martial and religious epic, an ancient and fateful holy work: the redemption of Iberia. Even through the twentieth century, we can follow the remarkable, feline activity of academics who have tried to keep in place a modest version of this historical fantasy, in which barbarous Muslims invaded Spain in 711 but did not alter its fundamental Catholic character and destiny, which came roaring back in 1492 to rightful prominence. In fact, with some few exceptions, some version of this story seems to have dominated teaching in Spain and held sway in the public imagination until the fall of Spanish fascism and the death of General Franco—he of the "National Catholicism"—in 1975. And beyond. As late as 2004, the prime minister of Spain, Jose Maria Aznar, could with a straight face declare how in the eighth century, "Spain was invaded by the Moors, and refused to become just another piece of the Islamic world."

It is a stunning centuries-long run of contempt, and it means that most of what we know about Al-Andalus has become available only in the last several decades. Much more will be discovered, but we walked our barrio in thankfulness to the many scholars who have begun to teach us about this splendid period. Let us, together, pass through one of the strange doors in the Albayzín and look into another age.

And where might we look? Let us, to begin, visit a workshop in Toledo in the thirteenth century.

THE REBIRTH OF BOOKS
IN THE CONVIVENCIA

The workshop is a room of stone provided by a Christian king, Alphonso X, known to history as Alphonso the Wise. At a large wood table piled with books sit two scholars, one of them reading aloud slowly from a text in Arabic, translating it as he speaks into Castilian; the other man listens and writes down his own translation, translating the Castilian into Latin. Aiding them in their task are editors and researchers, who come and go as needed. It is a slow process, and there are many pauses to clarify, to review, to dispute.

Many of the terms in Arabic have no exact equivalent, and a new word must be coined for the translation. It is laborious, intelligent, patient work; slowly the translation takes form.

What books do they translate? In Toledo principally, but also among the cities in the region where good libraries and royal patronage are available, the books in the hands of these men span a phenomenal range of subjects. First among them we must list Euclid's *Elements*, one of the key advances in human history, and one of the books in wide use in Al-Andalus. Euclid had been translated into Arabic in Baghdad by an assembly of scholars first organized by Haroun al-Rashid and carried on by his son, who created an academy called the House of Wisdom, a crucial source of books for Al-Andalus.

In the House of Wisdom worked Al-Khwarizimi, a ninth-century astronomer and mathematician who wrote his books principally in Baghdad. His name gives us the word *algorithm*, and he is honored as the father of algebra. Al-Khwarizimi's work on astronomy centered on the refinement of astronomical tables used to calculate and understand the motions of the heavens. It was none other than Adelard of Bath, seeking "truth based on reasoning and not doctrine," who translated into Latin the entirety of the tables, which were studied throughout Europe. But even more important was the book of Al-Khwarizimi's called *The Hindu Art of Reckoning*; that is, what we know as Hindu-Arabic numerals. This book is a straightforward description of a place-value system of numbers, with the use of zero demonstrated, and calculations in arithmetic set forth. It is an intellectual thunderclap, and it was translated into Latin in Toledo. This book, along with others such as Abraham bar Hiyya's *Book of Geometry*, which also taught arithmetic, would play a crucial role in bringing the Hindu-Arabic numbers into widespread use in Europe, and so transform the study of mathematics and astronomy throughout the continent.

And what about the extraordinary and anonymous *Epistles of the Brethren of Purity*, a mystical work meant to be a compilation of all knowledge, so as to bring the mind into the freedom of understanding, and so closer to the divine? This book dealt not just with math and logic, but with music and natural history, botany, geography, music, and psychology, all with the idea that we may be transformed by the harmony and beauty of the whole. The book was likely in Saragossa as early as the eleventh century, and at least two of the *Epistles* have anonymous Latin translations.

Other key philosophical texts were translated: Al-Farabi's *Classification of the Sciences*, which set out the discipline of philosophy as a whole and organized scientific study into six branches, from the sciences of language through logic, math, and physics, on to metaphysics and law; and for each of these studies he proposed a method. This, from a man who wrote as well on politics, sociology, ethics, medicine, and music.

And most famously among translated texts: the work of the Córdoban scholar Averroes, who wrote three levels of commentaries on the whole of Aristotle as well as a translation of and commentary upon Plato's *Republic*. All his books would be studied in Europe and kick off an intellectual revolution in philosophy, education, and theology. Even Dante in *The Divine Comedy* would find a place for the Muslim Averroes—in Limbo, where he mused alongside the pagans Socrates, Aristotle, Homer, and Euclid. It was a kind of All-Star team of indispensable men, curiously dispensed with by Dante into a kind of steamy vestibule of the Inferno.

In Limbo they had for company someone else translated in Toledo: the Persian genius Avicenna, whose *Canon of Medicine* was a work of genius that dominated medical practice and teaching for centuries in Europe and remains among the most illustrious texts in the whole history of medicine.

Scholars even translated the Koran, in a fit of curiosity about the culture politically dominant in Toledo for more than four hundred years.

These books are a small sample of the collection translated in Toledo, in Saragossa, and in other cities in Al-Andalus in the twelfth and thirteenth centuries. By these translations, much of the philosophy, science, and technology of the Greek world, and the advances and inventions of the Arab and Persian civilizations, were given to Europe. From the beginning of the twenty-first century, as we look back on the ecology of ideas as they moved from culture to culture, we stand in thankfulness and amazement at the effort. By their work, these men shared the best of the science and philosophy present in one of the most advanced cultures in the history of the Mediterranean: a recent evaluation among historians places Al-Andalus at its zenith no fewer than four centuries ahead of Latin Europe. The texts they translated are a crucial part of the foundation of the Renaissance. It is impossible to imagine the rapid development of the West in science, culture, and commerce without just this gift of knowledge. That it turned out to be a monumental and decisive transfer of power, as well, could not have been known to the translators.

Who were these men who labored in so concentrated a period in the history of Al-Andalus? They translated texts from Arabic, and their teams consisted of Arab and Jewish scholars, Spanish Christians, and a smattering of Slavs and Englishmen. Since they worked so beneficial a revolution in history, we might expect to recognize on sight so extraordinary a group. Let me recite at random the names of some of them: Hugo of Santalla, Hermann of Carinthia, Robert of Ketton, John of Seville, Daniel of Morley, Judah Mosca, Galippus, Guillen Arremon Daspa, Plato of Tivoli, Peter of Toledo, Gerbert of Aurilliac, Gerard of Cremona, Michael Scot, Abuteus Levita, bar Hiyya, Galip, Ibn Daud, Gundalissimus. So obscure a gathering of men! Many a common fungus is better known. Here are men who killed and tortured no one, made no practice of pomp or grandeur, nor promoted any hatred. Yet they played a pivotal role in human history, undertaking prodigious labors that uprooted prejudice and ignorance, concentrated twenty centuries of knowledge, and showed Europe a way forward based on reason, understanding, and calculation. Perhaps the day may come when these workers and their colleagues are those we name, recognize, and honor in place of the sordid lists of kings and soldiers that we suffer in book after book of history.

How was such a work possible, and why was it so splendidly done in Al-Andalus?

This is a question that begs a wildly complex explanation, so let us answer in one word: the *convivencia*.

In Al-Andalus, for eight centuries, communities of Muslims, Jews, and Christians lived side by side or intermingled the one with the other. There was no precedent for so extended an experiment in the history of Europe, and it has not been equaled since, for daring, brilliance, or productivity.

First, the religious background. As is well-known by now, Islam did not claim to bring a new faith. It claimed, rather, that Muhammad was the last of a series of prophets come to humankind with a revelation to speak to our hearts and awaken our souls. In the Koran

we find Moses, Abraham, and Jesus honored and exalted. This sensible idea, of a continuity of knowledge through the ages, meant that
Islam, especially in its early period, was predisposed to tolerance.
This tolerance was a matter of religious principle, not political con-
niving; that is, it rested on Koranic teaching and the direct statements
of Muhammad. To disclaim Jesus and Abraham would have been a
blow to Islam itself, since these teachers featured prominently in the
Koran. And not only did Christianity and Judaism have as founders authentic prophets, they had scriptures—they were "People of
a Book." As such, they merited protection and respect, and in the
first several centuries of Al-Andalus, they had it. Each religious community had its own law courts and religious practice and custom,
derived from Visigothic law in the case of the Christians and rabbinic
law for the Jews. But the center point of this system of tolerance was
simple: there were to be no forced conversions to Islam.

So it was that in this early period of Al-Andalus, from 711 to
1009, the three principal religious communities of the Mediterranean
settled down to live together: to learn new languages, trade, start
businesses, farm, travel, intermarry, and, slowly, learn from one
another. The project had its difficulty, conflict, animosity, and spasmodic, wretched violence. At times brutish attacks and murders
overcame the test and tradition of tolerance. But overall, during this
early period, and in fact during the nearly eight hundred years of
Al-Andalus, under Muslim emirs and caliphs and Christian kings,
and with the assistance of an active and powerful Jewish community,
the three great religions of the Mediterranean had their chance to
settle down together and make a go of it.

What happens when, under conditions of *relative* safety, such a
diversity of cultures has a chance at civility, at prosperity, at study,

at shared labor? To walk through our beloved Albayzín is to move among the centuries of medieval Spain, to observe the texture and detail of the *convivencia*.

THE *CONVIVENCIA* IN STONE, WORSHIP, AND POLITICS

First, an architectural *convivencia*: in the Albayzín, the Alhambra, and throughout Spain, the form most identified with Al-Andalus is the horseshoe arch. We see this emblematic arch as a graceful entrance to houses, to courtyards, to palaces. In the famous Mosque of Córdoba, it defines the exterior of the whole building, and inside, double horseshoe arches lead our vision skyward, along with our meditations. It is a rare shape, and one that is literally uplifting, because of a simple trick in its design. The semicircle of the arch is extended, so that the ends of the arch fall below the center point of the circle that defines the arch. Because of this simple layout, the whole form seems to be rising: it's a portrait in stone of sunrise. It gives the form a natural lightness and grace. And when the horseshoe arches are multiplied, as in the Mosque of Córdoba, we feel weightless in the force field of such strange beauty.

Universally, the design of these arches is identified with Islam and with Islamic Spain; but, curiously, in its origins it is not just Syrian, it is Visigothic. From this historical mix, Muslim architects and builders of Al-Andalus took up the design and brought it to full elaboration and prominence. The horseshoe arch is an architectural *convivencia*.

Yet even this plain fact makes us wonder: Who was a Muslim, and who a Christian or a Jew, and if we wanted to tell one from another, what might we look for?

When, in 711, the Iberian peninsula came under Islam, Muslims numbered in the hundreds, and only later in the thousands, and this among a Christian population of around seven or eight million and a Jewish population of several hundred thousand. A hundred years later, only about 10 percent of the population was Muslim; but as religious and cultural life became mingled, so the voluntary conversions increased slowly, so that after another two full centuries, Iberia had a population that was more than 70 percent Muslim. But as most of the converts had a long family history as Christians, there would have been an understanding of and natural insight into Christian doctrine and custom. It was, overall, so rich a mix that it called forth a whole new vocabulary: *mozarabs* were Christians under Islamic administration; *mudejars*, Muslims under Christian administration; *muwallads*, non-Arab converts to Islam; *moriscos* and *conversos*, the Muslims and Jews who had been baptized. The complexity increased with the centuries. Later, as power swung from Muslim to Christian hands, anti-Semitism increased, and the number of conversions from Judaism to Christianity rose, many of them forced on Jews with political pressure, threats, or violence. Or, in the same way, forced on Muslims who once were Christians. At the same time, some Muslims kept to their faith and were full participants in the culture. In addition, there were marriages between men and women of different faiths. All in all, the more we seek to understand the religions of the people of Al-Andalus, the more complex and bewildering it seems. The story is one of an iridescent and complex weaving and unweaving, all through the history of Al-Andalus. If we know anything about this tumultuous movement of faith and family in the communities of Al-Andalus over eight centuries, we know that the legacy of belief, ritual, bonds of friendship, family stories, religious feeling, and wealth all endured in one form or another, and wove into the life of the times myriad threads of sympathy and understanding.

The *convivencia* created one of the great cultures in the history of Europe, and in the history of the Mediterranean. In the far north of present-day Spain, as far from the power centers of Islamic Spain as one may get, in the settlement of Escalada, we found a tenth-century church, cold, austere. It was full of horseshoe arches, because it was built by monks who came from Córdoba. Even though it was built by Christians, in a place where they would not have been forced into any design, the builders were fully versed in decoration and construction in the style of the day, which was a collective creation.

All through Al-Andalus, we see these synthetic creations. In Toledo, the medieval synagogue of Samuel Halevi bears horseshoe arches, and everywhere arabesques and worked plaster similar to those that bejewel the walls of the Alhambra. Among the inscriptions in Hebrew are passages from the Book of Psalms and the Chronicles; but the inscriptions are not only in Hebrew—they are in Arabic, which most the Jewish population of Al-Andalus would have spoken fluently. And among the Arabic inscriptions, here in this Jewish holy place, astonishingly, are quotations from the Koran. What is more, we find incised in the stucco the coat of arms of Castile; so in addition to the Old Testament and the Koran, we have an explicit acknowledgment of close bonds with the Christian royal house. This place of worship shows us just how far the fusion of cultures proceeded. We stand within it and try the obvious thought experiments: Do we know a church with Jewish ornament and declarations from the Koran? Do we know a mosque with Christian painting and quotations in Hebrew from the Torah prominently displayed? It is easy to overlook the strangeness and hopefulness of the synagogue of Samuel Halevi. I hope we do not.

Not far from this famous synagogue—one of three remaining in Spain—is the mosque of Bab al-Mardum, also called Cristo de la Luz, which has an apse called the Church of Santa Cruz. It is packed with strange magic, like the cave of Ali Baba. Its façade is made of brickwork so delicate it looks sculpted, and exquisite small horseshoe arches, so evocative of Islam, are set along the upper story, as though trying to lift the whole edifice into the sky. This beautiful neighborhood mosque became later a chapel and oratory for the Knights of Saint John, and within it we see an octagonal ceiling like the inside of a jewel and a fresco of Jesus as the ruler of creation, surrounded by stars. It feels miraculous, this small chapel. It feels simultaneously Christian and Muslim, a place where we know Jesus to be an authentic prophet common to both faiths. It is a magnetic, complex treasure box of beauties.

What about the men and women of influence in Al-Andalus? Do we find, in their life and blood, the same deep envelopment in the *convivencia*?

One high point of the period is the early tenth century, that of the Caliph Abd Rahman III, whom we have met in our travels among the gardens of Spain. He is found in many history books as the exemplar of Islamic Spain, princely ally of the arts and sciences and relentless military genius who reigned for almost fifty years, built his incomparable palace, and presided over a time of increasing conversions to Islam. One thinks of a classically formed Arab prince, descended from the illustrious Abd al-Rahman I, another poet, lover of books, and devotee of gardens. But the caliph was hardly Arab at all. His mother was Basque, and his grandmother was from Navarre. Toda, queen mother of Navarre, was his great-aunt. He was blond and blue-eyed, stocky, and he governed with the help of Christians, who sought employment in his administration, and especially of Jews, among whom none was more powerful than Hasdai Shaprut. This learned man was master of Arabic, Latin, Hebrew, and Aramaic. As if that were not enough to accomplish, he was physician, advisor, diplomat, financial manager, and confidant of the caliph. And Hasdai, at the center of power in Al-Andalus, was himself a friend and patron of the arts and sciences, and he gathered in the court astronomers, mathematicians, and musicians. Such was Hasdai's love of language that he hired as his two personal secretaries poets of gifts so lustrous that we admire their work today, twelve centuries later. He was cofounder of a school in Córdoba for the study of the Talmud. At the same time, as an emissary from the Muslim caliph, this devout Jewish scholar traveled to Leon to propose medical treatments for the Christian King Sancho, who returned to Córdoba for his ministrations.

We do well, in the context of the Middle Ages, to pause before such prospects, since they bespeak so rich and rare an interplay between men, faiths, languages, and cultures, all to the benefit of the people of the Iberian peninsula. And we may ask the same kind of obvious questions that arose in the synagogue of Samuel Halevi. Where are the Arab leaders with learned and powerful Jewish ministers, who sponsor Jewish scholarship in the country where they live? The question sounds absurd. But if it was possible in medieval Spain, over a thousand years ago, are we to think it will be impossible, forever, in the decades and centuries to come?

And Hasdai is far from being the only example of the powerful Jewish-Muslim political force field in Al-Andalus. Take the example, a century after Hasdai, of a man we have already met, Ismail ibn Naghrela. This is a man whose name will be more familiar every passing decade. Another leader of the Jewish community in Al-Andalus, he was a refugee from Córdoba and, by legend at least, a spice merchant and scribe in Málaga. One pictures him dusted in spices and working in language to find a way to marry sensual delight and spiritual certainty. Through his eloquence, derring-do, and literary abilities, he rose to the notice of the vizier of Málaga. Later, he made himself so indispensable to the king of Granada that he was appointed the king's vizier and, astoundingly, the king's chief military commander. Imagine this: a Jewish leader for the military forces of a Muslim head of state. As if this were not enough, he was a Biblical scholar and a world-class poet, even penning lines from the battlefield. His verse is metaphysical:

> *Earth to man*
> *is a prison forever.*
>
> *These tidbits, then*
> *for fools:*
>
> *Run where you will*
> *Heaven surrounds you.*
> *Get out if you can.*

Or it is practical:

> *Luxuries ease, but when trouble comes*
> *people are plagued by the wealth they've accrued.*
> *The peacock's tail is spectacular*
> *But it weighs him down on the day he's pursued.*

Or it is erotic:

> *I'd give everything I had for that gazelle*
> *who, rising at night*
> *to his harp and flute*
> *saw a cup in my hand*
> *and said:*
> *"Drink your grape blood against my lips!"*

It is easy to imagine Naghrela, in all his lucid, adventurous power, in his palace on the Sabika hill, where the Alhambra now stands, and looking over to the thriving Albayzín.

Hasdai and Naghrela are two of the preeminent figures of the Jewish culture of Al-Andalus—the resplendent centuries known to history as the Sepharad. It was a culture of preternatural brilliance, with its doctors and astronomers, poets and viziers, scholars, translators, poets, mystics, and mathematicians. To mention one of them, virtually at random: in medieval European philosophy, there is the influential Avicebron, whose philosophical work was taken up by Aquinas, Duns Scotus, and Albertus Magnus, and who played a central role introducing Neoplatonism to the period. For centuries, no one knew precisely who this gentlemen was. A writer in Baghdad? A contemporary of Avicenna or Omar Khayyam? The best guess, for centuries, was that he was a Christian or Muslim philosopher. Then in 1846, a scholar working in the Bibliotheque Nationale de Paris noticed that the Latin translation of Avicebron's most influential book, *The Fountain of Life*, was taken from a book written in Arabic—by the Jewish Solomon Ibn Gabirol, an Andalusian philosopher and poet from Málaga. Gabirol's work includes *Kingdom's Crown*, a long, transcendent, unforgettable prayer that figures prominently in the literature of Hebrew. Gabirol's poetry remains part of Hebrew liturgy; and his challenging philosophy took on such core notions as divine essence and divine will, the creation of matter and form, universal soul, and the exact elements that compose the created order of the world. And so the philosopher Avicebron turned out to be a temperamental, independent genius, disfigured by a horrific skin disease, who lived much of his life wandering among the Jewish communities throughout Al-Andalus. He entered fully into his physical pain, and into his solitude and darkness, that we might have the good light and uncompromised power of his work.

To understand the *convivencia*, it is best to let the work of the period speak for itself: work on all fronts that took form brightly in this mixture of cultures, religions, and languages. I have been reading history for years, and I recall no astonishment so sharp as learning of the accomplishments of Al-Andalus.

THE NEW OLD WORLD
OF POETRY AND STORIES

Since we have learned of the poetry of Ibn Gabirol and Ibn Neghrela, let us listen to other poets of the period. The verse is far-rambling and marvelous in scope, written not from ideas, but from the good ground of experience, even at its most metaphysical. There is nature poetry, verses of searching love and raucous consummation, transcendent appeals to the heavens, bitter laments and longing, taunts, jibes, seductions, and wholehearted thankfulness. It's poetry meant to embrace the whole of life, to call the mind close to life.

As we named the translators who changed forever the course of European history, so let us name some of the Arabic and Jewish poets of Al-Andalus: Yehuda Halevi, Moshe Ibn Ezra, Wallada, Ibn Zaydun, Ibn Hazm, Ibn Khafaja, Al-Mutamid, Ibn Abd Rabbihi, Al-Ghazal, Ibn al-Quittiya, Avraham Ibn Hasdai, Yusef Ibn Zabara, Hafsa, Ibn Hani, Ibn Shuhayd al Andalusi, Yosef Qimhi, Avraham Ibn Ezra, Al-Sunawbri, Dunash.

Sound familiar? Before our move to Spain, I was wholly ignorant of nearly all of them. It is yet another example how work of merit rises slowly to prominence, dependent upon the whimsy of politics,

of taste, of cultural ignorance or presumption, of the vagaries of acci-
dent, and of our willingness to look into the past with hope, goodwill, and resistance to political and aesthetic propaganda. The names
of these poets are as familiar as would have been the names of, say,
Vermeer in 1800, or Vivaldi in 1850, or Emily Dickinson in 1886—
all three of them virtually unknown before, respectively, their painting, music, and poetry was rediscovered, understood, and cherished.
I name these poets of Al-Andalus to honor them, and as part of the
blessed rediscovery of them now underway at long last.

Here, to give you some savor of their work, is a sampling, what is
called in Spanish a *florilegio*: a gathering of flowers:

From Ibn Hani in an amorous mood:

Is it the darks of your eyes, or your father's swords?
Are these cups of wine, or your kissable lips . . .

Your eyes are our rendezvous . . .

A generous verse of praise from Ibn Shuhayd:

She's played adulteress to her men,
But what a lovely adulteress!

And from the same poet: he has grown old, he looks into the
gathering darkness, yet is still possessed:

But what is strange is that in my breast
A love kindles, like flying sparks of embers.
It moves me as death bores into my heart,
Excites me as my soul hangs in my throat.

From Ibn Hazm, long gone in love, from a poem called "The
Nature of the Beloved":

Do you belong to the world of angels
Or that of men ?
Explain it to me . . .

Blest be the One who . . .
. . . arranged that you
be marvelous natural light.

From the poet Ibn Khafaja, a lovely verse on longing:

Your love is firm, but I am full of consternation
At our ever fated separation
As if we were on a revolving sphere,
When I appear, you disappear.

And then the same poet, on a happier night:

He almost drank my soul, I almost drank his cheek.

Nature poetry was so well developed in Al-Andalus that there were established genres for poems about spring, about gardens, and about flowers. There was even a tradition of minute description, that studied in language the most humble things, like a medieval version of Pablo Neruda's witty *Odas elementales*. Take these lines, for instance, by Ibn Al-Quitiyya, about a walnut:

Its covering is composed
Of two halves so joined
It's a pleasure to see
Like eyelids joined in sleep.

A simple, beautiful line from the nature poet Al-Sunawbri:

The silence of gardens is speech.

Centuries before the Romantics of England, and yet more centuries before the powerful tradition of nature writing in North America, we have the poets of Al-Andalus in conversation with nature, seeking concord and hoping to attend, to learn, to understand. Here is Ibn Khafaja again, traveling through a mountain pass, and hearing the voice of the mountain itself:

It blocked every which way
The rushing winds and at night
It shouldered the stars

Arched over desert the mountain
Like some thinker
Weighing all the consequences

Clouds like turbans, black, wrap him
Lightning fringed them
With tufts of crimson

And mute as he was, languageless,
On my night journey I heard him
Speak to me of the mysteries . . .

We have been roaming among both Arab and Jewish poets, and it is worth knowing that the Jewish poets' shining work has its roots in the same blessed phenomenon: the *convivencia*. For Arabic had strongly developed vernacular forms, and the Jewish poets of the period used them as their schoolhouse. As one of the earliest

Jewish poets wrote: "Let Scripture be your Eden, and the Arabs' books your paradise grove."

And so the early Jewish poets made a deep study of Arabic prosody—the patterns of meter, intonation, rhythm, all the conventions of music and rhetoric present in the body of Arabic verse. They adapted those elements to Hebrew and made together a revolution. It is a period now called the Golden Age of Hebrew Poetry. It has also been called the Spanish Miracle. The best of these poets are now with us, thanks to the work of the poet, scholar, and translator Peter Cole. His beautiful collection, *The Dream of the Poem*, brings these poets into our hands and their light into our daily lives.

A few more offerings from Professor Cole's translations. First, let us return to Ibn Neghrela, the vizier, scholar, and military leader of Granada. Listen to this fierce vow, as he leaves a city lost to anarchy:

> *By God and God's faithful—*
> *and I keep my oaths—*
> *I'll climb cliffs*
> *And descend to the innermost pit,*
> *and sew the edge of desert to desert,*
> *And split the sea*
> *And every gorge,*
> *and sail in mountainous ascent,*
> *until the word "forever" makes sense to me.*

And an offering from a man we've already met, Solomon Ibn Gibirol, or Avicebron, also a poem of departure and defiance, as he is leaving Saragossa:

You who seek my peace, come near—
and hear the roar of my heart like the sea.
If your heart has grown hard it will soften
faced with the hatred that faces me.

Here in Granada, in the eleventh century, lived the poet Moshe
Ibn Ezra, ranked among the best of the epoch. His work ranges from
this bedazzled piece, called "Weak with Wine"—

We woke, weak with wine from the party,
barely able to get up and walk
to the meadow wafting its spices—
the scents of cassia and cloves:

and the sun had embroidered its surface with blossoms
and across it spread a deep blue robe.

—to the poems of his years of exile from Granada, separated
from his family and from an energetic and brilliant life in this beautiful city. It's called "The Dove":

Why is that dove in the highest branches
grieving now in the garden of spices?
His summer streams won't run dry,
the palm trees shade will always shield him,
and before him, in spring his fledglings sing
all the melodies he has taught them.
So cry, little bird, but cry for the man
forced to wander. His sons are far.
He cannot tend his young. He sees
No one who sees them—and sorcerers alone

Can he consult. Sigh for his wandering,
but do not bring your song to him;
Lend him your wings to fly to them
and delight in the dust and stones of their land.

This man could be our neighbor. He could be showing us the agony of exile in our own times, as he talks directly and intimately to us, across nearly a millennium. In Moshe Ibn Ezra's work, and throughout the work of the poets of Al-Andalus, we have their uncanny modernity, a clairvoyant engagement with the details of politics and daily life.

There is this rueful piece, from Avraham Ibn Ezra,

The heavenly spheres and fortune's stars
veered off course the day I was born;
If I were a seller of candles,
the sun would never go down.

And from Yosef Qimhi, this bitterness, called "Love for the World":

Man in his love for the world is like
a dog gnawing on bones;
He sucks the blood between his lips
and doesn't know it's his own.

From Avraham Ibn Hasdai, in a quatrain called "Wisdom's Mantle," taken from a longer piece called "Advice for a Future King":

As long as a man seeks out wisdom
wisdom will have him hold sway over men;

but once he thinks he's wearing its mantle—
know that it has just been taken from him.

The thirteenth-century poet Todros Abulafia has this playful erotic piece, called "The Day You Left":

The day you left was bitter and dark
the finest thing, you—and when I think of it,
it feels like there's nothing left of my skin.
Your feet, by far, were more beautiful,
the day they mounted
and wrapped my neck in a ring.

I would like, reader, to have you into our garden, and sit with you under the grapevine and beside the pomegranate tree, and read aloud with you a whole suite of selections of this poetry. I would wager that never, in the course of such a reading, would you say: how medieval! This is the poetry of men (and some women) who were centermost in the life of their times, plunged in the life of their times, with all its prosperity and learning, its beauty, irrepressible curiosities, songs and science and mathematical ingenuity, its religious exaltations, its stunning culture, and its spasms of violence. These poets offer us the very minutiae of their lives. Rather than the tedious religious dogma we find elsewhere in Europe, they work into the verses all they can of their days and nights, and nothing is off-limits. We can read poems of longing and praise addressed directly to God, and savory erotic speculations; subtle political advice and sage psychological observations; forlorn torments of despair and thanksgiving for a deliverance in love; the refusal to submit to fate and to bitterness, yet sometimes the anguished offerings of a learned man overtaken by events and trampled by sorrow.

In other words, these men and women write to us from their lives, which are our lives. Though they may have lived centuries ago, they are our neighbors. As we read, what grows in us is a feeling that is uncommon when we hold a book from the Middle Ages: a feeling that we are among friends.

Before we leave the literature of Al-Andalus, we should look together into a book of a man born near Granada at the beginning of the twelfth century, Ibn Tufayl. His profile is similar to many of the writers of this period—he had profoundly diverse interests and skills. He was a doctor of such renown that that he was court physician to a sultan of the period, Abu Yaqub, a lover of books who delighted in the company of men of learning. The sultan would spend hours musing with them about whether the world was eternal or created, about Aristotle and the Koran, about the source of the world's order. In all this, Ibn Tufayl played a crucial role, bringing men of science and philosophy to the court. It was a place of robust and wide-ranging inquiry. Ibn Tufayl was even assigned the task of writing commentaries on the works of Aristotle. He steered the assignment to a young, luminous protégé—also a doctor and philosopher—Averroes.

Ibn Tufayl not only placed crucial work in brilliant hands, he wrote medical treatises, gathered important astronomers in the court and promoted their mathematical challenges to Ptolemy, and wrote poetry and a number of works on natural philosophy. But the book of his that is still with us, and still will stagger a reader, is his short account called *The Journey of the Soul*. It is, in modern translation, all of sixty pages. I do not recall, in a lifetime of reading, so piercing a surprise.

It is the story of man named Hai bin Yaqzan (which means Alive, son of Awake), who as a baby is marooned on an island. He is discovered by a doe, who suckles him and protects him. The boy thrives and grows, and his world changes when the doe perishes. Assaulted by sorrow, Hai begins to explore and to reason, and as we listen to his reflections, we are taken on his journey, on this island, by himself, with only his own experience to guide him. Hai muses his way straight to heaven. Let us follow along, as we can.

His journey begins when, in attempt to bring the maternal doe back to life, he finds her heart. He realizes that she will not return, that what was animating and vital had departed forever, and he learns from ravens that he must bury her remains. But from his discoveries he comes into a kinship with the life of the island, and from a flare-up in a thicket of cane, he discovers fire and then cooking. He takes up a life as an amateur scientist, and in hopes of understanding the life around him, he practices dissection. We should remember—it is difficult to do so—that this is a twelfth-century text.

His investigations center on the heart and brain:

It became clear to him that every animal, although apparently a multiplicity—if one considered in all its apparent organs, senses, and movements—was really a unity . . .

Each such organ has other organs serving it and no action takes place in any organ except from impulses of spirit conveyed along routes called nerves . . . These nerves channel the spirit from the depths of the brain but the brain, like all the other organs, receives its spirit from the heart.

From his discovery of the nerves and the living unity of the body, he next concludes that the hearts of animals of the same species are so alike, they could be said to share the same spirit, and make among themselves a concord of forms. From there, he see that all animals,

however distinct their form, are so akin to one another that the like-
ness makes for a further unity, more enveloping and powerful.

He goes on to consider plants, stones, clay, water, and works out
the difference between form and essence, cause and effect, mass and
weight, then goes on to conclude calmly that the earth is round. In
all this, we follow him and have the privilege to share in a journey of
unabashed hopefulness: a man alone on earth, longing to understand,
seeking order in the world, and full of thankfulness for the chance.

Later, as he comes to contemplate the stars, the world of his
understanding comes into a more far-reaching unity.

> *. . . he realized that . . . all the bodies he had considered*
> *before, earth, air, fire, water, plants, animals, etc., were all*
> *within the firmament and not apart from it. In its entirety it*
> *was not unlike an animal organism, the luminous stars being*
> *the creature's senses . . . He realized that the whole universe,*
> *when he applied to it the same outlook that he had applied*
> *to objects of the earth, had the nature of a single being.*

From this exaltation he moves to matters of spirit—to the con-
sideration of the source and origin of life. He decides that just as he
is different from what he makes with the means and intelligence he
has, so our created world must be made by a power different from
the world. And such a formative power would not be physical, nor
comely, perfect, good, and beautiful, but rather is the source of such
qualities: the permanent reservoir of those qualities, from which they
take form in the physical world. And in these deductions, he comes to
his understanding of the divine, as Cause, Necessary Being, Creator.
And sees that he could not have such a conception unless there was
in him some essence, something that partakes of a permanent world.

Hai ibn Yaqzun sees that his task is to perform a great work—
to develop the finer part of himself—so as to learn and to witness
beauty, in hopes to understand the source of beauty. And just when
you think the story is going to go off into the ethereal, Hai does
something extraordinary: he turns with love and thankfulness to
the physical world. He wants to learn, yet only in unity with creation. And as the animals had a divine creation, and he is partly an
animal, he will imitate and care for animate creation. As stars are
pure and illuminate the earth, he spins in imitation of the stars, so
as to refine himself into a fateful purity. He hopes by his closeness
and his care for creation to bring himself into harmony with the
source of life.

He gives himself with kindness, in a spirit of service and of humility, in faith that he can witness the truth shown in the lovely details
of creation. The narrative is practical and lovely, even when he is
wondering how to eat:

> he would select only those things whose destruction by him
> would offer least opposition to the intention of the Creator
> . . . for example ripe fruit whose seeds would still be avail-
> able to reproduce their kind . . . or he would use vegetables
> which had not reached the limit of their growth . . . he
> would confine himself to those which were most abundant,
> and most capable of further reproduction and would be
> careful not to destroy their roots and seeds. He . . . would be
> careful never to wipe out a whole species.
>
> . . . he imitated the heavenly bodies by imposing upon him-
> self an obligation to help, whenever he was able, anything

hurt or injured or in need; and to remove or reduce any
impediment from which an animal or plant was suffering
. . . If he saw a plant being weighed down by the growth of
another plant, he would gently separate them . . . If he saw
an animal suffering from hunger or thirst, he did all in his
power to help.

When he spun rapidly enough all sensory things faded
away . . . Awareness of his essence, which is innocent of the
body, would then increase. From time to time he would be
cleansed of all impurities . . .

It is strange reading: a mystical ecologist in a text of the twelfth century. He struggles, he works, he loves, he carries out his work of care. And one day he is called, and vanishes into the truth, and nothing of him remains but what is permanent.

Immersed in this state, he saw what eyes have not seen nor
ears heard, neither has the human heart experienced.

It is his unity with the divine, beyond description and measure, "too fine to be clothed in letters or sound." In sixty-odd pages, we go from an abandoned baby on an island to a man of revelation. It is a classic of Al-Andalus: the journey of life transformed by work and love into a homecoming of soul.

We have had altogether too brief a sojourn among the poets and storytellers of these centuries; but now that you know them, reader, you can take their work into your own hands and travel with them.

THE BLESSINGS OF REASON UNITED
WITH THE LABORS OF FAITH

Let us turn to philosophy, for here too the labors of our compatriots in Al-Andalus helped to shape our minds, our books, our lives. The period has its logicians, its theologians and mystics, and we must choose among the riches offered.

We will visit Seville, in the year 1169, and attend to a judge at work in the city. Conflicts are presented to him; he questions, hears evidence, considers facts, offers judgment, often on cases of consequence. Some may involve debts between those of different faith, or the ownership of land or details of inheritance, or accusations of blasphemy or murder. He judges the most important cases, because he is the *qadi*—chief judge of this resplendent, powerful Andalusian city. All his life, he will be immersed in the daily life of the communities where he lives.

He is the young friend of Ibn Tufayl, and his name is Ibn Rushd; he will be called Averroes in the West. He has a long family history in Al-Andalus. Some generations back, his ancestors probably were *Muwallads*—Christians who had converted to Islam, becoming "protected ones." Many of his predecessors were judges or legal scholars, and as a boy, he is trained in the Hadith (the verified statements of Muhammad while he lived) and in the Koran and in theology. But that is not all: he studies, as well, the law, philosophy, medicine, and what we may call Arabic *belles lettres*.

There are numerous contemporary accounts of Averroes, and one reads them and wants him for a neighbor. He is accounted as generous, humble, soul-searchingly fair. And he carries these qualities to the court of the sultan, as well as to the people on any street. Though his ideas were attacked, sometimes viciously, he was never accused of the least dishonor. More than one account mentions his frayed clothes.

Frayed clothes or not, his work was a gift to history, and to all of us. It is not easy to portray the scope of that work, since he was not only the chief judge of Seville and later of Córdoba; he was also a renowned physician, in fact physician to the sultan himself. All the while, he carried on with his legal scholarship and study of the sciences and then marshaled his knowledge to make himself the greatest philosopher of Al-Andalus. What he learned, he set forth in more than eighty books.

What are his books? He begins with introductory books on logic, physics, and psychology and then turns back to medicine, studying Galen and the great Avicenna and writing a commentary: the *Kulliyat*, a grand, useful synthesis of the medical understanding of the times. This he follows up with a treatise devoted wholly to antidotes against poisons. Afterward, he deepens his studies in the law, writing over the years about the philosophy of law and developing a way to compare different legal theories throughout the history of Islam; his summary book, the *Bidyadat*, has been called "a monument of logical explication of Muslim law."

After being confirmed in 1180 as grand *qadi* of Córdoba, he took up the work that would become the basis for scholastic and theological study in Europe in the following centuries: the detailed commentaries on the entire work of Aristotle, and his separate commentary on Plato's *Republic*. It was not just the texts themselves, and the incomparable riches of Greek philosophy that Averroes delivered to Europe. His commentary is shaped by his own values: above all, his devotion to reason and science, and his decisive turn away from fundamentalism in religious faith.

In his day, the Koran ruled Islam, just as the Bible ruled Christianity. If we grant that there is truth in scripture, how are we to evaluate the truth we are led to by reason? Averroes answered this question, and his answer forged a hinge in history that opened a door into a new world. Averroes taught that reason leads us to a truth that has equal standing with that of scripture, and that can always be reconciled with scripture. This sounds simple, but it is a momentous declaration of intellectual and spiritual liberty. For if the course of reason can lead us to truth, and we may follow that course wherever it may lead us, then the work of the mind may take up with fierce energy and freedom any subject at all in the world. We may follow a course of observation, and study, of logic and exploration. And we may do this in full faith and conscience, knowing that to seek the truth through reason is a blessed enterprise.

What if the truth we find by reason is in conflict with the truth we find in scripture? Averroes taught us the answer: if there is a conflict, then we must reexamine scripture and seek a new meaning in the text that will be in harmony with the truth of reason. It follows that the sacred texts must be open to interpretation as time passes, and as we investigate the world, examine nature, and test experience, then scripture will be made richer and more complete by our attempts to bring it into concord with the conclusions of reason.

To many of us, these ideas are familiar and straightforward, and it is easy to forget that someone, sometime, had to conceive them. Averroes did so, in Córdoba and Seville in the twelfth century, and sent history off on another course altogether. He offered more than a political declaration of independence. He proposed a declaration of independence for the mind itself. He taught that the world had a rational organization, and that it was our responsibility to understand it. It was more than our responsibility, it was a spiritual obligation, since we are endowed by the heavens with reason, and so must use our reason to light the torch of understanding and hold it high that all around may see.

And that was not all. Averroes wanted more for us than freedom. He wanted us to consider the consequences of freedom. Having brought reason and revelation into harmony by claiming equal status for reason and proposing a more fruitful and wide-ranging study of scripture, he asked us also to consider the *use* of reason: What, after all, is the point of philosophy? And he answered: it is to use the understanding we gain in service of the whole human community. In this way, as knowledge of the world is gained from personal and empirical studies, the benefit is to everyone, and the free practice of philosophy takes on a real, material beauty, because by its nature it must be shared.

This is the new world sketched for us by a judge in frayed clothing in Al-Andalus. He worked to honor an idea about why we are created: we are created to know, to learn, to observe and study, to attend carefully to the reality shown to us in the workings of nature and of society. And he taught that our reason, working openly and in liberty, can lead us to truth that benefits humankind and works in concord with spiritual understanding.

The ideas of Averroes shook the world. He addressed a key juncture in human experience, and he gave us his answers. Suddenly, humankind had a chance and a work that had been always present, but never set forth so clearly by someone of his religious authority. The challenge he set forth riled Islam and Christianity, since it sets aside the infernal habit of fundamentalism everywhere: a fixed, literal-minded reading of scripture. Averroes addressed directly the fundamentalists of any religion: they were encouraged to study and obliged to read their sacred texts anew, with a flexibility of mind and an openness to the world around them, so as to explore how they might align their holy books with the open conclusions of science and study. We have been, in the ensuing centuries and in the present day, treated often to the horror visited upon societies when this teaching of Averroes is forgotten. He foresaw a plague of ignorance and barbarity, and he worked for a world in which clarity and freedom coexist with religious practice, for the benefit of all.

The day would come when the books of Averroes would be burnt by his fellow Muslims. But that is another story.

MAKING NUMBERS, UNDERSTANDING THE STARS

Given such engagement with the power of reason, what progress was made in Al-Andalus in science and mathematics?

It was a period of rambunctious investigation. We take for granted the use of Hindu-Arabic numbers, whose ease of calculation made possible the tremendous advancement in science and technology in the last many centuries. But that system came to Europe from the Near East. As the system was tried out in the Arab world in the seventh and eighth centuries, the forms and names of the numbers evolved by fits and starts, as books were written to try to codify the rules of this new method of making quantitative sense of the world. As these texts were translated in Al-Andalus, the system was used, discussed, studied, and developed. And as we work every day with numbers, in whatever walk of life, we would do well to remember the prodigious labor of translation and calculation in Al-Andalus. We are all in their debt; in fact, the numbers 4, 5, 6, 7, 8, and 0 all took on their final form, the one we use today, in the books of Al-Andalus.

Once again, we are indebted to the indefatigable translators of Alphonso the Wise, who turned the essential Arabic texts into Latin, allowing for their rapid spread through Europe. Not that it was easy: the numbers took on the name Toledan numbers, and they were popularly regarded as strange and potent, the medium for magical powers. We need only consider the story of Gerbert of Aurillac, a French Christian who became Pope Sylvester II. He learned his Hindu-Arabic numbers early, in Catalonia in the tenth century, and his knowledge so flummoxed his compatriots that he was thought to have sold his soul to the devil. In the bargain, he learned his math, and, as a bonus, the ability to fly through the air. He also, by popular repute, constructed a talking head that he kept on his desk. The head could prophesy and, happily, solve mathematical problems. These labors he undertook when he was not with his mistress, a witch. Reading such accounts, we sense how one could go far in the Middle Ages, once in possession of basic numerical prowess.

Leonardo of Pisa, known to many as Fibonacci, is the man usually credited with the most thorough introduction of Hindu-Arabic numbers to the West. Yet he took much of his work from Abraham Bar Hiyya, a twelfth-century Jewish mathematician of Al-Andalus who wrote on arithmetic, ratio, proportion, and geometry and their use in commerce and surveying.

Once in use, how was the new number system put to work in Al-Andalus? With curiosity, with élan, with aggressive experimental devotions. In astronomy, scientists began refining devices to assist in the study and measurement of the heavens, chief among them the astrolabe. These lovely instruments have been handed down to us: built of brass, they are early and efficient examples of a working analog computer. They were understood and improved in Toledo, in Seville, and in Granada, where there was active interest in astronomy and astrology, and they were used for calculation of latitudes and longitudes of the sun. You can calculate the times of sunrise and sunset and determine the position of stars on any date and time of the year, as well as the altitude of the sun on a given date and time. All this nicety of calculation can of course be related to the signs of the zodiac and positions of the moon and planets. So the astrolabe could be used in a host of ways—to navigate, to set the times for prayer, to cast a horoscope, and the like. All in all, not bad for a medieval computer, all of six and a half inches in diameter. They are beautiful and useful, and even Geoffrey Chaucer felt moved to write a treatise on them, for his young son Louis.

One of the major contributions of Al-Andalus was the so-called universal plate, whose addition meant the astrolabe could be used at any latitude. It is pictured in the *Book of Astronomical Knowledge*, which came, once again, from the school of translators of Alphonso the Wise. From his court, as well, came the famous astronomical tables that revolutionized the study of the subject in Europe when they were translated by Gerard of Cremona at the end of the twelfth century. They were a synthesis of tables taken from the work of Arabic astronomers working principally in Baghdad. But the astronomers of Al-Andalus added corrections, editing and polishing, all due to their scientific practice. Ibn Al-Zaqullah, a brilliant instrument maker and astronomer, studied and measured the position of the moon for thirty-seven years and the sun for twenty-five years. The tables themselves permit calculation and prediction of planetary motions, eclipses, conjunctions of the planets, meridians, and with one in hand an ephemeris could be written out, setting out the positions at any time of a given heavenly object. The original tables were compiled in the twelfth century and continuously sharpened with additional observation. For three centuries, this work was the foundation for astronomical study in Europe. Even Copernicus had a copy on his shelf. They show us a moving example of the *convivencia* of Al-Andalus: the work of Arabic astronomers, with the ardent sponsorship of a Christian king, refined and extended by two Jewish scholars, whose work in 1483 gave to the world the final version of centuries of collaborative labor.

The Alfonsine tables were not the only showing of mathematical expertise. Another astronomer, Ibn Mu'adh, wrote the first book in the West on spherical trigonometry. In Saragossa in the eleventh century, Arab scientists assembled a wonderfully complete library of classical work on mathematics, from Euclid forward, as well as the texts of the great Arab mathematicians like al-Kwarizimi. With these achievements in hand, they carried on their own studies on conic sections, the ideas of ratio and proportion, and number theory. All this work, in part or in whole, directly or by quotation and summary, found its way to Western Europe and had a most salutary effect on studies there for the ensuing centuries.

What is enlivening is the close bond throughout the period of scientific study and public service, for these were practical men and women. They wanted not just to think things. They wanted to do things, to invent, to serve, sometimes with outlandish derring-do. Take, for example, the ninth-century poet Abbas Ibn Firnas, who climbed a building in the beloved Rusafa, the country palace and botanical garden built by Abd Rahman I. Once at the top, Firnas

donned a silk suit with feathered wings and jumped off, one of the
first known efforts to fly. Alas, he had forgotten to stitch on a tail,
and his weight was a bit much for the lift given him by the frantic
beating of his wings. The injuries he suffered, however, did not deter
him. He went on to build a clepsydra—a water clock—for timing the
hour of prayer. He turned one room of his house into a planetarium
and perfected a method of cutting quartz. I regret to report that the
poetry of this enterprising gentleman has not come to light. But one
never knows what surprises the libraries of the world might yield. I
live in hope.

WATER, A BOUNTY OF FOOD, ORANGE BLOSSOMS, AND ROSE OIL

Abbas Ibn Firnas was not the only venturesome inventor. Rusafa,
with its early collections of plants from the Middle East, gave rise
to centuries of botanical study and experiment. This work looked
into the qualities of a wide variety of plant species and explored as
well the nature of given regions—what we would call bioregions—in
order to discern the best methods of cultivation. These studies invigo-
rated the agriculture of Al-Andalus. And as one or another approach
was tried, the results led to more experiment and understanding, in a
rich and vigorous exchange of experience, observation, and analysis.

Let's see how this worked: take, for example, a book given
by the Byzantine emperor to the Andalusian caliph, Abd Rahman
III, who ruled with the crucial help of his scholarly Jewish prime
minister, Hasdai Ibn Shaprut. The book is the *Materia Medica* of
Dioscorides, a first-century physician who wrote up the first great
manual of medicines derived from plants. An Arabic version was

already available, but the naturalists and linguists of the court wanted to reconfirm their knowledge and extend their range of language, and they promptly requested a Greek scholar from Byzantium. So arrived the monk Nicholas, who joined a group whose work was to synthesize, extend, and adapt the material to the Iberian peninsula. It is yet another instance where, by the energies and openness of the age, the doors of understanding swung wide; for from that original group of workers, and their students and collaborators, we see the vigorous development of agriculture, botany, pharmacology, and medicine.

In agriculture, what moves us is the sheer collaborative zeal over the years of the people of Al-Andalus. For a given bioregion, agronomists would plant botanical gardens in order to study the qualities and composition of the soil. They assessed the water available and pressed into action technologies adapted from Roman agriculture, combining them with ideas brought to Spain from Syria and arid North Africa. To bring new land into cultivation, they needed to distribute water more widely and efficiently. They built the great *noria*—large water wheels—in fast-flowing streams. The wheel was fixed with clay pots, which filled with water as the current turned the wheel; the water was then spilled by gravity into troughs, which carried it away for irrigation. Or they used the *qanat*, a method developed originally in Iran, which allowed for the delivery of water to cropland without any pumping. First, they would locate an upland aquifer, which was tapped by means of a horizontal tunnel through which water would flow into channels connected to cropland. In addition, a series of vertical wells were dug that ran downhill from the high end of the tunnel at the main water source. These secondary wells allowed access to the tunnel and provided air for those who cleaned and maintained it. Once in place, the *qanat* would deliver cool water reliably year round. It was a nice piece of civil engineering—cooperative, durable, simple, but requiring close study and careful labor.

Even today, many melodious terms still in use in modern Spanish agriculture come straight from Arabic; among them are *acena* or *noria* (water mill), *acequia* (irrigation ditch), *zubia* (small channel), *almunia* (farm), *almazara* (oil mill), *azahar* (orange blossom), *aljibe* (cistern), *azud* (waterwheel), and a host of others.

Such botanical study and practical engineering gave rise to the robust and diverse cultivation of Al-Andalus. The period is full of small landholders who often owned adjacent land in family groups, each of whom had its specialty and its customs. But with the use of soil science and botanical study, the understanding of crop rotation and fallowing land, the southern half of the Iberian peninsula enjoyed centuries of extraordinary fertility and diverse production. The production is so various and adventurous that reading about it makes one want to go to the kitchen and cook. Of course they grew grains, wheat and barley for bread. But they also cultivated spices and exotic aromatics—mint, cumin, licorice, marjoram, dill, caraway, saffron, garlic. There was a plentitude of fruits in production beyond our beloved pomegranate: the fig and date, lime, orange, lemon, pear, and grapefruit. And, by the recipes we have, some excellent watermelon. And I am happy to report they did not neglect the legumes, including french beans, chick peas, and lentils. As if this were not enough, near cities and in kitchen gardens they grew cucumbers, carrots, leeks, and eggplant. And of course we have already seen the heartfelt interest in ornamental plants for the family gardens, the roses and water lilies, violets and chrysanthemums.

As all this exuberant agriculture went forth, the scientists studied the initiatives, the experiments, and the techniques and tried to summarize their learning in handbooks, manuals, and compendiums. One of these is by Al-Tighnari, a poet with an interest in linguistics who, naturally enough, embarked on a series of agricultural experiments and joined forces with the agronomists and botanists who had gathered in Seville in the late eleventh century. His book, wonderfully entitled *Splendor of the Garden and Recreation of the Mind*, is dedicated to the governor of Granada, where recreation of the mind is carried on to this day. Another strange and splendid book is the *Calendar of Córdoba*, which shows us the work of the land according to the Christian calendar of months (with the Syriac and Coptic names of each). We have shared part of it with you in our look into the history of our garden. It's a wonderful read. Not only do we have details on the times of sunrise and sunset, the constellations and even the length of twilight, we have a most delicious and persuasive description of the life on the land. Let us look into, say, April, in the tenth century:

> *The month when . . . rose water, rose oil, rose syrup and*
> *rose preserves are made; violets are picked for the making*
> *of syrup and oil; or they are pickled; syrup is made from*
> *rue-herb; there are cucumbers. The palms are artificially pol-*
> *linated and the palm leaves are cut. The early grapes begin*
> *to form, the olive trees blossom, and the figs come out; the*
> *Valencian falcons hatch out their young ones; it takes thirty*
> *days for them to grow their feathers. The fawns are born.*
> *Supports are made for the lemon trees and jasmine cuttings*
> *are planted in the ground. The wild carrots are ripe and*
> *harvested for the making of jam; and then there are poppies,*

pomegranates, ox-tongues and the leaves and petals of the
dyer's weed from which juice is extracted. It is also the
month when henna, basil, cauliflower, rice and beans are
sown; the green gourds and aubergines are dug out of their
forcing beds; small melons are sown, and also cucumber.
Peafowl, storks and many other birds lay their eggs and
begin to brood.

This is poetry, pressed into action as an agricultural manual. The description of each month is so detailed and affectionate, and so full of a sense of wonder, that one wants to take the whole text and read it aloud, month by month, to friends. It makes one want to keep bees and make wine, watch falcons and gather rose petals. It is yet another example of the practical labors of the period, where the result was a book people could love and use in their daily life on the land.

Just such enlivening engagement is seen throughout the agricultural enterprise. What impresses is the willingness to try things out, to sift through results, to carry on for years in search of the best solution. And then to summarize the results so that other people could use them. And so we have attempts not just to list plants, but to classify them into varieties and families, and note their preferred climate and characteristics. There were detailed descriptions of a whole set of agricultural tools, sixty in all; they even used the astrolabe to level land in preparation for planting. They used their botanical learning as well, to enrich their crops, showing for instance the most detailed knowledge of grafting, which is an art, as anyone who has tried it will know. But it is essential to master it if one is to breed hardy, consistent varieties of fruit trees. In grafting, one takes the scion wood—a cutting from the tree whose qualities you want—and joins it to existing stock. One can splice the scion in, or insert it into a cut directly in the trunk, which is called wedge grafting. This art was practiced all over Al-Andalus, deftly, and with care and cumulative refinement of technique. It's one small bit of agricultural practice, but evocative of the devotions of the period.

It is this spirit of sustained experimentation that we find everywhere. In this way, a science could be refined, transformed, and integrated into the life of the times. Take, for instance, the coming of Dioscorides' *Material Medica*, where more than one thousand kinds of medicines are discussed, most of them derived from plants. We saw how this work led to the importation of monk Nicholas, for the teaching of Greek. But the book gave rise to study of plants and herbal remedies throughout Iberia. As decades passed, more and more plants were collected and studied. Remember this line from the *Calendar of Córdoba*: ". . . juice is extracted from two different kinds of pomegranate and mixed with fennel water to make a thick ointment for the treatment and prevention of cataracts and other diseases of the eye." Now, I have not tried this, but the description makes me want to, especially because we can go out every year into the garden together to harvest pomegranates. Be that as it may, over time the scope of herbal treatments branched out, plants were collected, medicines made, illnesses studied. By the mid-thirteenth century, one Ibn Al-Baytar put together an up-to-date list of plants for use in the healing arts: more than three thousand of them, with his comments and recommendations. And this effort was just one of the period's devotions to pharmacology and the practice of medicine.

THE STUDY OF HEALTH,
A HERITAGE OF HEALING

The art and practice of medicine was a telling part of the repertoire of many a polymath of Al-Andalus, from Hasdai Ibn Shaprut to Averroes. Such work was linked with chemistry, the kindred study of alchemy, just as astronomy was the kindred study of astrology. In the preparation of medicine, Andalusian physicians were building on the work of Persian polymath Avicenna, whose magisterial works on medicine were well-known, and the work of Al-Kindi, a ninth-century Arab genius who wrote on philosophy, mathematics, and physics, in addition to medicine. His best-known utterance is as close as we have to the spirit of Al-Andalus, at its best: "We must not hesitate to recognize truth and assimilate it, even though it may come from earlier generations or foreign peoples. For the seeker after truth there is nothing of more value than truth itself . . ."

Al-Kindi brought together mathematics and chemistry to produce a set of principles meant to guide the making of medicines. It was a complex business but a remarkable advance in pharmacology. It meant that in the preparation of medicine, physicians could calculate exactly the quantity of each element in a mixture, so as to give the dosage proper to the malady being treated. A Christian physician from Valencia, known as Arnald of Vilanova (who had a reputation as an alchemist and magician), translated many of these Arabic texts and combined them with Latin teachings and his own experience into a book meant to be a textbook of pharmacology. Arnald taught at the School of Medicine in Montpellier, in Barcelona and Paris, in addition to other adventures and shenanigans. He served as physician to popes and kings, and he wrote the first widely circulated book about the art and medicinal benefits of drinking wine. He seems to be the one who first proposed that before tasting wine, one should have a few pieces of bread; though, curiously, he thought such tastings should occur in the morning. He also recommended wine as a good treatment for dementia. We hope and pray it may be so.

But for originality, we must deliver the palm to Abu al-Qasim Khalaf bin Abbas Al-Zahrawi, known in Europe as Abulcasis. He was born in a village near Córdoba in 936, and so would have had access to that city at a time of such prosperity and learning that, all the way from Germany, the Benedictine nun Hroswitha, a poet and a dramatist, called the city "the ornament of the world." Of the details of the life of Abulcasis we know little, except for the most important particular: he gave fifty years of his life to learning and practicing medicine, with the aim of gaining a comprehensive knowledge of the field, so that he might share it. And so he did, in a book called *The Method of Medicine*, all thirty volumes of it.

It is a remarkable presentation. He touches on his experience as a physician, discusses physiology, and demands that doctors have a sound knowledge of the whole human body, "the uses, forms, and constitutions of the parts . . . the bones, nerves, muscles, their numbers and origins; and also the blood vessels, body arteries, and veins, with the locations of their sources . . . for he who is not skilled in as much anatomy as we have mentioned is bound to fall into error that is destructive of life." He follows all this up with clinical descriptions of various maladies, the whole gamut of them, from melancholy to apoplexy and convulsions, to arrow wounds and compound fractures, and all this along with resoundingly sane advice to question, observe, and contemplate the patient seeking care, "since many patients cannot express their troubles."

His treatments are of striking detail. For nervous convulsions in children, as an example, the doctor has some soothing ideas: ". . . grease his body with milk together with sesame oil or oil of violet . . . give him four portions of she-ass milk daily with almond oil and sugar . . . the nutrition of the patient must include barley, sugar, and almond oil. Also, chopped white meat, tender and fresh, is given together with honey." For the common cold, he recommends a concoction he made of camphor, musk, and honey. I have no idea of the efficacy of such ministrations, though the cold remedy sounds to me like a sure thing. But I have little doubt about the care and thoughtfulness of the doctor.

But the doctor is not through with his exposition. For there in Córdoba, in the tenth century, Abulcasis, in the last book of his treatise, writes the chapter that has dazzled doctors and medical historians for the last millennium. It is the first detailed treatise on surgery, and the medical zeal and the scope of procedures discussed is extraordinary. He discusses how to clean and treat a wound and cauterize it to stop bleeding and prevent the spread of infection. He would cut away dead or unhealthy tissue to promote healing (what is today called debridement) and then stitch the wound up with catgut, wool, or silk. To protect the sutures, he binds up the wound in cotton. He writes about repairing damage to bones and joints, shows us his best method to restore a dislocated shoulder or to set a broken bone in a cast. He would operate on the spinal cord. He figures out a way to dissolve bladder and kidney stones, and he describes tonsillectomy and tracheotomy, and a way to extract a rotten tooth or excise a growth from within the respiratory system with a special hook. He did eye surgery, making delicate incisions in order to repair exotic malformations called entropion and ectropion, in which one or another eyelid is turned inward or outward unnaturally, interfering with vision and causing constant irritation. And he tried to work out a way to remove cataracts.

To do all this complex and dangerous work, he used a host of surgical instruments, many of which he invented himself. In histories of medicine, one may find iconic drawings of the tools he used. Looking over a page of them, one wants, of course, to run for the hills. But in fact the illustrations mark a turning point in the history of medicine, and we can see there many familiar tools. We see surgical needles and scalpels, forceps and tooth extractors, catheters, curettes (a sharp-edged spoon for taking out a growth or other tissue from a body cavity), and retractors (to hold back the edges of a surgical incision). Here is a small sample.

The work of Abulcasis was translated into Latin five times and spread throughout Europe, serving as an essential reference text for the Middle Ages and the Renaissance. There is some competition for the title of "the Father of Surgery," but the title seems to have settled on this one busy physician of Córdoba.

One more curiosity on this, which any of us feel when looking upon the surgical tools of Abulcasis: What about the need for anesthesia? No one seems to know for sure what techniques were used, but they would have been essential to the success of these surgical interventions. There are clues which tantalize: Avicenna, whose medical texts were studied throughout Al-Andalus, used such plants as mandragora, cannabis, nightshade, henbane, and opium. All these plants have powerful and dangerous effects if the dosage is not controlled. But Abulcasis had strong and exacting pharmacological standards, to judge by his careful clinical observations. Surely he had learned from Avicenna, and from his fellow practitioners, and experimented with various mixtures, depending on the patient and the malady. And though we do not know exactly which compounds he settled on, the most common anesthesia he mentioned used inhalants from sponges, the so-called *spongia somnifera*, to relieve the suffering of his patient. Dried ingredients from narcotic plants were dusted over the sponge to the dosage required, and it was then moistened and held for the patient to inhale. I would certainly have been wary, but I certainly would have been willing as Abulcasis came near with his assortment of scalpels and scrapers, his probes and tissue clippers, ready to begin his incisions.

To Abulcasis is credited one other tradition, and it is the one that always comes to mind when trying to understand his life and practice: the tradition of taking flowers in hand to those in sickness. It is a simple gesture, but in it we feel the graceful and generous spirit of this good doctor.

WHERE SONG WILL LEAD

A recovering patient, in a surround of flowers, might well have hastened her recovery by listening to the musicians of Al-Andalus. It is an extraordinary period for music. And it is music that has proven its worth by the vigor of its survival. One superb scholar of this music, Dwight Reynolds, tells us that "the Arab-Andalusian musical legacy . . . ranks as one of the oldest continuously performed art music traditions in the world." And no one writes about it without a focus upon the grand, outlandish figure of the African singer Ziryab (which means blackbird), who arrived in Al-Andalus in the year 822 like a cultural thunderclap. He was tall and lean, with dark olive skin and considerable grace. No one seems to know the real story of his background in Baghdad, in the magnificence of the Abbasid court. But there are common themes in the wild tales: he was so gifted a musician that he offended his own teacher by surpassing him with ease and élan in performance, or that he gave offense by his ideas or conduct to potentates in one or another court. One has the sense of a man overflowing with musical genius and myriad opinions.

When he arrived at the court of Abd al-Rahman II, he set about remaking court society, as if he were some cyclonic force of fashion come to a new and rustic culture. It is almost comical, twelve centuries later, to read about it, for it seems he hypnotized the whole society. He introduced bleach and instructed all and sundry how to vary the color and style of their clothing to accord with the four seasons. He brought recipes and the idea of serving food in courses and using tablecloths and glasses, and such is his influence that he is even given credit for introducing exotic foods, such as asparagus. Lest he be associated only with asparagus for all of history, he promoted bathing in the morning and the use of toothpaste and deodorant. If this were not enough, he even founded a school of cosmetology and was a cheerleader for short hair and shaving.

All this was in his spare moments. For his central work was always music. He had a repertory of more than ten thousand songs, which drew upon poetry and history and the deep musical traditions of the Middle East, in which he had such intensive training. He concentrated his knowledge in a school of music he founded, where he invented new methods for training the voice and which was full of students he taught himself, including all ten of his children, eight boys and two girls. One of the instruments they played was the 'ud, which became the lute of the Renaissance. It was Ziryab who is credited with a redesign of the lute, using thinner and finer woods, distinct materials for different strings (from lion's gut to silk), and the addition of a fifth string, to represent the soul, even as the standard four strings represented the four humors natural to the body. This fifth string, alas, was discarded by later musicians, who brought their own souls.

Yet music had its performers even before Ziryab, and centuries afterward. I mean the widespread and well-documented qiyan, who were highly trained professional female singers, often referred to in histories, curiously, as singing girls, as though they were the warm-up act at a local school. They were not. They were the main event. We even know the names of some of them, so let us use them, since we want to honor these extraordinary figures. Qumar was a young woman trained in Baghdad, and three others—Fadl, 'Alam, and Qalam—were trained in Medina. All these singers performed in Al-Andalus, and the story of Qalam is emblematic of the times. For she is not Arab at all, but from northern Spain, either Basque or

Navarrese. She was taken in a military raid at a young age, enslaved, and then packed off all the way across the Mediterranean to Medina, where she was pressed into a course of studies in Arabic poetry, singing, dancing, and calligraphy. From there, she returned to perform in Al-Andalus as a much-praised favorite in Córdoba in the courts and country houses of Abd Rahman II. All these improbable arduous journeys, and her star turns in Andalus, were in the ninth century.

These gifted women, young and mature, turn up everywhere as musical performance and training developed in Al-Andalus, which offered a regime of studies of real rigor and scope. A girl would learn as many as five hundred examples of a complex form called the *nawba*, which moves in rhythm from languorous to swift and has four movements altogether. She learned to play a whole set of instruments, and the skills in song and movement that fit the piece and the performance. She learned the arts of improvisation, to the extent that one singer is credited with a two-hours-long outpouring of variations on one line of one song. She even learned shadow puppetry, and at graduation—there were certificates that described her attainments—she was a fully formed artist. When she was sold, she brought the sweep of her talents to the life of a court or to a wealthy family. These remarkable women were so valuable that their possession, whether by capture or purchase or trade, was a natural part of military and political maneuvering. It is among the ways that medieval warfare in Al-Andalus differs from modern warfare: nations at present do not attack a rival in hopes of winning a retinue of singing girls for their own country. If only the prizes of war could offer such joy and such beauty, we might see that it would be better to stay home with such women, and learn from them, and not go to war at all. Better yet, given the way these women had demonstrated their dedication, discipline, stamina, and learning on so many fronts, they might be excellent candidates for heads of state.

Most histories of European poetry feature the troubadours, the famous first singers of vernacular poetry in Europe, a poetry whose influence was of the most remarkable power and consequence. That influence reached throughout Europe, and later to America. The troubadours have fascinated everyone from Dante to Ezra Pound. The man often named as the first such poet, William IX of Aquitaine, grew up in a court in Southern France—an area heavily influenced by Al-Andalus—in the company of hundreds of these highly trained young women. Their music, their Arabic poetry, court songs and street songs, all the emblematic and sensuous poetry enlivened by the *convivencia*, must have had (one can only imagine) the most vivid and seductive influence on this capable and intelligent young man. Later in life, he would join the first Crusade, stay on in the Holy Land, and by all accounts deepen his knowledge of Arabic culture. Later, back in his court in Europe, he would manage to be excommunicated twice and to write the first lyric poems in European history, so decisive in the history of verse. I hear singing girls in them.

And to speak of singing: we cannot leave the music of Al-Andalus without visiting the *Cantigas de Santa Maria*, the uncanny collection of songs produced in the reign of Alphonso the Wise, who, as we recall, was otherwise busy, not just with his kingship, but with his school of translation; that is, busy with some of the most consequential work in recorded history. The *Cantigas* comprise more than four hundred songs with Mary as their protagonist and tell stories that show her on earth, at work, intervening hither and yon in human affairs, with power and meticulous judgment and unexpected whimsy. I urge the reader to seek out recordings of this music. And we should here dip into the stories, for they give a savor of the era, its religion, imagination, and art.

Let us begin with Mary's miracles, for she swoops in miraculously for all manner of interventions. In many of the songs she brings the dead to life, especially dead children and occasionally stillborn babies. As if that were not enough, she can revive dead horses, even mules. She'll even return lost hunting falcons for those who favor her with their worship. In one transport of scholarly zeal, she brings back to life a sick boy, and he straightaway begins quoting scripture and reading Latin. She even zips over to a battle in Constantinople, sinks the ships of the Moorish navy, and saves the city.

My favorite is her sojourn in Sicily, where the volcano is erupting. Mary approaches some worthy fellow and suggests he compose a song in her honor. Happily, he was able to produce an acceptable rhyming ditty, and, satisfied, she obligingly turns and quiets the volcano. These are not powers usually associated with bursts of lyrical poetry. But perhaps, learning from the *Cantigas*, we should reform our ideas.

Then there is Mary's formidable and surprising powers of forgiveness. In one song, a beautiful nun (these nuns figure frequently in the *Cantigas*) is courted by a rich and virtuous man. She decides to go off with him and says a final prayer to the statue of Mary, who promptly steps off her pedestal and blocks the way from the chapel. This happens a second time. The third time, the supple young nun dodges around the Virgin, goes off with her beau, and with him lives happily and deliciously, bearing many children who, sure enough, are also beautiful. The family is rich, and her husband makes her independently wealthy, just as he had promised. Mary bides her time but eventually comes to remind the former nun of her convent, to which she returns. Her husband then repairs, obligingly enough, to an abbey himself. We pray it was one nearby.

Then there is the practical Mary, ready to help. She's especially ready to help a sinner who will honor her with prayers, vigils, devotions, songs, or whatever. She redeems thieves, gamblers, rapists, and other criminals, who are cleansed of their infamies. There seems to be no one beyond forgiveness: in one remarkable song, a beautiful noble woman sleeps with her godfather and bears him three children, all of whom she murders. Then, in despair, she stabs herself, but misses the mark. She next swallows spiders, trying to die. Finally dying, she repents and asks the Virgin for forgiveness. Mary comes posthaste, saves her, and then, astonishingly, makes her more beautiful and fit than ever. And straight to the convent she goes. There is no further word of the amorous godfather.

And this is not the only instance of her sympathy for infanticidal women. In one song, a Roman woman whose husband had died goes to bed with her son, becomes pregnant, and kills the child when it is born. A devil masquerading as a diviner tells the emperor, who summons her and attempts to find out the truth. The incestuous murderess prays straightway to Mary, who confounds the devil, leaving the emperor without proof and the woman exonerated. It is a most remarkable tale, and the message seems to be: whatever you have done, no matter how abominable, call on Mary.

She is also the one to call for a cure. She cures the paralyzed, lepers, the lame and halt, the disfigured, the crippled. She restores sight to the blind, hearing to the deaf, speech to the mute, and she's especially good on the removal of kidney stones, reported to be the size of hen's eggs. She will even remake eyes that have been gouged out and heal the wounds suffered by a knight who fought a dragon.

For the most arduous of these cures, she has a magic potion: the milk of her breasts. It is a half-naked Mary who comes to the rescue of the most needy cases, for with her most exalted potion she can remedy any malady, any at all. I do not know of any other song sequence where mother's milk is so often pressed, literally, into action. All this surprising worship culminates in a song about John of Chrysostom, who is blind, lost, and has fallen into a patch of briars. He takes the occasion to ask Mary, who has come to cure him, what Jesus loved most on earth. Mary goes away, and John continues suffering but has a vision in which Mary comes to show him just what Jesus loved most: her breasts. John, of course, is then cured and heads off for heaven not long after.

Yet Mary has her vengeful side. Woe betide those who will not do her bidding, or those who make her jealous. A priest who steals silver from a cross, gives it to a woman, and then lies about it is blinded, and his nose is made to grow all over his face. And we will not even discuss the fate of the priest who stole some fancy altar cloth to make himself underpants. Consider, instead, the fate of the young man who puts a ring on the hand of a statue of the Virgin and pledges fidelity to her. Her hand closes over the ring. Later, he marries, and Mary, having none of it, gets right into bed with the couple, lying between the bride and bridegroom, disrupting the wedding night and rebuking the young man for abandoning her. He realizes immediately that having the Mother of God in bed with you and your bride is not a propitious sign that consummation will be yours. He goes off to the wilderness and ends up a hermit in a pine grove. It is but one example of the sexual mischief of Mary. The songs are replete with lustful priests and knights. Many a concubine or nun is left behind for the greater glory of the Virgin. One sorry knight prays to Mary for help in controlling his lust, which has led him as much into bed as onto the field of battle. Mary summarily makes him impotent. And in one barbaric song, yet another beautiful nun—has ever a country had more beautiful nuns?—is about to run off with a gallant and handsome knight and is saying a last prayer in the chapel. The statue of the Virgin begins to weep, and Jesus, next to her on the cross, wrenches a hand free and slaps the nun. And she loses her beauty, because Jesus's hand carried its nail with it for the slap.

Such agonies are rare, what with the cures, miracles, and mercy. And the occasional sweetness. One song relates how a monk sat down in a lovely garden by a fountain and asked Mary to give him a fore-taste of paradise. A bird began to sing with such finesse and power that the priest listened and listened . . . for three hundred years.

And another tale relates how an archdeacon was composing a song for the Virgin and had it complete except for one crucial rhyme. He prays to her, the perfect rhyme is delivered, and the statue of Mary leans forward to thank him. And that is why that statue leans to this day. It is a story to give hope to minstrels and sonneteers everywhere.

Accompanying many editions of the *Cantigas* are beautiful illus-trations of the musicians who performed these songs. They show us so much about daily life in the thirteenth century that whole books have been written using those images as reference. In them we are reminded of just what instruments were played. Just as in agricul-ture, in administration, and in science and mathematics, fields which have many Spanish and English words of Arabic origin, so in music many common instruments have the same origins. We have seen how the lute, indispensable to Renaissance music making, derives from the ʿud; so the rebec, from Arabic *rabab*, offered a way of using the bow that led to the emergence of the viol family, whose instruments are fretted in a way similar to lutes. And there are a host of other examples, all together making up a healthy portion of musical instruments of Europe. What calls our attention, then, in the images, is the very familiarity with those instruments. They were part of life in a way that was open, intimate, prolonged, and cherished. The Christian cultures knew these instruments because they were so often in their hands.

WE HAVE BEEN traveling among the regions of Al-Andalus, and through its history, visiting provinces of mind and experience: the poetry, the science and mathematics, philosophy, agriculture and botany, medicine and music. It is an extraordinary picture, a joy to study, and it leaves us with awakened admiration for the men and women of medieval Spain, who ventured so far in their investigations. When we first moved to the Albayzín, I had never heard of many of the people I write of now, such was my ignorance of the period. But we had the simple need to understand where we lived, and what I expected to be a sojourn among some few books turned out to offer long, fascinated journeys with brilliant companions into just-discovered country. This recent work by many scholars— Spanish, European, and American—on medieval Spain is called the "historiographical revolution," which is a long name for beginning to get it right at last.

THE ARTS OF LOVE

Among these many surprising and useful books, none has been more stunning than a scholarly and comprehensive study of a manuscript called G-S2, found in an obscure set of codices (folios 75v–104v) in

the Library of the Royal Academy of the History of Madrid. The
book is by the esteemed scholar Luce López-Baralt and is titled *A
Spanish Kama Sutra*. The manuscript she studies, written in 1609, is
a treatise on the arts of love.

We recall the startlingly erotic poetry of the period, written not
only by men, but also by some women, who set down poems of
open sensuality and independence. It makes us wonder about the
sexual practices of Al-Andalus, and of course we can never know.
But we have this one manuscript, and it is full of details and ideas,
suggestions and guidance. It is a book of erotic counsel, theology,
and poetry, all at once. There is absolutely nothing like it, nothing
at all, in Spain, or in Europe of the period. And so in keeping with
our theme of *convivencia*, as we come to the end of our look into
Al-Andalus, it is fitting that we address the most ardent *convivencia*
of all: that of a couple in love, in one another's embraces.

Most of us are familiar with the history of misogyny worldwide,
a calamity which has infected philosophy and theology, with heart-
breaking results for women, denying them education, liberty, and the
chance to develop their minds, their gifts, and their art. Even today
in much of the world these attitudes persist, a plague and a disgrace
to humankind. In the West, in particular, that misogyny was bound
up with female sexuality, and Professor López-Baralt sets out for us
the conceptions of women that dominated thinking in the West since
Aristotle. I will follow her summary.

Aristotle thought that a woman is a defective man, a kind of
failure of nature. She cannot produce semen, and therefore needs a
man, the more authentic human, to produce a child. This inferiority is part of a natural incapacity in practical and spiritual matters.
And when we add to this rank idiocy of Aristotle the Old Testament

story of Genesis, in which Eve is responsible for Original Sin, and that sin is associated with sexuality, we have the makings of a theological disaster.

Make it they did: beginning with Saint Paul, the fathers of the church addressed sexuality with consistent attitudes that moved within a restricted range: from suspicion to condemnation to repugnance, for sexual love in general and women in particular. It is a remarkable spectacle, one that has been studied in detail by many scholars; yet their analyses and summaries sustain the most lively incredulity as we read our way through the original texts of such influential and learned theologians. How could they have believed what they wrote, when their ideas are so at variance with the experience of so many men and women alike? How could they refer to women with such scornful contempt? How could they deny the joy and the hopefulness that comes to any of us who give ourselves to the prolonged and various pleasures of the one we love?

Deny it they did. Better than to summarize their attitudes is to let them speak for themselves. Saint Paul famously said that it was "better to marry than burn." Marriage, in this view, is an inferior state for a man, since the practices of sexual love distract him from service to God. And so from the beginning, the body is distinct from the soul and is a source of weakness and dissolution. Gregory of Nisa thought marriage a "dismal tragedy," and Jerome wrote, "The truth is that, in view of the purity of the body of Christ, all sexual intercourse is unclean." Tertullian, for his part, saw no intrinsic difference between fornication and sex within marriage, since intercourse was essentially shameful. Combined with the ascetic and ferocious solitude of the desert fathers, these early thinkers set down a foundation of ideas: that virginity is superior to marriage, that celibacy is required for service

of God, and that sex is contaminated with sin. The Christian preacher
and philosopher Origen, in the early third century, thought that sexual love stilled the spirit and that the embraces of the beloved were a
pathetic substitute for the only embrace that counted, the embrace of
the soul by Jesus. Origen himself, rather than suffer such temptations,
went to be castrated. In the late fourth century, Ambrose, not to be
outdone, wrote that marriage made women filthy and that a wife was
like a prostitute of one man. If a married couple yielded to sexual
desire, then it was of the utmost importance that their coupling be so
strict and mechanical that it held no pleasure whatsoever.

All this leads to Augustine, the most influential of thinkers in this
field. The ideas of Augustine about love and sex have been the subject
of countless books and commentaries, and rightly so, since upon the
foundation given him he constructed a house of ideas. The house has
stood and weathered a thousand assaults through the centuries, and
in orthodox Christianity at least it still is a formidable presence.

Augustine associated sexuality directly with original sin. The
shame of sexual love, by his reasoning, derives from the fateful disobedience in Genesis, after which Adam and Eve had the first sexual
desire (there having been none, according to Augustine, in Eden).
Sexual desire, after the Fall, was no longer a matter of will; it was
spontaneous and uncontrollable. All this being the case, every child
is conceived in sin and is in some way marked at conception, since
every man carries the contaminated seed of Adam. We should recall
that this corruption, expressed in the flesh of every one of us simply
by our being born, has an easily identifiable cause: the yielding of Eve
to the temptations of the Devil in the Garden of Eden.

We can see from this very brief sketch of Christian teaching how
such ideas led naturally to the beliefs and practices we would expect:

the requirement of celibacy for priests; the insistence upon the shame, if not depravity, of sex within marriage; the counsel against sexual pleasure, which alienates us from God; the natural inferiority of women; and the exaltation of virginity.

I trouble to sketch these ideas, since they would have been fully in play in the early seventeenth-century Spain, in which there lived a young man—we do not know his name—who attended Catholic church, but, as well, practiced in secret the rites and offered the prayers of Islam in company with other Muslims. And this, in Inquisitorial Spain. These men learned Arabic and parts of the Koran. They lived in constant threat of arrest, torture, and execution.

This young man read the literature of the day—Cervantes, Garcilaso, Góngora, Fernando de Rojas, and first, and most, Lope de Vega. He loved the work of Lope and memorized a host of his sonnets, as well as passages in Spanish of most of the other writers he held dear. In 1609, when Philip II expelled by proclamation the remaining Moriscos in Spain, he was among the miserable and despised exiles. Eventually he would find his way to Tunis, and there settle. And come to write, in Spanish, a treatise on marriage and sexual love that stands as the most astonishing and beautiful in the history of the language of the times. Though it is written in Tunis, it is, like its author, so casually mystical that it draws directly from the work of Sufis who had written on sexuality; and it is so incorrigibly Spanish that it is laced with sonnets from . . . Lope de Vega!

However remarkable its content, it is a patient exercise in explication. The writer reviews the characteristics of a man who should marry. He should be someone concerned about virtue, secure enough in his work to be able to support and care for a wife, and he should be amorously inclined. This last qualification alerts us immediately

that we are not reading a lecture from, say, Thomas Aquinas. Our
Spaniard goes on to review the qualities such a man should seek in
a wife, such as physical and moral beauty, piety, modesty in public, and capacity to bear children. He even has explicit recommendations for the marriage celebration, which, poignantly, follow in
many details what we know of such ceremonies in the Morisco communities of Al-Andalus. And then, to the obligations of marriage, in
which the evocative and passionate ideas of our author begin to take
shape: for he offers his arguments on behalf of the sexual rights of a
woman, her rightful claim on the amorous energies of her husband,
and her presumptive liberty to explore with him the whole combus-
tible range of her pleasures. There is even a passage of advice for a
woman whose husband is neglectful, because he is too often con-
sumed in prayer and contemplation. She has a right to the physical
love of her husband, and her right is founded not merely in the fact
of marriage; rather, his amorous devotions are a spiritual necessity, a
gentle directive from heaven, a duty to God.

We are taking leave, we sense, of Augustine. Our Spaniard has
not the least hesitation to head off into erotic detail. His theme is
consistent. A husband must recognize that a wife has the same sexual
rights and privileges in the nuptial bed as he does himself. His counsel
is clear: a husband must in his erotic offerings show a considerate,
knowledgeable attention to his wife, so that trust and pleasure can
live together. Imaginative adoption of a host of sexual positions is
recommended, though a husband must never ask his wife to take up a
position uncomfortable to her. He must in his loving of her bring her
to full, intense, transformative satisfactions, and he must make sure
that her climax occurs at the same time as his, or if not, that her climax always precedes his. Wholehearted exploration in bed, the slow,

attentive use of hands and mouth, all the fine variety of embraces, the transports of playfulness, the most candent and conscious devotion: all this is, by the good lights of our Spaniard, natural to marriage. It is celebratory, tender, reverential treatment of sexual love, and as we come to know the book, what grows in us is a wonder it exists at all. And as if all these surprising and delicious offerings were not enough, our Andalusian has yet more suggestive counsel to offer.

The first sentence in Professor Luce Lopez-Baralt's five-hundred-page study of the *Kama Sutra Español* says it best: "*Nunca lo había-mos oído en literatura española: el sexo nos lleva a Dios*": we have never heard it before in Spanish literature: sex bears us to God. Our Spaniard, writing in Tunis, makes just such a claim. When a couple gives themselves to their mutual delectations, when their envelopment in the pleasures of one another is unreserved and trusting, what they feel is far more than pleasure. Their devotion does more than burnish the body. It awakens the soul. The sensual, with such radiance and unity in bed, is more than sensual: it is transcendental. The experience is a special dispensation of God, and it means that sexual love might be understood as an ecstatic and initiatory prayer. It gives us directly and unmistakably a foretaste of paradise. We move outside of time, in a benediction of flesh that is natural to human life. Alone among the human appetites, erotic love, rightly practiced, can bring us spiritual refinement, and our shared pleasures are both joyful and sacramental.

It is one vision of life, of marriage, of sex, written by a Spaniard in exile in Tunis early in the seventeenth century. It is a vision of unusual gentleness, sustained beauty, and devotional heat. It brings together desire and knowledge, sense and spirit, sex and soul; and instead of shame, we have his song in favor of erotic life that is a flourishing and deliverance.

Al-Andalus and 1492:
the Plate Tectonics of History

*W*E HAVE BEEN in swift passage through the work of Al-Andalus, so surprising in its variety and accomplishment. The more time spent with the texts and the historians of the period, the more we come to admire the uncommon energies, exploratory zeal, and systematic rigor of the men and women of the time. Hardly a worthy human endeavor was left aside: we have visited their music and poetry, philosophy and mathematics, medicine and astronomy, agriculture, governance, gardening, and the arts of love.

Our look into such work has not allowed us to linger as we might. If we had such time together, we might look into the work of the eleventh-century Córdoban Ibn Hazm. When the caliphate disintegrated, he was forced into exile and occasional imprisonment. But he was a man of his times: highly educated, a sometime vizier, a religious scholar, student of law, and poet. He had the privilege of being, until the age of 14, raised in the harem, where his studies seemed to have enlivened him considerably. The women taught him poetry, composition, and the Koran. And so, later on in life, he thought himself the right man to write a book called *The Dove's Neck Ring*. It is an essay on love, which takes as its starting point the idea that those in love reunite parts of a soul divided at creation, so that love is a concord of life in this world that re-creates a sublime and original unity. It is a notion that speaks to the power and fatefulness of love, and its unpredictability. Ibn Hazm wants to give us love as it is, in men and women he has known. He writes openly that women's desires are equal to those of men, and even that women may have prophetic abilities. He wants to show how our lives play out in love, in our gestures and longings, work and concealment, signs and language; in our dreams, by our secrets, with song, in bed. The book even has a chapter charmingly entitled "On Falling in Love While Asleep," which goes to show that none of us is ever safe.

We should, before we take our leave of Al-Andalus, touch on the transformative current of mysticism that ran through the centuries of the period. Mysticism, in a sentence, is the principle that a man or woman with the right initiative may in this life come into unity with the divine. In Judaism, this principle took form in the Kabbalah, a study that came into prominence in Al-Andalus in the work of Moses de Leon, another far-rambling scholar who finally settled in Ávila. He is the author of the *Zohar*, the rich book which established the Kabbalah, a method by which the inner reality of the Torah may be studied. The student, using the framework offered in the *Zohar*, may work his way through levels of meaning in the scripture, each level more sacred than the next, so as to reach an enveloping reality from which all life is derived. The resulting knowledge allows the student to be of secret help on earth and a force for harmony everywhere. Of course, the search for such knowledge requires such inner capacity that it is not recommended that the study begin before age 40. Be that as it may, Moses de Leon's *Zohar* (that he wrote, or he conjured, or had revealed to him) is of course supposed to be based on much more ancient texts of the second century and be reflective of secret practices of antiquity. But some scholars think that the wily Moses de Leon dreamed up the whole art in Al-Andalus. This is a period when dreams were given life and released into the world. Whatever the case, it is in Al-Andalus that the Kabbalah was given definitively to the world.

And we cannot touch upon mysticism in Al-Andalus without bringing to center stage the work of the Sufis, an influential and extraordinary group. Poets, scholars, paupers, scientists, doctors, beggars, historians, jokesters, hidden and public men and women, this group created in Al-Andalus and throughout the Middle East one of the most distinguished records of accomplishment in the world. The Sufis hold that in this life, we may seek to purify the heart, perfect the mind, and learn the purpose of all life. Such work can only be undertaken because of love, by means of love, for the purposes of love. If a student makes real inner progress, then the honor of her conduct and her fidelity to learning leads inevitably to a luminescent, uncommon understanding; from such understanding, she has her practical chance to serve life, in love, with rare prescience. The distinguished historian L.P. Harvey has suggested that Granada itself owes its origin to the Sufis, and the Albayzín and the wider city have been the site of many Sufi schools. We shall have in this writing further occasion to learn of the work of the Sufis, after we visit the walls of tiles that are among the most uncanny beauties of all Granada.

We should note that the Christian mystics who rose to prominence in Spain—two examples are Saint Teresa of Ávila and John of the Cross, both of the sixteenth century—drew upon the mystical work of Al-Andalus in their search to say what they understood of their own spiritual experience. Take, for example, the famous seven mansions of Saint Teresa of Ávila, which we encounter in her mystical essay *The Interior Castle*. In that book, she describes the soul as made of crystal (or diamond) and having seven rooms that we may visit as we search for God. The conception seems to derive from two directly related Sufi texts, the *Maqamat* of Abu'l Hasan al-Nuri, which has the same journey through the same seven dwellings, also concentric, and the mystical seven valleys of Faridudin Attar's famous *Parliament of the Birds*, so magnetic a text that even Chaucer took a crack at writing a book of the same title and theme. It all bespeaks the cross-pollination of religious writing and experience, and Saint Teresa, one of the most famous Christian mystics of Spain, was of Jewish ancestry. It is as if, in the mysticism of Al-Andalus, we witness a *convivencia* of souls.

Saint John of the Cross, a monk, poet, and mystic, was a close associate of Saint Teresa. He, also, was from a Jewish family who had converted to Christianity. In a life of wandering, in which he was persecuted, imprisoned, and tortured by his fellow Christians, he managed to write some of the most compelling mystical poetry in Spanish. His poetry draws on Sufi imagery and on the Hebrew *Song of Songs*—more spiritual *convivencia*. It is intensely erotic and addresses the chance that we may (as the Sufis also held) die consciously in this life and move by love into unity with the beloved. The ecstasy of two devoted lovers, in his powerful verse, is at once a resurgence of soul— a departure from oneself into another and a better world.

As to the influence of mystical and religious texts on Christian writing, in 1919, the renowned Spanish Arabist Miguel Asín Palacios set off a firestorm by showing how Arabic texts, especially the *miraj*—the ascent of Mohammad to heaven from Jerusalem—were almost certainly a source for Dante when he organized *The Divine Comedy*. And it turns out that Dante's teacher, Brunetto Latini, spent two years in Al-Andalus, in the court of Alphonso the Wise, the very place where texts about the *miraj* were translated. It is certain Lattini read them. Today, after nearly one hundred years of polemic, Dante scholarship has come round to the idea that a number of important Arabic texts were available to Dante when he composed his Christian epic.

And one last word on mysticism: I pray that some scholar some day may tell us what on earth happened during the visit of one luminous gentleman to Al-Andalus: Francis of Assisi, who was there in the years 1213–15. One of the most bold and independent of saints was present in the country which, more than any other in Europe of the period, was awash in heady currents of mystical insight and practice. What might he have learned?

And if we may, before we leave our brief account of the spiritual and practical genius of Al-Andalus, let us touch on one last domain: color. Contemporary accounts of the life of the period mention the brilliant colors of clothing seen on the streets, so that against the whitewashed houses figures moved brilliantly, like flowers in the wind. It is yet another example of the Andalusian genius of collecting and refining the best of their cultural heritage, whatever the region or language where it was found, and whatever the religion of the people in possession of such knowledge. So from knowledge gathered from Arabic, Hebrew, Greek, and Latin sources, they learned how to dye cotton, flax, palm fiber, hemp, wool, and leather. On the Iberian peninsula, they lived in the fine slanting light of the Mediterranean and put on clothes of indigo, gold, tropical green, crimson, lapis lazuli, all using both mineral and vegetable dyes. Most valuable of all was the uncanny *byssus*, a silken material obtained from a mollusk, close in appearance to the pearl oyster, but found off the coast of Tunisia and southern Iberia. The filaments are golden, unforgettably soft, and were woven into garments so precious that they were forbidden to leave the country. Seen in full sunlight, the cloth changed color subtly but continuously, its lusters in strange harmony with the weather and the angle and intensity of the light. It is a fabric that could stand in for Al-Andalus itself, which offered over the centuries so rare and various a range of beauties in response to the changing lights of time and chance and opportunity.

PEACE AND CROSSFIRE OF THE *CONVIVENCIA*

The history of Al-Andalus is now more open to us than ever before, as a result of the labors of scholars, principally the work of the last forty years. There were many superb scholars who wrote previously, but the more recent work, seen as a whole, is extraordinary. To the lay reader, it is like watching the excavation of buried treasure, lost under layers of confusion, ideology, propaganda, ignorance, religious animosity, indifference, and hot debate. But treasure it is, and with every further investigation, the facts of *convivencia* become more intricate and complex. Two things are clear: the *convivencia* was no utopia and was subject to breakdown, violence, rivalries, suspicion, and stalemate, and second, its accomplishments were magnificent, undeniable, and transformative of European life. As to Al-Andalus itself, we are still learning how interfaith relations played out in political, professional, and domestic life. One way to gain the flavor of it

The Alhambra at twilight, with the famous *Torre de Comares* in the foreground and the Sierra Nevada along the horizon. © ROBERT BLESSE

The Alhambra aglow, as seen each night from the Albayzín. © STEVEN NIGHTINGALE

A closeup of the whirling, sidereal *muqarnas* of the ceiling of the *Sala de las Dos Hermanas* in the Alhambra. Titus Burckhardt calls them "a honeycomb whose honey consisted of light itself." © JOSE VAL BAL

The Albayzín as seen from the Sabika Hill, high in the Darro Canyon, east of the Alhambra. © ROBERT BLESSE

A closeup of the center of the Albayzín, with its complexity of terraces, balconies, windows, and flowers.

© JOSÉ VAL BAL

The hill of the Sacromonte above the Albayzín, where the famous lead tablets were found bearing the Seal of Solomon. © STEVEN NIGHTINGALE

The church of San Pedro at the base of the Albayzín, with the Alhambra soaring above. © JOSE VAL BAL

The Albayzín at night, with its illuminated windows and mystery. © JOSE VAL BAL

The Church of Saint John, in the lower Albayzín, with its fine Almohad tower. The church has been recently restored. © JOSE VAL BAL

The thriving *Calderería Nueva* in the Albayzín, where Arab merchants from north Africa sell goods from around the world. © JOSE VAL BAL

A street near our carmen in the Albayzín, with its vines, cobblestones, and come-hither narrow passageway.
© STEVEN NIGHTINGALE

A beautiful terrace in the Albayzín. It has the traditional offerings: grapevine, flowers, railing, woodwork and open sitting area. © STEVEN NIGHTINGALE

The entrance to a typical carmen, with fountain, *alberca*, flowers, lanterns, brickwork, grapevine, and dappled light. The *Alcazar* of the Alhambra rises in the distance. © STEVEN NIGHTINGALE

A watercolor of a beautiful and historic carmen in the Albayzín, recently restored. © RICARDO BELLIDO CEBALLOS

A watercolor of the Darro canyon at the base of the Albayzín, showing early fall colors and one of the low bridges. © RICARDO BELLIDO CEBALLOS

A classic torreón of a lovely carmen, with sitting area, flowers, and irresistible hammock. © STEVEN NIGHTINGALE

Tile work over the entranceway to a house in the center of the Albayzín. We came to think of our neighborhood as a barrio of stars. © STEVEN NIGHTINGALE

A street in the Albayzín engulfed by bougainvillea. © STEVEN NIGHTINGALE

In a small garden in the Albayzín, a young fig tree growing aside a flourishing mock orange. © STEVEN NIGHTINGALE

In the Albayzín, wherever there is support, roses will climb and bloom and, given the chance, grow over the roof and onto the street. © STEVEN NIGHTINGALE

Windows of colored glass found now and again in the Albayzín. The morning meant green and blue streaming light in the room. © STEVEN NIGHTINGALE

Lemons and oranges growing over a wall in the afternoon light of the Albayzín. © JOSE VAL BAL

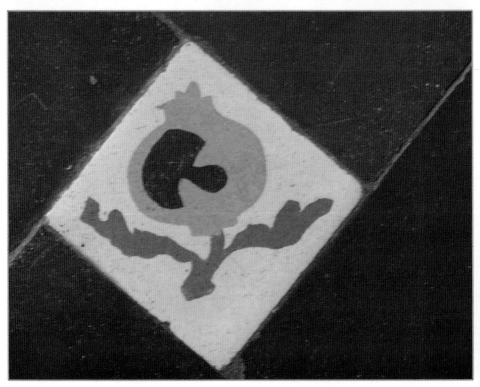

An *olambrilla*—an example of the small painted tiles often inset into terra cotta floors in the Albayzín—this one of a pomegranate. © STEVEN NIGHTINGALE

The legendary double arches of the Mezquita in Cordoba. Standing among them for any length of time can give rise to a feeling of weightlessness.

The poster advertising the *Concurso de Cante Jondo*—Contest of Deep Song—organized by García Lorca and Manuel Falla in 1922. It was planned for the *Placeta de San Nicolás* in the Albayzin, but the big crowds obliged a move to the terrace of the Alhambra.

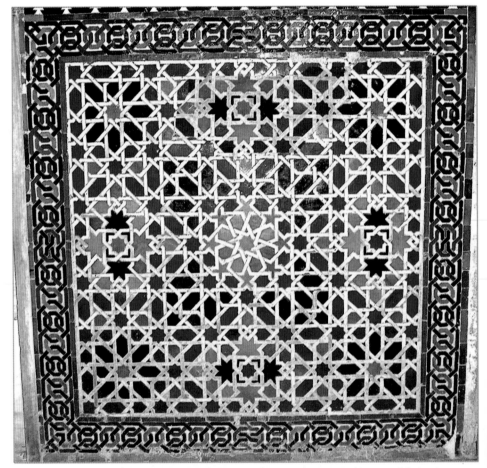

A wall of tiles in the *Torre de Comares*. The whole pattern here, in relation to its history and design, is discussed in depth in the chapter entitled "A Few Notions of Geometry and Revelation." The tile work is meant to offer us the chance to understand patterns of conception and creation, refine our perceptions, and develop new capacities of mind. © STEVEN NIGHTINGALE is to consider a spectrum of facts through the region, and throughout the centuries of Al-Andalus. Consider, for example, the partnership in diplomacy during the reign of Abd Rahman III: a Muslim, he appointed a Christian ambassador to the courts of Byzantium and Syria and to the court of Otto I of Germany, and he appointed, as well, a Jewish ambassador, the formidable Hasday ibn Shaprut, to the Christian courts of Navarre and León. In the time of Shaprut, such was the willingness to exchange ideas and the facility with languages that we learn a Jewish scholar went so far as to expound the Talmud, in Arabic, to the caliph himself. And we have seen how, in the twelfth-century school of translators of the Christian Alphonso the Wise, the work was done by teams of men of all three faiths, working in Arabic, Latin, and Spanish. In commerce, Muslim traders, with silks and timber, saffron and paper, roamed all over the Mediterranean but traded also with the Christian north. Christian prelates complained that the young of their faith were too enthusiastically speaking Arabic. And they were criticized, as well, for fasting with Jews on the Jewish religious ceremony of the Day of Atonement. Be that as it may, anyone who could would seek out an Arab or a Jewish physician, such was their reputation during many of the centuries of Al-Andalus. Not only did they serve as physicians to caliphs and emirs, but we know of one Jewish doctor who tended to the privileged and powerful nuns in the cloister of Las Huelgas, owner of rich farmlands, refuge to royal widows, and center of local Christian power.

Historians have gathered, as they can, the facts of the ground from the nearly eight centuries of the commingling of faiths. There were interfaith marriages. In some settlements, the faiths lived together; in others, in separate sections of town. But they certainly traded together. Muslims cultivated vineyards, which were undoubtedly used to supply wine to Christians. And Muslims are known to have visited monasteries to sample the latest vintage, and even to be arrested with their Christian drinking partners for disturbing the peace after too enthusiastic a tippling together. Muslims might work for Christians as grooms or muleteers. Muslim women might visit churches, though they were advised against it because they might "fornicate with the clergy." A Christian could come from a Jewish family. A Muslim might hail from a Christian family. And some families might have more than one faith in their ancestry. It is recorded that one Alphonso Fernández Samuel instructed that he be buried with the Torah beside his head, the Koran on his breast, and the Cross at his feet—a kind of one-coffin show of *convivencia*. Jewish prayers were intoned to the music of popular Muslim songs. In Murcia, gifted Muslim musicians and jugglers were invited to participate in Christian religious festivals. Muslims brought Christian food and customs into their religious festivals, where men and women celebrated together. They even liked the *churros*, a long fried sugary donut that the reader may buy today in the Albayzín, in say, Plaza Larga, any day of the week. Try it with a *café con leche*.

Muslims and Christians were in business together, in one case owning an inn in a Jewish quarter of the town of Borja. A Muslim and a Jew might come together in an enterprise to lend money, a kind of interfaith private banking. And if we consider the irrepressible energies of commerce in Al-Andalus, and the remarkable scope of talents offered, we can easily imagine any one worker wanting to sell his products to anyone who might have an interest, whatever their faith. Are we really to believe that the baker and the blacksmith, the silk weaver and the paper merchant, the carpenter and the spice peddler, the vendor of vegetables and the maker of painted ceramics or metal pots, all working in the rambunctious markets throughout Iberia, sought to restrict their clients exclusively to those of their own faith? It is absurd to think so. Commerce, the daily and necessary trading that all of us count on, is a unifier, a leveler, a maker of community and understanding. It is what we do together. A crowded market, singing with energy, is a thing of practical and cultural genius. The roles of buyer and seller have no faith but the faith that in a market, we have the chance to offer our work and knowledge to one another, the faith that our lives can be of mutual enrichment. The regulated commerce of Al-Andalus, with its market inspectors of weights and measures, regulations for cooked food and thread count in textiles, and supervision of craft guilds, provided so superb a model that it was adopted by Christian municipal governments in later centuries. Even today in the Albayzín's Plaza Larga, over the beautiful gate called the Arco de las Pesas, you can see upon the walls the measures and weights overseen by the inspectors. From this careful, efficient regulation come the Arabic roots of so many market terms: *almacén* (large market, warehouse), *almotacén* (market inspector), *alcaicería* (silk market), and *almoneda* (auction sale). And supporting all this rough-and-tumble commerce was the strictly regulated currency, the famous gold *dinar* and *dirhams*, with their fixed weights of gold. It served as the currency for Iberia and the Maghreb (the North African coastline), used by Christians in the north, Muslims and Christians, and by everyone in Al-Andalus.

Let us close this rambling exploration of the minutiae of the *convivencia* with a quote from a writer known as the Blessed Ramon Llull, a Catalan of the thirteenth century. As a young man, his principal interest seems to have been amorous escapades with women of beauty and knowledge. One day, writing a love poem, he had a vision of Jesus and embarked thereafter on a program of self-education

whose ferocity can hardly be believed. A Christian, he studied Arabic
for nine years. He translated a book of the seminal Muslim theologian Al-Ghazali. He studied the *Zohar* at length, and to his study
of that complex Jewish mysticism he joined a long study among the
Sufi poets, whom he credits outright as the inspiration for one of
his books about the nature of love. He traveled about Europe trying to convince popes and the powerful to begin schools of Eastern
languages in Europe. He was captivated by the science of calculation
and tried to devise a thinking machine, whose use would let anyone
work with key theological concepts, all arranged in a system of logic
with rules of calculation that used algebraic formulas and relied upon
combinatorial diagrams. It was meant to be a virtual, practical science of the sacred that a man or woman could use to guide decisions
and approach the truth. And on the way to such exalted domains, the
Lullian art could solve any other problem that came round the bend.
His first work on this calculator of the soul is wonderfully titled *On
the Brief Art of Finding Truth*. If the reader wants to drink deeply
of the heady brew of Al-Andalus, she should seek out this arcane
labor of a man of genius. Ramon Llull went on to write more than
two hundred forty books—translations, poetry, books on medicine,
mystical treatises. In his spare time, he was a Franciscan monk who
traveled extensively in North Africa seeking conversions. Reading his
work, we naturally enough ask: conversion to what, exactly?

One of his books is called *The Book of the Gentile and the Three
Wise Men*. It concerns a gentile who is a philosopher yet has no belief
or knowledge of God. He is facing death, is disconsolate, and sets
himself to wander in a beautiful forest, where he meets three wise
men: a Jew, a Christian, and a Muslim. They are friends and offer
to teach the Gentile the facts of faith and the glory of God. They are

ably assisted in this work by a very beautiful woman whom they find drinking from a clear spring in the forest. She, as we might have expected, turns out to be Intelligence, and she helps them use Llull's theological art in a course of instruction. At the end of the course, the Gentile is to choose one of the three faiths for his own. So do the three wise men argue eloquently and powerfully for their own faith, and after a few hundred pages, the Gentile, having given the closest attention to all three, comes to his moment when he must choose which faith he would take as his own. And he does *not* choose. And the three wise men, at the end of a long and exhausting exchange, say goodbye to one another in an extraordinary passage that has to be read as a whole to be believed. Here it is:

> *While the wise man was speaking these words and many others, the three of them arrived at the place where they had first met by the city gates; and there they took leave of one another most amiably and politely, and each asked forgiveness of the other for any disrespectful word he might have spoken against his religion. Each forgave the other, and when they were about to part, one wise man said, "Do you think we have nothing to gain from what happened to us in the forest? Would you like to meet once a day and, by the five trees and the ten conditions signified by their flowers, discuss according to the manner The Lady of Intelligence showed us, and have our discussions last until all three of us have only one faith, one religion, and until we can find some way to honor and serve one another, so that we can be in agreement? For war, turmoil, ill will, injury, and shame prevent man from agreeing on one belief.*

Each of the three wise men approved of what the wise man
had said, and they decided on a time and place for their
discussions, as well as how they should honor and serve
one another, and how they should dispute; and that when
they had agreed on and chosen one faith, they would go
forth into the world giving glory and praise to the name of
our Lord God. Each of the three wise men went home and
remained faithful to his promise.

Seven hundred years later, reading this, we feel the incorrigible sweetness of it. These are three men who have been engaged for hundreds of pages in a far-reaching debate about the virtues of their own religions. The claim here is that such debate, the open search for truth, can be an occasion for honor; it can itself be a work of knowledge, peaceful and respectful, that we pursue together.

It is a vision of a better world. The *convivencia* was a dangerous experiment. It proceeded by fits and starts, setbacks and abominations, strange alliances, unexpected advances, and practical ingenuities. Its achievements, only recently come into focus, were without precedent in Europe. It is a schoolroom where we might learn, we who even now are failing disastrously to live together at a time with much more dangerous weapons and with billions of lives at stake. And we might start by learning from its fate, when in the fifteenth century, Al-Andalus, with all its accumulated knowledge and accomplishments, met King Ferdinand and Queen Isabel. The two monarchs brought to the Iberian peninsula a will to power, a formidable union, a sense of messianic destiny, and, in 1480, their own specially designed government agency: the Holy Inquisition.

HATRED ADMINISTRATIVE AND
METICULOUS; ARM-WRESTLING THE POPE

Let us visit Toledo, the city of the legendary thirteenth-century school
of translators of Alphonso the Wise. The year is 1486, on a Sunday
in early February. The Inquisition has identified some seven hundred
and fifty Christians from *converso* families—men and women who
have converted from Judaism—who are suspected of backsliding, of
maintaining Jewish beliefs or practices of any kind in their daily life.
This is the scene, as recorded by a historian of the day, and quoted
often in the most authoritative of modern histories of the Inquisition:

> *On Sunday the twelfth of February of 1486 all the reconciled*
> *[of seven parishes] went in procession. They were about 750*
> *in number, men and women. The men were all together,*
> *wearing nothing on their heads or feet . . . They bore unlit*
> *candles in their hands. The women were in a group, without*
> *any covering on their bodies, their faces and feet bare like*
> *those of the men, and with the same unlit candles. In the*
> *group of men were many of prominence and high honor. In*
> *the terrible cold and the dishonor and disgrace they suffered*
> *since such a crowd turned out to watch them (many people*
> *from other districts had come to see them), they went along*
> *sobbing and howling, and tearing out their hair, more for the*
> *dishonor they received than for their offenses against God. In*
> *this way they went in tribulation through all the city where*
> *the procession of Corpus Christi goes, until they arrived*
> *at the cathedral. At the entrance to the cathedral were two*
> *chaplains, who made the sign of the cross over each one's*

forehead, saying, "Receive the sign of the cross, which you denied, and being deceived, lost." Then they went through the church until they arrived at a scaffolding put up by the new door, and on it were the official Inquisitors. Nearby was another scaffolding where they said Mass and preached to them. After this a notary rose and began to call out each one by name, saying, "Is so-and-so here?" And that person raised his candle and said, "Yes." Then the notary read aloud publicly all the ways he had judaized. The same thing was done with the women. When all this was over they announced publicly to them their penance, and ordered them to go in procession for six Fridays, scourging their naked backs with cords of hemp, going without covering for their feet or heads. And they were to fast on each of the six Fridays. And they were ordered also to never, for all their lives, hold public offices such as alcalde, alguacil, regidor, jurado, or be messengers or public scribes, and those of them who held those offices were to lose them. And they were not ever to be able to work as moneychangers, shopkeepers, spice sellers, or hold any official position whatever. And they could not wear silk, nor clothes colored such as scarlet, nor any gold, silver, pearls, or jewels. And they were unworthy to be witnesses. It was ordered then that if they relapsed into the same error once more, and did again what had been attributed to them, they would be condemned to burn. And when this was finished at two o'clock in the afternoon, they all went away.

This procession went through the middle of Toledo, the city that had been the very university of all Europe. It was a city, not long before this scene, graced by the presence of some of the most beautiful synagogues, churches, and mosques in Spain. In this context, the procession described takes the breath away from any reader: some of the most distinguished citizens of the city, all of them Christians converted from Judaism, men and women, stripped and paraded in bitter cold before their neighbors. They are humiliated, sentenced to further humiliations, deprived of current and future work, forbidden certain clothes and adornments, and informed they would be burned alive for a second offense.

What, pray tell, had they done to merit such punishment?

It is a question that goes to the heart of the Spanish Inquisition, and it is easy to answer: they had done nothing whatever.

We can understand this by looking at the origins of the Inquisition in Spain. First, a review of the facts. The Inquisition, as organized originally by the papacy in 1231, was under the control of the Vatican. The Inquisition's power was established in a papal bull, which is an official declaration carrying the full weight of the papacy. The bull endorsing the use of torture came in 1252. Ferdinand and Isabel, beginning their own Inquisition in 1480, did something unprecedented: they set out to make the Inquisition a personal, special, strategic royal project. In a bull of 1478, Pope Sixtus IV had given them the crucial authority: Ferdinand and Isabel could appoint all the inquisitors themselves. Now they dominated an institution with uncommon potential that could be shaped into a potent ministry of power and control. The monarchs oversaw the rules of this special new court. They appointed the inquisitors, they set their salaries, and they coordinated their work with the military. It was an extraordinary move, given that the Inquisition was, of course, a strictly Catholic institution meant to identify and punish heresy. But

Ferdinand and Isabel, with canny political willfulness, had remade
this Catholic Inquisition in their own image. The first burnings were
in 1481, and the monarchs, beginning with their supervision of the
first inquisitors, had a new and well-funded base of power whose
writ extended throughout Spain. It extended, most importantly, into
regions where royal power was otherwise weak or suspect.

The system worked like this: anyone could denounce a family
member, a neighbor, or any other citizen to the Inquisition. Once
denounced, the accused might hear at night the knock on the door
that meant immediate arrest. It is a knock that echoes through centuries. The accused would be taken straightaway to a secret prison.
He was not allowed any money, paper, or visitors. He was not told
the charges against him. The accusers' names were kept secret. The
Inquisition demanded a confession, and the accused was shown the
devices of torture that awaited those who refused to acknowledge
their crimes. But of course those arrested, knowing neither their
accuser nor the charges against them, had no way of knowing what
they were expected to confess. After three demands for confession,
the accused was read a list of charges (carefully edited to conceal the
witnesses' identity) and required to answer on the spot.

Yet this sudden and mysterious imprisonment was only part
of the process. For after the arrest was made, all the goods of the
accused were seized. A thorough inventory was compiled posthaste,
from gold and coins right down to items of kitchenware. Values
were assigned. A notary examined and verified the figures. *And then
the costs of imprisonment of the accused were paid from his own
assets.* As the time in prison accumulated, the goods of the accused
would be sold at public auction. Sometimes an entire family would
be imprisoned during this period. But even if they were not, the

families might starve to death or be thrown into the street to beg, since the family was now without income and all its goods were being sold off. No provision was made to support the family of the accused until 1561.

If the accused had not confessed satisfactorily, and the accusation was grave, then the tribunal turned to torture, infrequently but systematically. Anyone of any age could be tortured. The inquisitors, specialists in human torment, had looked carefully into the wretched cabinet of savagery and chosen three tortures. In all of them, the accused was stripped down. In the first, the rack, he or she was tied down and stretched into progressive agonies. The second was the strapado: with wrists tied behind the back with a rope suspended from the ceiling on a pulley, the accused was hoisted high with weights on the feet, then dropped suddenly. The pressure ruined muscle and nerve and pulled shoulder joints from sockets. The third was called the water torture, and its details are well-known, since with shame I note that in the administration of President George W. Bush and Richard Cheney, the practice was officially adopted in military interrogations in the United States of America, where it is known as waterboarding. I do not know whether President Bush decided with special excitement that his administration should adopt a medieval torture that had the professional blessing of the Spanish Inquisition. Perhaps he felt it gave him more historical gravitas and luster. Whatever the case, during the Inquisition, this torture, like the others, was attended by a whole battery of officials: inquisitors, a notary, a secretary to record what was said, the torturers themselves, and occasionally a physician. If there was a confession, then it had to be repeated in prison the next day. If it was not, the torture began again.

If the accused did not die under torture or die in prison, he still could be sentenced to burn at the stake for heresy. If condemned to die, the victims were informed the night before, which made appeal rather difficult. They went to the auto-da-fé—the public ceremony to announce judgments and punishments—wearing a yellow garment called a *sanbenito*, painted with crosses, flames, and devils. They wore also the *corozo*, a pointed hat that is a prominent feature today in Spain in the promenades of men during the celebration, if that is the word, of Semana Santa—Holy Week in the Christian calendar. The condemned, after their exhibition, condemnation, and sentencing, were then, as was said, "relaxed" to their executioners. It is one of the most detestable uses ever made of a verb, even though our language has been, over the centuries, recruited often enough into the service of hatred. Those condemned in absentia were burned in effigy. Those condemned who had already died had their corpses dug up and burnt.

The lesser punishments were to do penance, which could be a fine, banishment, service in the galleys, or wearing the *sanbenito*, with all its florid images of judgment and punishment. It was a public sign of shame and ignominy, and a penitent might be forced to wear it a short time, or for life, though that sentence could be commuted. After the time was up, the *sanbenito* was hung in the church to mark the disgrace of the family. For the more severe sentence of reconciliation, the prisoner got a long prison sentence, banishment, forced galley service, or flogging; in addition, the prisoner and his family usually had all their wealth confiscated. Galley service, of course, supplied the military with men who could be worked to death, or who succumbed to the disease rampant in the ships. As to flogging, the sentences were often between one and two hundred lashes. Men and women, young and old, received this sentence. They were stripped to the waist, mounted on a donkey, and whipped through the streets. During the course of this punishment, those in the street were able to scorn the sufferers, hurl stones at them, and shout execrations.

I recount all this because, as famous as is the Inquisition, its methods and rules are still not widely known. In the popular imagination, we recall grisly stories of heretics tied to stakes and having gobbets of flesh ripped from them with tongs heated in a fire, before the victims were burned to death. But this grandstanding of the executioners is, I suggest, not the real key to understanding the Inquisition. What this rare institution offered is a finely calculated formula for hatred that any society, anywhere, might use for its own purposes. The formula worked because of its closely fitted, potent assembly of elements. Taken together, they are: anonymous denunciation, secret prisons, confinement without charge, seizure of wealth, family disgrace, torture, popular ceremonies of punishment and humiliation, and public execution. To this list we must add one more, the absolutely crucial piece: sponsorship and control by the highest power in the land. For the Spanish Inquisition had this essential component: it was the creation of Ferdinand and Isabel.

We come, then, to one of the hinges upon which turned the history of Spain. In 1482, only a little more than one year after the first burnings, Pope Sixtus IV, upon receiving a series of reports of Ferdinand and Isabel's Inquisition, understood what was happening. And he had had enough. He issued another bull, one of the most extraordinary ever to come forth from the Vatican. We read it even today with admiration. For the pope was forcibly taking back the Inquisition, which had been, after all, his to begin with. He was on to Ferdinand and Isabel, and he told them the truth:

. . . the Inquisition has for some time been moved not by zeal
for the faith and salvation of souls, but by lust for wealth,
and that many true and faithful Christians, on the testimony
of enemies, rivals, slaves, and other lower and even less prop-
er persons, have without any legitimate proof been thrust
into secular prisons, tortured and condemned as relapsed
heretics, deprived of their goods and property and handed
over to the secular arm to be executed, to the peril of souls,
setting a pernicious example and causing disgust to many.

Pope Sixtus had a solution which a modern-day civil-rights activ-
ist would recognize. Bishops, who were responsible to Rome (rather
than to Ferdinand and Isabel) had to oversee the inquisitors. The
accused had to be informed of all charges against him. All accusers
had to be clearly identified. The accused must be allowed a legal
defender. Episcopal prisons only must be used. And any sentence
handed down could be appealed directly to Rome.

Pope Sixtus had issued in clear and forceful terms a bull designed
to correct the practices of the Inquisition that made it a source of
terror and a demonic instrument of royal power. The bull all but sev-
ered the insidious connection between the Inquisition and Ferdinand
and Isabel. It meant that the Vatican could control the institution
and stop the monarchs from using it as a political tool. It is open
to question whether the Inquisition would have become, instead, an
instrument of terror of the Catholic church. But the proclamation
was a political move of drama and consequence, since it restored
control of the institution to Rome and so gave to the Vatican the
measure of power it needed to influence politics and civil society in
Spain. Sixtus, with his bull, had stopped the new Spanish Inquisition

in its tracks by doing away with some of its most diabolical practices. His eloquent declaration had the potential to change the history of Spain, as it reorganized in the decades before and after the capture of Granada in 1492.

Ferdinand understood that the whole royal initiative was at risk, and he responded to Sixtus with righteous fury. He brought political pressure on the pope through key Spanish bishops. He professed amazement. He wrote that the bull could not be authentic. He claimed, falsely, that the pope had given a general pardon to *conversos* in Spain, whatever their offenses. He said the "concessions" offered by Sixtus were due to the "cunning persuasions" of the *conversos*. He flatly declared his intention to defy the bull. And he asked aggressively for the bull to be revoked and full powers over the Spanish Inquisition to be entrusted to him and his queen. An essential question of power hung in the balance. Ferdinand and Isabel had to subdue the pope or lose control of the machinery of accusation, torture, and confiscation.

The months rolled on. We will never know the full extent of the political flame-throwing, the exchange of threats and promises, private meetings and messages, and the acid tension between Rome and the Spanish Crown. In October, only five months after he asserted rightful control over the Inquisition in Spain, Pope Sixtus IV caved in. He suspended the bull. Ferdinand and Isabel had faced down the Vatican. They resumed complete control over the Inquisition in Spain. To add cream to their victory, their control was confirmed in yet another papal bull the next year, which took the definitive further step of appointing as inquisitor general the choice of Ferdinand himself, a man who had been the confessor of both Ferdinand and Isabel, Tomás de Torquemada. Working with the sovereigns,

Torquemada would appoint new inquisitors, establish their duties, and create permanent courts in most major cities where *conversos* lived. The combination of papal blessing and royal power meant that no region could resist, though many knew well what terror was coming their way.

The Spanish Inquisition lasted until 1834, a three-hundred-and-fifty-four-year run. It is useful to reflect on what it was and what it was not. To do so is to step into the tempestuous pool of Spanish history, with its violent waves of opinion and durable scholarly animosities. But just as with the history of Al-Andalus, enough time has passed, and enough work has been done, so that the facts on the ground might be assessed more accurately.

The picture is complex. It is important, given the infernal reputation of the Inquisition, not to overstate its influence and its scope. Such is its strange power, even today, that it has been portrayed as a monolithic, pervasive force responsible for just about every atrocious event in Spain in the centuries just after the fall of Granada. It was not such a force. Some writers have put the deaths ordered by the Inquisition at sensational figures, as if it were some cosmic death squad, but the final toll of men and women burnt at the stake, after much scholarly sweat and estimation, comes in at around ten to twelve thousand. And this in a period when religious wars convulsed whole societies, with much higher death tolls. The banning of certain books, via the famous *Index of Prohibited Books*, was not uniquely an initiative of the Spanish Inquisition, which was following the lead of the Vatican and other Catholic countries in Europe that had published their own indices. And the institution, though it was designed by Ferdinand and Isabel to have authority throughout Spain, did not in fact have a marked and dramatic presence everywhere in the country. Some less-populated areas might go a good long while without suffering the ministrations of the Inquisition, so that its local impact was slight. For some of the years, or even decades of its existence, the auto-da-fé was not much in evidence, whether due to temporary financial difficulties of the tribunal or an unfortunate lack of new victims. When victims were available, not every one was tortured, and only a small percentage of those arrested were burnt alive. Nor was the Inquisition a universally acclaimed institution. Many Spaniards fought against it, wrote against it, and resisted its influence, often at terrible risk to themselves.

All this being the case, we need to marshal the facts and try to get a clear look at what it meant for the country that created it at the time it was created, and what it has meant since.

We must remember, first of all, the context: Al-Andalus. It cannot be repeated often enough: three great faiths lived together, studied together, did business together, made war as allies and companions of one another, and learned one another's languages. Muslims and Jews governed together; Christian kings governed Muslim and Jewish subjects. An earlier King Ferdinand, the third, the father of Alphonso the Wise, in the thirteenth century called himself, accurately enough, the "King of the Three Religions." At his death, his tomb in Seville bore inscriptions cut into fine marble, as befits a king. But not merely one: there are four inscriptions, in Latin, Hebrew, Arabic, and Castilian. The Hebrew and Arabic texts refer to Spain as, respectively, Sefarad and Al-Andalus, and use dates computed and adjusted according to Jewish and Muslim calendars. And each inscription uses the ceremonial and rhetorical language of its own religious tradition, all in honor of one of the great kings of Al-Andalus. It is one of the most moving and beautiful tributes to any man in the history of Spain.

King Ferdinand of the fifteenth century and his powerful Queen
Isabel did not honor their ancestors, nor did they celebrate, con-
serve, and bear forward for the benefit of Spain the genius of their
own people. This was a king and queen who had fallen heir to the
most rich, various, and distinguished intellectual heritage in medieval
Europe. They lived in the midst of the Renaissance, a cultural awak-
ening built on the foundations provided in large part by Al-Andalus.
No country in Europe was in possession of the resources of mind and
wealth as Spain in the fourteenth and fifteenth centuries. What did
they do with their inheritance, at one of the most promising moments
in European history?

Ferdinand and Isabel had extraordinary political skills, organized around a central principle: the concentration of power. And
that will to power, in all its skill and purposefulness, its energy
and shrewd, ferocious ambition, was nowhere more evident than
in their remaking of the Inquisition into their personal ministry.
Recall that for these monarchs, the principal struggle was to unify
Spain beneath their banner. It was a country divided by geography,
language, culture, and religion, fragmented by a temperamental
nobility and proudly independent regions. By what means could
Ferdinand and Isabel extend, consolidate, and enrich their power?
The answer, of course, was by any means possible. But they needed
an institution whose writ would run throughout the country, and
whose power was fierce, unquestioned, and historic, yet an institution that could be wholly subjugated to royal power. It was a
political puzzle of the first order. With the Holy Inquisition, they
had a robust solution. For even in those cities of Spain where the
monarchs were weak, the Catholic church had a presence, power,
resources, and authority. It was their main chance. Ferdinand and

Isabel seized the Inquisition, held it, defended it, dominated and used it, and then left it to history and to Spain.

It was the perfect instrument. Since the accusers were secret, every man and woman was vulnerable to the most absurd and groundless denunciations. Since the accused paid for his or her own imprisonment, torture, and punishment, each of them might be confined and tormented to the limits of their wealth. Since the confiscated wealth of the accused paid for the Inquisition, with a healthy share given to Ferdinand and Isabel, it was in the interest of the church and the court to target powerful *converso* families with large fortunes. Since the officers and associated staff of the Inquisition were exempt from accusation, from any civil or criminal procedure in secular courts, and even from some taxation, they could, and did, engage in profiteering, fraud, larceny, and criminal assault, all while enjoying perfect legal immunity. It is hard to imagine a more masterfully designed instrument of power, and any of us reading this history would be glad to say that is the end of it.

But it was not the end. The reputation of the Inquisition is not merely that of unspeakable injustice. It has a reputation as fiendish, and it is worth understanding why. Beyond the perfection of its design by Ferdinand and Isabel as a tool of power, they made two enduring changes in what we might call the template of hatred. First—and this is crucial—the Spanish Inquisition gave the work of hatred a *deep-rooted, durable administrative form*, with a considerable staff, written procedures, excellent record-keeping, close bureaucratic control, and solid government support and recognition. It was an institution built to last. And second, *they made their ceremonies of humiliation and punishment into public festivals of political glamor, popular fanfare, and performance art*. They were held on feast days, Sundays and holidays, so everyone could attend. Members of civil, municipal, and religious bodies were all formally invited. The ceremony was magisterial, what with the lurid costumes, the solemn pageantry, the sonorous declaration of punishments, the theatrical and remorseless condemnations, and the delivery of victims to the crown's custody to be burned alive. The Inquisition made these events a natural part of the fabric of power in Spain. Important families vied to be seen at them; there was competition over the best seats; tailors and dress-makers were recruited to make the apparel that suited so august and celebratory an occasion. The well-connected and powerful, bedecked and bejeweled, all turned up in specially designated seats, near to the sumptuously dressed clerics. Anyone who wanted to be on the side of power, who wanted to give extra margin to their own security, or who just wanted a piece of the action needed to be present and noticed—not least by their neighbors. Tens of thousands of people attended these events, which were held in the biggest public square available. The auto-da-fé, as the decades progressed, took on more flamboyance and grandeur and came to be held in celebration of important royal events. In 1560, an auto-da-fé in Toledo was sched-uled to celebrate the marriage of Phillip II and Isabel of Valois, a macabre accompaniment to nuptials if there ever was one. Phillip II went on to be a royal enthusiast, presiding over no fewer than five baroque auto-da-fé, with minutely organized pomp, Mass, and the flagrant procession of the despised and condemned. The mind reels.

Scholars have noted the perfection, if that is the word, of this cal-culated governmental form. It has been demonically influential. One historian, Joseph Perez, has noted an obvious modern sequel, Stalin's technique of arrest and show trials in the Soviet Union. The similar-ity of key elements is there for all to see: the secret accusation, the sudden arrest and imprisonment, the use of torture, the insistence on public confession, the ruination of the family of the condemned. It is an accursed heritage. But it is only part of the story, since Ferdinand and Isabel had a comprehensive plan for power. The Inquisition should be seen not as the single tool, but one of many, the sum of which achieved for the monarchs the religious and political unity they sought. In 1481, the Inquisition had begun its persecution and burnings. In 1492, the monarchs took control of Granada, expelled the Jews from their kingdom, and flattened the Jewish quarter of the city, and then, as we have seen, they set in motion a series of laws and proclamations which taken together amounted to ethnic cleansing of the remaining Muslims. The prosperous Muslim and Jewish families who *did* convert to Christianity—and they were numerous— still remained in mortal peril, since they could be denounced to the Inquisition at any moment. In this way, national power and control was sustained and enforced by Christian fundamentalism.

All this accumulation of control and wealth had, of course, its costs, since Ferdinand and Isabel had to win allies among the nobility and to recruit, supply, and maintain a large standing army.

To pay these costs, the monarchs went into debt—often, in dark irony, to Jewish or *converso* families—with Isabel hocking her royal jewelry now and again. To pay off Christians for their political and financial support or for military exploits, and to reward the church for its partnership, they distributed land and booty from their conquests. And in all this, their actions, as they conceived them, meant something well beyond the material and political domination of Spain. They were resplendent with a meaning that lifted them onto another plane altogether, the plane of the fantastical storyline that accompanied the workings of their power. They had a prophetic mandate to dominate Spain, conquer Jerusalem, and restore the world to the True Faith. It was by such blessing that Ferdinand, as we have seen, styled himself "King of Jerusalem." He and his queen saw resonant, singular, divine meaning in their history: they were the principal players in the last act of history. By means of their nobility, in accordance with prophecy, with the energy of destiny, they had brought salvation to Spain and would see the Kingdom of Heaven come to earth.

What were the consequences of this grandeur? It is the ideal occasion for what-if history, since at the beginning of the sixteenth century, Spain looked to be at the beginning of one of most influential empires in history, with one of the most remarkable chances at knowledge and power ever presented to a country.

THE CATHOLIC MONARCHS RE-CREATE SPAIN IN THEIR OWN IMAGE

It was a pivotal moment in history. Ferdinand and Isabel knew it to be one. They unified Spain, and they looked to the future. Of course they wanted, by the alliances they made with the marriage of their children, to provide for the continued ascendency of their country. Their one son, Prince John, died as a youth. They had had one surviving child, Juana (the unfortunate woman known to history as Juana la Loca—Juana the Mad). Juana married Philip the Handsome, an Austrian Hapsburg, the only son of Emperor Maxmilian the First, Holy Roman Emperor. Philip engaged in a seething fight with Ferdinand, his father-in-law, for power in Spain. He chose the wrong adversary. One day, at age 28, some hours after quaffing a glass of ice water, he sickened and died. Rumors of poison circulated immediately. We shall never know for certain, but we do know that Ferdinand had shown for decades a refined genius for murder from a safe distance. As to Juana la Loca, she showed a profound if not perverse interest in the corpse of her husband, part of the reason she was locked up in a castle for the rest of her life. But after the deaths of Isabel (in 1504) and Ferdinand (in 1516), the first son of Juana la Loca, Charles I, became king of Spain. Three years later, he was crowned Holy Roman Emperor. So did Spain come to be in legal and royal possession of many of the countries and territories of Europe, including Sicily, the Kingdom of Naples, Sardinia, large portions of France (including Provence and Burgundy), Austria, Bohemia, the Low Countries, and Luxembourg. And to all this, of course, they added their incomparable territories in South and Central America and the Caribbean. It is difficult to overstate the magnificence and promise of such a position. And Spain, among all the countries of Europe, had an extraordinary advantage: it was the only country that could bring to the management of these vast domains the most advanced technical, scientific, mathematical, and commercial culture in the whole of the Mediterranean: the culture of Al-Andalus.

It was not to be. Spain chose another course: descent into centuries of war, economic stagnation, rampant corruption, bankruptcy, and scorching misery. So unprecedented was the opportunity, and so elevated its position, that the full collapse required generations to play out. But the road down through the decades and centuries was a precipitous one, and economic and cultural historians have given us a map of the way: the plain facts of what Spain did with what they had.

Just as the Inquisition supplied the world with a template of hatred, so the governance of Spain, beginning with Ferdinand and Isabel, provides a distinct template for national failure. That template has a fixed set of elements. Prominent among them are the union of the state with fundamentalist religion; a preference for debt-financed military solutions to political problems; the destruction of the country's manufacturing base, in favor of the production of raw materials and precious metals; a marked decline in the quality of education; and the abandonment of small-scale diversified agriculture in favor of large estates. There are shelves of books with the details, so I will touch on a few instances of each element. But it is staggering how many of them were set vigorously in place by Ferdinand and Isabel: it is a testimony to their power to shape the destiny of Spain in their time and for centuries afterward.

As to the unity of church and state: the Inquisition, of course, being so politically useful, bonded the Catholic church closely to the crown. Part of the spoils of war were given directly to the church, especially the large estates owned by "Catholic military orders, monasteries and convents, brotherhoods and cathedral churches." And the church associated itself directly with merchants and commercial undertakings—even initiation into guilds was sewn with religious ritual. Given the church's influence at court and the ability of the Inquisition to seize the wealth of whole families, it became politically wise, if not essential, for an ambitious family to build their stature and connections in the church through gifts and legacies. By such means, the church was able to gain more real estate, and as the revenues from such land enriched the church, the institution gained yet more power at court. At the same time, a material part of the seizure of assets from those accused by the Inquisition went directly to the Crown, who used the wealth to reward noble families for political or military help, though the Inquisition often claimed the confiscated wealth for itself, to fund its expensive operations. It meant that the

Crown did not enrich itself unduly, but engorged its power further by such financial coordination, which extended even to Ferdinand and Isabel's taking a portion of the ecclesiastical tithe. And the messianic vision of the two monarchs dovetailed perfectly with the flammable rhetoric of a militant church working for the salvation of all human-kind in the triumph of the True Faith at the end of time.

From 1492 forward, it is hard to pry apart church and Crown. They found their embrace mutually enriching, and they wielded power in rough synchrony. An excellent example is Ximenez de Cisneros, the friar whom we have met in Granada, as he was burn-ing the university library and the books of the Albayzín. In 1492, Isabel had chosen him as her confessor. He proved to be a man with an extraordinary talent for administration, though he was said to be of "warlike and even disquiet condition." And so he was: he wore a hair shirt, scourged himself with gusto, got lost in ecstatic trances, conversed with celestial visitants, and recoiled at the idea of stay-ing in a building where women had resided. In 1495, Isabel took the next step and made him archbishop of Toledo, the most power-ful ecclesiastical position in Spain, the so-called "Third King." In 1507, Ferdinand made him Inquisitor General and a cardinal. Such was his power that he took control of all Spain twice, as regent for Ferdinand in 1506 and for Charles I in 1516. All this vigorous unity of church and state was stamped onto history early on, when in 1494 Pope Alexander (the Spaniard Rodrigo Borgia) gave Ferdinand and Isabel the title of *los Reyes Católicos*—the Catholic Monarchs. The pope meant to celebrate the fall of Granada, the working of the Inquisition, the expulsion of the Jews, the discoveries of Columbus, and the religious orthodoxy of the king and queen, and all this for all Christendom. It was a designation that they would pass on to their descendants. And the unity of church and state would prove of the most startling durability in Spain, a kind of fatal embrace not undone until the death of Francisco Franco and his government of "National Catholicism." The emblem of the Falange, the fascist political party that supported Franco, was the yoke and a bundle (*fasces*) of arrows. They are none other than the personal emblems created by Ferdinand and Isabel as the standard of their fundamentalist reign, half a millennium earlier. More than once during our life in Granada, coming upon public demonstrations of the far-right wing in contemporary Spanish politics, we saw the same emblem, on a flag, waved with incendiary pride and excitement from a balcony.

As to Spain's debt-financed military efforts for political ends, and the devotion of public funds to those ends: it is a classic story of how imperial leaders can redirect the economy of a whole nation. Learning from Ferdinand and Isabel, and from his grandfather Maximilian, Charles I had the right pedigree for empire: he was archduke of Austria, king of Spain, and Holy Roman Emperor. He followed *los Reyes Católicos* in seeking a worldwide Catholic empire with Europe as its center and Spain as its epicenter. Just as the Inquisition worked to arrest and punish nonbelievers, heretics, infidels, and Protestants, so did Charles determine to bring the cleansing power and religious purity of Spain to all the people of his continent. He would go to war with Holland, France, England, Italy, and anyone who asserted a political and religious life independent of Spain. Now, to pursue a continent and a world with such dynastic and universalist ambition means paying the bills. And so Charles and his successor Philip II had to find a centerpiece for their financial policy, and they did: gold and silver. From the New World, beginning in the early 1500s, precious metals began to arrive in magnificent quantities. Spain could, of course, have invested such wealth in education, manufacturing, and development of agriculture, national transport, scientific work, and commercial ventures meant to enrich the country over the long term; that is, the country could have transformed its windfall into an impregnable economic foundation for prosperity. Yet, with its colonies producing such a bounty of precious metals, it seems that the court considered Spain already rich. And so the metals, principally the silver, were put to another use: as security for loans the country sought to pay for its operations, above all for its extravagant military adventures in service of empire. Within its own country, Spain sold short- and long-term government bonds to its own people, to aristocrats, cathedrals, merchants, rich peasants, men of business, monasteries, and anyone else in the country with capital who wanted a dependable source of income. Outside of its boundaries, Spain sold its bonds to German industrial groups, to Italian and Flemish bankers, and to Dutch financiers. When the borrowing needs outstripped the silver available for security, Spain borrowed more money, this time secured by tax receipts in Castile and custom receipts from its trade with its own colonies. The bonds were called *juros* and carried interest of 5 to 7 percent.

What were the facts on the ground, as they come into view during this macroeconomic escapade? It is not just that Spain used its precious metals principally to secure debt, rather than seeking productive investment within its own borders. The real effect was much more broad: in borrowing money from its own citizens, Spain diverted capital away from the investment needed to build a vigorous economy at home. These citizens did not, in general, gather talent, assess the needs of their neighbors and their city, adapt the rich technological heritage of Al-Andalus to the needs of their time, draw

upon the accumulated operational skills and market and manufacturing intelligence of Al-Andalus, and then embark upon new enterprises. They felt no pressing need to make any such efforts. The vigor
and prestige of the market was in remarkable disrepute. For those
with social prestige and capital assets, a life of commerce, of working, making, inventing, buying, and selling, risked a perilous decline
in personal dignity and social status. Why take such risks when an
investor could easily earn a generous income by loaning money to
his own government? What is more, the principal and interest paid
to international financial centers in Europe was very unlikely to be
reinvested in Spain; rather, the funds flowed outside the country
to bankers and families who were perfecting the strategic, technical, and market expertise needed to profit from Spain's urgent need
for cash and the demand of the Spanish colonies for manufactured
goods. It is the most terrible irony that the precious metals of the
New World, finally, drove the commercial enrichment of Europe and
ignited its technological advances, since it helped to finance the very
scientific and market development that Spain chose not to undertake
for itself.

The money spent on perpetual war could never be recovered.
And with every decade, Spain dug itself in deeper, since a country
with a failing economy could not attract investment even from those
among its own citizens who might have the talent and interest to
make such investments. As if all this were not calamitous enough,
through the late 1500s and 1600s, Spain increasingly had to import
even the most basic materials—paper, textiles, hardware, and the
like—and, as a result, the country ran a current account deficit with
all its adversaries. It is painful to read about, this story of a country
that worked a lengthy national confidence trick and swindled itself

out of its own silver. The end of such financial connivance is the obvious one: the loss of technical and intellectual ability, a momentous decline in the productive capacity of the nation, and the dismal, inexorable impoverishment of its citizens.

The years rolled on. When Charles I got into desperate financial trouble, he simply went forth to the great port of Seville and seized for himself private shipments of silver. He offered compensation, of course: more *juros*. In their indispensable economic history of the period, Stanley and Barbara Stein say it best: "In 1557, for example, 70 percent of military operations against France were financed by American silver. The next year, 85 percent of total state borrowing was guaranteed by the same source." By 1559, the "accumulated pubic debt reached a figure of 25 million ducados": a figure, they note, which was a breathtaking sixteen times annual revenues. Perhaps Charles I was exhausted by his forty years of military aggression in which he even managed to sack Rome itself, or weary of the demands of the country's creditors. In 1556, he retired to pray in a monastery in Ayuste, where he passed the time trying in vain to synchronize the clocks in the building. Alas, in the country he left behind, the interest clocks were ticking on the money he had borrowed. He left his country so crushed with debt that his son, the pious Philip II, would run out of money and default on his own people three times, in 1557, 1575, and 1596. Not being content with repudiating his own countrymen, in the same years, he defaulted on Spain's foreign creditors as well. His successor, Philip III, would default three more times, in 1607, 1627, and 1647, on debt owed to foreigners. I cite all these dates because they are a portrait in time of the decline of the Spanish economy: the richest and most accomplished nation of the European Middle Ages, the centermost of scientific advancement and commercial vigor, became, within a century and a half after the fall of Granada, the deadbeat of the continent.

To make sense of this decline, we should recall the wealth of Al-Andalus, based on commerce of inventiveness and energy, with a wide variety of manufactured goods and a diversified and progressive agriculture. It is worth looking into the material energy of the culture, constructed over centuries, that Ferdinand and Isabel inherited. The eminent historian Daniel Levering Lewis, writing of Al-Andalus in the tenth and eleventh centuries, gives us the heart of the matter:

> *Despite the esteem of the soldier's profession in creed and rhetoric, the reality of Muslim Andalucia was that most people had little desire to go to war—even Holy War. To a large extent, the business of Al-Andalus was business, in great contrast to Carolingian Europe, where warfare comprised most of the business and the raison d'etre of a specific caste was the perpetuation of war.*

This business of Al-Andalus, how vigorous was it? And how was it organized? Unless we understand these things, we can have no way to see what might have been gained or lost when Ferdinand and Isabel and their successors remade the Spanish economy by their own lights; that is, we need to understand the history of the economy they inherited, and which they determined to use for their own purposes. What we see, when we look into the commerce of Al-Andalus, is an economy based on trading throughout the Mediterranean, the open adaptation of ideas and techniques from other cultures, careful market regulation in the cities, and the use of technology to add value to raw materials through small- and large-scale manufacturing.

By the 900s, traders had a flourishing business in Al-Andalus, making markets in precious stones and textiles, books and spices, timber and wool, pearls and dye, ceramics, leather, and paper. Some of them were merchant-scholars, who went not only to buy and sell goods but also in search of knowledge, whether it be immediately practical or not. What metaphysical knowledge they brought back to the Iberian peninsula I presume is still with us all. And once again, these traders of Al-Andalus were not exclusively Muslim or Jewish. Until 1212, Muslim and Jewish entrepreneurs oriented toward the Middle East undertook most of the trading voyages and financial management, and then the activity, for political and military reasons, swung to Christian traders oriented principally toward Europe. In both periods, Al-Andalus was in lively communication and exchange with other countries and cultures.

But whatever the faith of the traders, we have record of the practical knowledge pressed into action: the horizontal loom, for example, three centuries ahead of its use in the rest of Europe. The techniques to make glazed and polychrome pottery, also unknown in the rest of Europe, came into beautiful use—their painted designs bore witness to a cosmopolitan culture, since they showed origins in China and Syria, in Iraq and Persia. Iron was worked to such demand that in one district alone in Málaga, there were twenty-five iron-smiths. The agriculture and mining industries used fine steel made in the country. Metalwork in bronze yielded buckles, oil lamps, and bowls, and we have still the shining astrolabes of brass that concentrated so much astronomical and mathematical understanding into a single instrument. Near Valencia, there was a paper factory that supplied not only Al-Andalus, but the export market. But beyond all that, we have numerous accounts of the robust, inclusive, ebullient market life. We can read a description of such markets; this one in our own Granada, the Alcaicería, has

> *... so many streets and lanes it resembles the Cretan*
> *Labyrinth, and it is even necessary to tie a thread to the door*
> *so as to be able to find the way back. Its shops are innumer-*
> *able, wherein is sold every kind of silk, woven and in skein*
> *plus gold, wool, linen, and merchandise made from them.*

There were spice merchants and money changers, cobblers, smiths, tailors, carpenters, shield makers, a hive of artisans practicing a rich variety of crafts, book sellers and wheelwrights, as well as vendors of fresh produce and cooked dishes. These markets throve in every city we know of in Al-Andalus. This activity was overseen by market inspectors, public health officials, and guild supervisors, with such success that for centuries most of the Spanish words connected with market regulation were taken directly from Arabic. All this retail activity, combined with the large capital projects throughout the peninsula in agriculture and fortifications, in house building and road building and military supplies, meant that the economy of Al-Andalus was complex and, to use current terms, a producer of value-added goods by efficient use of intellectual property: some of the most advanced technology in the Mediterranean. And it meant that wealth and work was distributed more widely, since so rich a suite of skills and goods were in demand. We are painting in broad strokes here, but the commercial zeal of the period is unmistakable. This gift for making and doing, for experimentation, for enterprise, for testing ideas and techniques in the marketplace where the citizenry of the period had their say: it is a recognizable formula for prosperity, and for centuries it worked to lift the standard of living in Al-Andalus well beyond anything that could have been imagined in the rest of Europe.

To return to Ferdinand and Isabel and the economy they and their successors created: it is one of the most useful periods of economic history to study, since the policies they adopted hold the same elements any nation must consider today as it seeks its own thriving. The changes made by *los Reyes Católicos* had deep effect, durable form, and extraordinary scope. First, the king and queen, with their campaign of forced conversion and then expulsion of their Jewish subjects, combined with their cumulative ethnic cleansing of their Muslim subjects, mounted a frontal attack on some of their most productive and enterprising citizens. Though the *convivencia* had its violent and contentious periods, there is no longer any doubt about the prosperity of the period, nor about its genius in science and culture. But the monarchs, once in possession of Granada, enforced policies contemptuous of their Jewish and Muslim subjects, policies that (to put it mildly) diminished their status and wealth and increased the risk to their fortunes and their families. Those who were expelled lost most of their assets, and Spain forfeited their talent and energy and knowledge. Those who did convert did not thereby gain full entry into Christian society, since the new focus on "blood purity" divided Spanish society into New Christians (anyone converted from Judaism or Islam) and Old Christians. The New Christians were former Jews (*conversos*) or former Muslims (*Moriscos*). As New Christians, even if they had prominent roles in society and did useful work, they had inferior social, political, and economic prospects. Worst of all, they had to live with the daily risk that they might be denounced to the Inquisition. So the campaign of forced conversion and expulsion struck two fierce blows at the economy: it limited the financial capital available for productive uses, and it undercut the work and damaged the prospects of a portion of its most productive subjects. This malign result accompanied an even more perverse social change: a dramatic shift in attitudes toward work. Since commerce was associated with subjects whose faith had been declared inferior to Christianity, and since those very subjects, as New Christians, suffered social disadvantages and political decline, it made sense that commerce no longer enjoyed its former prestige as a way to give meaning and value to a life. It is a most curious change to the material and psychological foundation of a whole society. Slowly, with the decades and centuries, market participation and trading took on a stigma, and gainful labor a tarnish of dishonor. The valor of military deeds, the exalted security of a victorious faith, and the adventure of the colonies all took center stage. In any society, energy and capital are invested for desirable returns, and such investment is decided in the climate of the times. In the decades after 1492, to build a career of wealth, status, and prestige, of honor and dignity, many men and families concluded that there were three avenues: the military, the church, and the court. There the energies of the country were concentrated; men went where the action was. As for money and trading, making and inventing, technical progress and market expertise, in the ensuing decades and centuries, all these fields came to be specialties of countries directly in competition with Spain: England, Holland, Italy, France, Flanders. Of course the troops and mercenaries of Spain still had to be paid, and goods for the country still had to be bought. For such needs, Spain had its gold and silver and its debt.

As we watch Spain change after 1492, we see an economy that moves in reverse, back to a more primitive form concentrated on precious metals and basic commodities, especially wool. It is symptomatic of an economic revolution, since Al-Andalus in its most prosperous period was a net *importer* of wool and a dynamic exporter of textiles. Though Castile had a resurgence of its textile industry in the 1500s, it did not last. Manufacturing of a whole range of fabrics moved to other countries, especially Holland and England. What did last in Spain is sheep-raising, which was concentrated in the Mesta, the council that controlled the industry in Iberia. It was allied closely with the Crown, to whom it paid generous taxes, and in return it was granted extraordinary privileges (called *fueros*) to graze private land throughout Spain. It was an alliance that endured for centuries and gave Spain a commodity, merino wool, in which it could specialize. Yet it meant that Spain regressed to a supplier of raw materials, which calls for little learning and provides employment at a subsistence level for everyone but the owners of the herds, who were mostly from noble, politically connected families. In addition, it produces no finished goods for the market at home, nor for the colonies abroad, where demand was growing apace. What is more, we know from modern ecological study what such gigantic herds—more than three million animals—meant for the land of Spain: the animals ate Iberia alive.

This concentration on sheep and wool production went along with a concentration of land in large holdings. It was another momentous change. Much more is known now about agriculture in Al-Andalus, but the key event was the transition from dry agriculture in classical Mediterranean form—grapes, olives, and grains—to irrigated agriculture that supported the production of fruits and vegetables of the richest variety. When a family in Al-Andalus brought water to dry land, they could become proprietors of that land, and so small landholders proliferated, cultivating the land according to soil and climate, to family need and market demand. The familial control, the flourishing permitted by irrigation, and the progressive introduction of new techniques of cultivation and new crops all meant that the cities of Al-Andalus were likely to be surrounded by a fecund rural space teeming with variety—what is today called polyculture. Such diversity in planting does not replace the natural habitat, but it imitates it more closely: it conserves soil, retains water, increases yield, and boosts crop resilience. It is labor-intensive, and the landholders needed to plan and coordinate, because they were tied together by the irrigation systems that gave their land fertility. And just as Spanish words connected with commerce tend to have Arabic roots, so the Arabic words for common work in agriculture gave rise to a whole vocabulary that survives today in Spanish. Here are a few of them: *acequía* (irrigation ditch), *alberca* (small pool), *azude* (floodgate), *acenas* (water mill). And the words for hundreds of vegetables, fruits, and spices often have Arabic roots as well: examples are *aceituna* (olive), *albaricoque* (apricot), and *azafran* (saffron).

But *los Reyes Católicos*, with most of Spain at their disposal after the conquest of Granada, worked closely with the Mesta. Irrigation systems, with their gates and ditches, their complex of fields and community participation, cannot survive an uncontrolled invasion of grazing animals. The damage is just too severe and unpredictable. Thomas Glick, a sober and meticulous scholar, notes in a fine one-sentence summary:

> The ordered landscape of Al-Andalus, responding to an agrarian system tightly interlocked with an urban artisanal economy, had no place for the kind of rapacious, land-devouring pastoralism that later came to characterize the Mesta, whose herds ran rampant over many a settled community in the later middle ages and in early modern times.

An equally momentous decision of Ferdinand and Isabel was their granting large holdings of land to noble families and financial and political allies. These lands became the famous *latifundia*, enormous tracts whose owners had virtual fiefdoms, meting out justice, collecting taxes, and naming administrators. From those estates, as well, they could gather manpower to be pressed into military service. The *latifundia* often undid the diverse small-crop mixtures, and wherever the cooperative irrigation systems fell into disuse, the land reverted to the dry farming of the Roman and Visigothic periods, producing once again grain, olives, and grapes. The local and regional power of the *latifundia* increased over time, and in the 1500s and 1600s when the Crown, desperate for revenue, sold off some of their own lands, the owners of such real estate amassed yet more wealth and influence. Overall, as time went on, the pattern of land use in Al-Andalus, with its rich variety of crops and linked assembly of family plots and cooperative control, metamorphosed into vast landholdings with one of three formidable and dominant owners: noble families, the Crown, and the church. The church, in fact, held land within all its separate institutions: cathedrals, monasteries, convents, military orders. It did not pay taxes, which was a disaster for the public treasury, especially given Americo Castro's estimate that at one point, the church "came to possess almost half the arable land in Spain." All in all, it was an agricultural revolution that altered profoundly the landscape and ecology of all of Spain. Riding across the Iberian peninsula today, it is hard not to conclude that the cumulative changes imposed after 1492 and intensified thereafter had a long follow-on effect. Those changes began to transform the land into the condition we see it in today, with a lamentable and dangerous expanse of biologically depleted soil and a countryside engulfed by monocultures.

Education declined in quality in Spain from the time of Ferdinand and Isabel, principally because of the closure of the educational system to ideas from the rest of Europe and the rest of the world. Spain was, of course, at war with most of Europe at one time or another. The Reformation, as a religious movement, was thought to be an abomination. And in the sixteenth and seventeenth centuries, the Catholic Counter-Reformation took hold. Just as books and ideas from Protestant Europe were suspect, so too the achievements in mathematics, science, philosophy, and medicine of Jewish and Arabic scholars carried a taint of heresy and inferiority. Though they had been a living part of the intellectual heritage of Spain, their influence, their languages, and their books all declined dramatically in esteem, distribution, and influence. After all, their people had been forcibly converted or expelled, and their faith and cultures had been eradicated, as far as possible. In addition, the Inquisition also censored books and managed to ban over a couple of centuries of works by Catullus, Martial, Ovid, almost all chivalric novels, and any books that doubted or attacked Catholic dogma. It banned Boccaccio's *Decameron*, all books written by Jews and Muslims, and eventually Copernicus and Kepler, the latter, of course, because they proposed a new astronomical model that came, ominously, from Protestant countries. Catholic countries did not necessarily escape. Even Dante's *Divine Comedy* was banned, rather mysteriously. Then, later on, those dangerous Frenchmen Voltaire, Diderot, Montesquieu, and Rousseau.

Earlier, in 1605, the Inquisition had taken another step, decreeing that booksellers keep a register of their clients, so that a check could be made on the reading habits of Spaniards. What effect all this fierce, suspicious oversight had on the actual studies of the Spanish public is a subject of controversy, but it is safe to assume that it did not encourage over time a spirit of critical inquiry and adventurous research, of independent thinking and open-minded embrace of the best work of other cultures and religions. These were the centuries of Leonardo da Vinci, Tycho Brahe, Copernicus, Galileo, and Kepler; of the rapid development of mathematics in the work of Descartes, Fermat, Pascal, Newton, Leibniz, and Euler; of the ascent of medical and biological science in the results of Anton van Leeuwenhoek in Holland and William Harvey in England; and the affirmation of the scientific method in the work of Francis Bacon. The labor of these men and their many eminent colleagues in England, Holland, France, Italy, Germany, and Switzerland prepared and carried forward what we know as the Scientific Revolution. What part had Spain in this decisive advance in human knowledge? In an attempt to answer this question, I passed a spell of days with encyclopedias, timelines, and histories in science, in a wholehearted effort to find the eminent Spaniards in science in the years from 1492–1900. I could not find a single mention within that period of any scientist of Spain known today for a pivotal invention or discovery. And this, in the country of Europe that had built a foundation of knowledge so formidable that Al-Andalus was known as the "Schoolhouse of Europe."

Education suffered also from the practice of book-burning. In the decades following upon the famous conflagration in Plaza Bib-Rambla by Xavier de Cisneros, there were massive burnings of books in Seville, Toledo, and Barcelona, where it was reported by a Jesuit that "on seven or eight occasions we have burnt a mountain of books at our college." We should note that the practice was carried on as well in the Americas, where in 1562, a mere seventy years after the fall of Granada, the 25-year-old Franciscan priest Diego Landa encountered the Mayans of the Yucatan. The Mayans were a people who could make a decent claim to be another of the "People of a Book," that is, cultures who merit the protection central to the legacy of Al-Andalus. For their books were among the principal treasures of their culture: constructed meticulously of durable plant fiber, bound in wood or leather, radiantly illustrated, with pages that folded out in a kind of lexical revelation. They held stories of Mayan history and the deeds of their gods on earth, and they set forth mathematical and astronomical tables, their records of observation and calculation. They held, in fact, virtually the entire written cultural heritage of the Mayans. Friar Diego Landa burnt every single one he could find, offering us his notes in return:

> These people also used certain characters or letters, with
> which they wrote in their books about the antiquities and
> their sciences; with these, and with figures, and certain signs
> in the figures, they understood their matters, made them
> known, and taught them. We found a great number of
> books in these letters, and since they contained nothing but
> superstitions and falsehoods of the devil we burned them
> all, which they took most grievously, and which gave them
> great pain.

Landa was censured in Spain and then duly promoted to bishop of the Yucatan and returned to the New World. In later years, three surviving Mayan books have surfaced. They are wondrous. I cite this instance because it is a chain of events resonant with the outlook of the period.

THE SEISMIC MONARCHS

That outlook took its cue, its form, its detail, and its future from Ferdinand and Isabel, and for their politics the moment of truth is 1492. One can imagine their grandeur and their hope as they took possession of the Alhambra, and from that phenomenal venue envisioned a world of piety, justice, virtue, and prophetic majesty.

There is some fundamental way that in 1492, in the palace we look upon from the Albayzín, history hung in the balance. The war and politics of the monarchs had come to their climax. It is as if the pressure of their worldview had been pressing against the world of Al-Andalus in a kind of plate tectonics of history. In Granada, the pressure reached an unendurable limit, and history let go, and the energy released remade the world of the sixteenth century with changes so violent we still feel the effects in our own time. As we studied the period, we came to see that it is impossible to understand the Albayzín, Granada, and Spain itself unless we see the politics, learning, and faith of the monarchs in direct relation to Al-Andalus. Too often, Ferdinand and Isabel have been seen independently of the eight hundred years of history that created the country they governed. This has been so because of the glamor of the discoveries of Columbus, the convenient way the fall of Granada marks the end of an epoch, and the rarity of vivid and comprehensive historical studies of Al-Andalus. And, it must be said, it was so because of the lustrous, if not mythic, success of the propaganda of Ferdinand and Isabel, their successors, and their church. But it is time to bring together those monarchs and the world whence they came. Columbus is no longer so glamorous, nor can we dismiss Al-Andalus so conveniently,

since historians in the last decades have brought clarity, energy, and
reality to Al-Andalus, really for the first time. All this being so, we
can work anew in hope to understand more clearly who Ferdinand
and Isabel were, what they did, and how we might learn from them.
As I tried to do so, I gained a sense of how benighted I had been in
my facile acceptance of the taking of Granada in 1492 as a moment
in which the energies of unity were released in Spain to the benefit of
all. To be sure, there was a release: of the energies of despotic leadership exercised with finely tuned political savagery. It was a dark and
humbling study.

Part of what it meant was that we needed to look again at the
very terms that have been applied to the history of this pivotal period.
Take, for just one example, the term "reconquest." If you read of the
history of Spain and of Europe, you will come incessantly upon this
term. It is used ad nauseam and ex cathedra, a bolted-down part of
the story of European history. But it seems increasingly plain that
"reconquest" is a kind of one-word propaganda stunt, a linguistic
bunco game, and, most of all, a code word used to glorify destruction and expulsion. Take the gently phrased declaration of the superb
historian Thomas Glick: "indeed, the notion of re-conquest involves
from a historiographical perspective a number of anachronisms and
anomalies." Such are the delights of reading history! Or take the
magisterial work of the world-class scholar L.P. Harvey, who points
out the incoherence of the whole notion:

> The European Conquest of the Americas is in some areas
> separated from our present day by a mere one-third of the
> chronological gap that stretched between the Spain of the
> Expulsion and the Arab conquest. Yet the Americas as we

know them are felt as a firm fait accompli of history, an
omelet that no one ever expects to be unscrambled. Nobody
imagines that America's white and black inhabitants will one
day be eliminated in favor of the peoples of the First Nations.

In other words: If eight hundred years from the Declaration of Independence—over a half a millennium from now—in 2576 AD, the Mohawks and Algonquians once again settle throughout New York state, will this be a "reconquest"? And what about the Kickapoo in the Upper Great Plains, who might ride into St. Louis and take up residence under the golden arch? The Shasta and the Klamath Indians of the Pacific Northwest, who might find Portland and Seattle, with their fine bookstores, very much to their liking? And the Ohlone of San Francisco, who will find the bridges useful, no doubt? Would they, in the name of "reconquest," feel justified in the expulsion, after eight hundred years, of those who followed a non-Indian faith, followed by the forcible erasure of eight centuries of American culture?

Eight hundred years cannot be erased by a word. In any case, there was no "Spain" (the word did not even exist) before 711 that rose again, like some Gothic monster, to take up the sword. In fact, Christians ruled peaceably and effectively with Muslim and Jewish officials, allies, and subjects. Muslim regimes in Al-Andalus sometimes fought one another with Christian help (for example, El Cid himself). Christian regimes sometimes fought one another with Muslim allies. So there was no prior, pure, monolithic Christian culture that could have "reconquered" a Muslim and Jewish country. It is, like so much, a cumulative invention of the chroniclers and political operatives of late Christian Al-Andalus and their colleagues since, who did not write history so much as gin up a rich mix of outright fabrication and military fantasy, laced with a hearty dose of religious bombast.

We have in this account lived alongside the scientists and traders, the rulers and inventors of Al-Andalus. It is worth repeating as often as possible, since it is a fact so often swept into a dark hole, that Al-Andalus was governed by Christian kings as well as Islamic caliphs and emirs, often with the assistance of powerful Jewish aides and counselors. So there was rich precedent for Christian rule of a society of mixed faith. If we bring together that society with the politics of Ferdinand and Isabel and their successors, then we are more likely to be able to assess clearly their influence, their institutions, and their reign as a whole.

The policies and politics of Ferdinand and Isabel brought dramatic change, change that uprooted centuries of economic and cultural institutions and drove deep and lasting roots for new ones. Reading about their reign, one thinks of how rare it is to learn of two rulers whose actions marked their country, and our history, so profoundly and indelibly. It is all the more reason we need to know the long-term result in detail. We have seen already, less than one hundred years after the fall of Granada, the way Spain defaulted on its domestic and international debt. From there, despite a brief industrial resurgence in the early 1600s based on New World gold and silver, the decline accelerated. We have a clear portrayal from two scholars who have made the most exhaustive study of the period, Stanley and Barbara Stein. They are writing about the end of the 1600s, just two centuries after the fall of Granada:

> . . . the shadow of Spain had contracted virtually to the country's borders. The metropole lacked a developed artisan

*industry, its agricultural and pastoral sectors were marked
by low productivity, and principal exports—aside from the
reexport of silver—were raw materials and some processed
food. Internal communications were rudimentary, domestic
demand was limited, and the Spanish merchant marine and
Navy were insignificant.*

We see, in the material life of Spain during the reign of the
Catholic Monarchs, how swiftly a dynamic and prosperous economy
can come to static ruin. It was a ruin that glittered with precious metals and the glory of empire, but it was ruin nonetheless. Ferdinand
and Isabel ruled with such abundant success that they have long, and
rightfully, been recognized for their decisive effect on the history of
Spain. But because of the work of two recent generations of scholars,
we understand now much more fully the culture and economy they
destroyed. Even more startling is how obvious that destruction of
the Spanish economy was to *Spanish* political economists from the
1500s forward; startling because, for all their acuity and analysis,
they could do nothing to alter the almost-surreal obsession of Spain
with its past: *Its past, that is, as if it began in 1492.* Once again, let
us quote the magisterial Steins, reviewing the work of the Spanish
political economists of the time, the so-called *arbitristas*:

> *Spain's decline had multiple facets: economic and political
> as well as religious, social, and cultural . . . When an early
> arbitrista concluded that Spain was poor because it was rich,
> he touched on the peculiar contradictions that give rise to
> the notion of a nation "bewitched," living outside reality . . .
> Although the term decline (decadencia) rarely appears in the*

*literature of the time, late-seventeenth-century arbitristas gen-
erally agreed that Spain, once prosperous and powerful, had
slipped into stagnation and poverty, political impotence, and
even institutional decay.*

*What had been inherited and developed in the fifteenth and
sixteenth centuries, particularly under Isabel, Ferdinand,
and their grandson Charles V, remained enshrined, almost
sacralized. Change toward something new, an innovation,
was in principle unacceptable.*

I do not think it can be said that Ferdinand, Isabel, and Charles V
destroyed the economy and culture of Al-Andalus. But they did give
that culture and the practice of *convivencia*, already in deep peril, the
final political bludgeoning from which it could never recover.

It is a most useful and instructive history to study. In sum, Spain
became a country of seigneurial privilege, with inviolate state and
ecclesiastical bureaucracies of entrenched power. A landed religious
and secular aristocracy came to control vast areas of the country but
provided only subsistence labor. Herds of sheep with up to three million animals were the economic centerpiece of the Iberian countryside. There was no dynamic and sustained creation of a middle class
devoted to commerce and production in the country, citizens who
could use the technical advances of Al-Andalus and of contemporary Europe to initiate new enterprises and seed national industries.
Instead, the country produced raw materials for other countries of
Europe that had developed their economies with sophisticated banking and credit facilities, laws governing and enforcing contracts, trading networks, supply chains, market intelligence, effective partner-
ships with governments, and joint-stock companies, all riding upon a

heady current of technical and scientific progress. Spain's silver and gold, for the most part, passed through its hands to enrich the rest of Europe. And in a most bitter irony, the growing material needs of Spain's own colonies were supplied largely by the very countries whose economies had used Spanish wealth to build their own commercial expertise. In an equally telling irony, the Spanish state came partly to rely for financing on Sephardic families it had expelled from Spain, whose descendants had become major financial powers in Holland. It is as if Spain traded in its whole economy for a patrimonial and military culture that enriched a narrow class, guarded its power jealously, held stiffly to its religious traditions, conjured a history that began in 1492, and blundered over decades and centuries into a bizarre failure that enriched all of Europe at the expense of Spain's own citizens. Such was the political prowess of Spain that it managed to miss, in whole or in part, the Enlightenment and both the Scientific and Industrial Revolutions. It is as if it sold off for pennies the winning trifecta ticket of modern European history. These three revolutions in understanding and accomplishment were built largely upon the achievements in the sciences and humanities of Al-Andalus. It is one of the strangest episodes in continental economic history, this metamorphosis from Al-Andalus to a country of colonies and precious metals, of military aggression and economic failure. It is, to use a term from the mystics, a teaching story.

A COUNTRY OF JASMINE AND DISASTER

To read Spanish history is to embrace a hornet's nest. If the reader is looking for an argument, any of the economic and political history I have related will do the job. Not only can you argue with many

Spaniards but with many academics, and not just about economics. There has been, over the last many decades, virulent kerfuffles among professors that are remarkable to follow for the lay reader. To recite the facts of Al-Andalus, in some company, will draw the most incendiary reaction. There will be bitter attacks on the notion that the *convivencia* meant anything and charges of "utopianism" and outraged recitations of the massacres of Jews and Christians and the internecine battles among Muslims that occurred in Al-Andalus. Some will tell you that the *convivencia* was just not authentic, that it was a coalition of the unwilling, that its reality has been so much swollen by praise that it should be considered a kind of magical thinking. Among such interlocutors, it is often heresy to celebrate any good thing happening before 1492. I have been surprised by the vehemence and bitterness of such reactions. Whatever dismissive contempt they carry, such views are increasingly in the minority, since it is no longer possible to deny that Al-Andalus was an advanced society—scientifically, economically, and culturally. Nor is it possible to deny that Spain largely squandered the knowledge, the power, and the commercial energies of Al-Andalus. The real question, for me, is why this controversy continues to awaken such hot anger. It does, I think, because the history of the period, as it has come into view, does not advance incrementally our understanding. It transforms our understanding. It asks us to look deeply at the Middle Ages in Europe and to extend our study and sympathy to a rare experiment in culture whose work and discoveries all of us can justly celebrate, and with that celebration, share in them.

Yet in the popular imagination, the old, fixed prejudices are still at work. One can, for instance, pick up popular treatments of the history of Granada and encounter references to the "perfidious Jews."

In distinguished museums, one reads how in 711, Spain "suffered" the invasion of the Arabs. At other times, I have been accused of outright deceit. Once, riding with my family in a taxi in Granada to a lecture to be delivered in the Xavier Cisneros auditorium, I joked to the driver that we did not plan on burning any books. I received an instant, snarling reply that Cisneros did not burn any books (or perhaps one or two, he said), and that any such event was the fabrication of "English historians," whose willing pawn I was. Yet the book-burning, of at least five thousand volumes, is an incident attested to from numerous sources, including Cisneros's own biographer. And the short summaries I have given in this book of the accomplishments of Al-Andalus could be, and in fact have been, expanded into multi-volume works.

The slow, cumulative massing of facts is now undeniable. Ferdinand and Isabel, and their successors and allies, gave Al-Andalus its death blow. Though their image is still that of triumph and righteousness, the Catholic Monarchs might be seen more properly as exterminating angels: flying in their own mythic light, winged with power, and lethal. The question now is how long might it take to see a deep change in popular understanding, a metamorphosis, a correction of the common narrative—a change, that is, in our comprehensive sense of the history of Spain. Because the Spanish Civil War is so agonizing a memory for Spain, and because of the rather straight line from Ferdinand and Isabel to fascist Spain, it may take a long time for enough detachment and perspective to clear the way for the transformed history that we have now in our hands.

I remember a lunch, early in our years in Spain, on the country estate of some wealthy Spaniards. Upon learning of my interest in Spanish history, I was shown from their library a book from the period of the Spanish Civil War titled *Jews, Masons, and Other Scum.* Soon afterward I was entreated to consider how blessed a salvation Gen. Francisco Franco and the Falangists had brought to Spain and heard an argument that Adolf Hitler had been unfortunately misjudged. The most sincere offers of help with my work were made as I read my way through books during our sojourn in Spain.

So many years later, I have come upon a passage that addresses such a view of history and ties together the fall of Granada with the aftermath of the Civil War, about four hundred and fifty years later. The passage is in *The Spanish Holocaust,* by the esteemed historian Paul Preston. We should note that he is one of those English historians so unpopular among certain taxi drivers. Preston is discussing the imprisonment of women after the victory of Franco's soldiers in the Civil War. It is a brilliant and careful book, and hard to read. He relates to us, for instance, how after the rebel military victory in the city of Zamora, pregnant women and nursing mothers were executed just for having a family member associated in any way with the Spanish Republic. Some of the women had merely cleaned houses of Republicans.

> *. . . the suffering of women in the prisons had dimensions unknown in the male population. Many of the women arrested were pregnant or had very young children with them. Mothers of children older than three were not allowed to take them into the prison . . . Older women were forced to watch while their sons were tortured and sometimes murdered.*

> *Rape was a frequent occurrence during interrogation in police stations. Transfer to prison and concentration camps was no guarantee of safety. At night, Falangists took young*

women away and raped them. Sometimes their breasts were
branded with the Falangist symbol of the yoke and arrows.

The yoke and arrows: symbol of Ferdinand and Isabel. We cannot ignore this survival of the emblem of the Catholic Monarchs,
burnt into the breasts of women just eighty years ago. The same
emblem is found on the Grand Cross of the Imperial Order of the
Yoke and Arrows, the highest decoration bestowed by the Franco
regime. And bestowed it was, in 1938, on Reichsführer SS Heinrich
Himmler, whose Gestapo colleagues provided crucial training for
Franco's political police. In 1940, Himmler would be welcomed to
Spain, where his opulent tour included rides through San Sabastian
and Burgos, their streets awash with swastikas.

It is a warning to all of us: once widespread imprisonment and
torture become embedded in a culture, they can survive for centuries, accompanied by their symbols. It happened in Spain, but not
because of any dark strain or special weakness in the Spanish temperament. It happened in Spain because such conduct is possible in
all countries, in all societies, at all times. No one has written more
eloquently about this than Primo Levi, the Italian chemist who survived Auschwitz. He, who has seen the full scope of human barbarity, tells us: "We must be listened to . . . It happened, therefore it can
happen again: this is the core of what we have to say. It can happen,
and it can happen anywhere."

In Granada, the plazas where we went to buy ice cream for our
daughter are the same ones used for the condemnation and burning
of innocent men and women a half a millennium ago. In our beloved
Albayzín, there are two streets named after prisons, the Carcel Alta
and the Carcel Baja: the upper and lower prisons. And just down our

street in the barrio, there is a Plaza de la Cruz Verde: the Plaza of the Green Cross. The green cross is the symbol of the Holy Inquisition. Upon the side of the Cathedral of Granada, you will find, even today, a chiseled name—the only citizen to be so honored on the entire face of the cathedral: José Antonio Primo de Rivera, the founder of the Falangist Party of Spain. And down in the commercial district of Granada, you will find a monument dedicated to the same man. He is the principal martyr of the fascists. In 1934, he urged the military to revolt against the government, writing to senior military command-ers that they were "the only historic instrument to achieve the destiny of a people." He went on: "This will be the decisive moment: either the sound or the silence of your machine guns will determine whether Spain is to continue languishing or will be able to open its soul to the hope of dominion." In 1935, speaking privately to a core of fascist leaders, he urged that they should "prepare to revolt, counting, if possible, on the military, and, if not, on ourselves alone. Our duty is, consequently, and with all its consequences, to move toward civil war." And Jose Antonio was the man who stated clearly enough in the same year:

> We regard Italian Fascism as the most outstanding politi-
> cal development of our time, from which we seek to draw
> principles and policies adapted to our own country . . .
> Fascism has established the universal basis of all the political
> movements of our time. The central idea of Fascism, that of
> the unity of the people in the totalitarian state, is the same as
> that of the Falange Española.

It is a measure of the complexities of recent Spanish history, its vainglorious alliances and its adulation of power, that such a name should figure upon the side of a cathedral dedicated to the worship of the Prince of Peace. It is the central Christian monument in one of the most famous cities in Europe. It is not far from the enormous statue honoring Isabel. I passed these monumental tributes almost every day, but with an anguish informed by the history of Spain, by the joy of our life in the Albayzín, and by our unreserved love for our adopted country: its music, its poetry, its people. Talking to a Spanish friend one day, after looking through a book of historical photographs of the country, at one point he put the book down and looked off into the distance. "We must write another book," he said. "Here in my country, these last centuries we have written the encyclopedia of suffering."

With the founding of a new European democracy after the death of Franco in 1975, Spain turned away from such darkness. Its democracy, in the view of this one American, is troubled, complex, disputatious, detached occasionally from facts, sometimes timid and sometimes bold, sometimes brilliant and sometimes corrupt. That is, it's just like every other democracy. It belongs to the people of Spain, and may every blessing and beauty come to their aid as they move forward together.

We have been one family living in one neighborhood in Granada. Nothing could have led us to think that the Albayzín would course so vividly with the currents of history. It speaks of jasmine and disaster. And nothing could have prepared us for the goodwill and loving-kindness of our neighbors, their helpfulness and the sweetness of their natures, as we struggled to make our way in a country not our own. If they are the future, then Spain will one day be first among nations.

A Few Notions of Geometry
and Revelation

*F*ROM THAT LONG-AGO night of rain, when we walked with dog and baby to our rubble-strewn house, after the months of construction as our life took form here, we came to live with books and conversation, red wine and ebullient company, the music of Spain and mood of the Albayzín, languorous and celebratory at once. And we lived with a castle in the sky before us, the Alhambra. It floated there as improbably as a fortress in one of the fantastical tales we read to Gabriella every night. The terrace off our *torreón* looked straight toward the castle, and each night, it seemed a conjuration. I was never sure, when we went to bed, if it was still going to be there in the morning.

As a hive holds cells of honey, so does the Sabika hill, rising before us across the canyon of the Darro, have a history of holding constructions of the most intricate beauty. After looking into the history of our neighborhood, we were hardly surprised to find that the Alhambra has one of the city's most bizarre stories. In 1492, after Granada was starved into surrender, Ferdinand and Isabel used it as their own, with Isabel swishing around in gorgeous Arab robes. Then, after their departure, the palace began to disintegrate all through the early 1500s, even though the despised Moriscos were forced to pay tribute to maintain it. As the Inquisition and ethnic cleansing lay waste to the Morisco community, the tribute began to fail, and in 1571, Philip II decided to direct some of his income from sugar cane works near Seville to pay for repairs. Still, in 1590, part of the palace burned down, and as the years rolled on, the governors of the barrio and the palace cast about, rather wildly it seems, for ideas to use the space. So, noting the beautifully tiled chamber where ambassadors to the court of Granada were once received, they decided that it would make an superb ammunition dump.

So it remained for decades, until in the early 1700s a new Philip, this time the Fifth, decided that the palace and its royal district no longer needed its own governor, with his noisy band of servants. So he dismissed him. This governor, a duke who liked the palace and the servants, wanted to depart with a flamboyant gesture, so he burned down his fabulous residence.

A good deal of the royal barrio lay now in ruins, but one group with canny temperament and a good eye for real estate moved in: the gypsies. So, a bit more than two hundred years after the conquest of Granada, a gypsy encampment thrived in the palace of the sultans and of Ferdinand and Isabel. Visitors, of course, thought it picturesque to have donkeys and guitar-strumming gypsies wandering with them through an august and crumbling ruin.

But the dedicated administration of Spain and Granada were not done exploring how they might use the palace and its grounds. As the 1700s went their way, the palace looked like an ideal place for a military hospital—it was dirty, but it had big rooms and nice views.

Then the governor of Granada, musing perhaps on the fine time his predecessor once had, decided that he, too, would move right in and sport about in the ruins. The palace still being full of incomparable woodwork set into geometrical patterns as complex as the tile work, the new resident governor began to rip it out and use it for firewood. Wanting to have his milk and meat close at hand, he also set his farm animals to roam throughout the complex, adding another complement of animal droppings to the already rich mix. And even then, the ingenuity of city officials had not exhausted itself, for the rooms where dwelt once the wives of the sultan were selected as the ideal venue for the salting of fish.

In other words, the palace complex came to look rather like the Albayzín of the same period: a ruin full of gypsies. Through the monument, animals wandered, and moss found a foothold among the trash and weeds. Virtually no one thought that the extraordinary Albayzín would survive, and by all accounts, the legendary palace of the Alhambra was turning into rubble and dust.

As the centuries wore on, the reputation of the Alhambra, as though by strange radiance, came to penetrate most of Europe, because of the fictional flights and visits of the English, Americans, and French. They used the palace as a basis for fantasy, with full doses of sexual intrigue, genies, tragedy, and frothy romance. Let us roam over a few centuries and look at the names of some of the writers and composers who treated us to fantastic stories of the place: in 1672, the English poet John Dryden wrote a play about the conquest of Granada; in 1739, the French composer Joseph Pancrace Royer wrote a famous ballet about the sultan's amorous wife, who met her lover for secret couplings in the rose hedges. Not to be left out, in 1829, Victor Hugo published a long, over-the-top poem on the same subject, called "Les Orientales," full of genies and exclamation marks, and in the late 1800s, Claude Debussy wrote two moody pieces about Granada and the gates of the Alhambra. All these writers and composers over several centuries had one astonishing thing in common: not a single one of them had ever been to the Alhambra, nor to Granada, or even anywhere nearby. Even the twentieth-century Spanish composer Manual de Falla, who eventually lived near the Alhambra, went right ahead and wrote music about the gardens there, well before he ever visited them.

Fortunately, other writers, scholars, and composers *did* visit, and it is partly to their work that we owe the unlikely preservation of the Alhambra. In 1840, the 19-year-old French poet-to-be Theophile Gautier sauntered straight in to the Patio de los Leones, cooled his wine in the fountain, and bedded down for the night. But two other nineteenth-century visitors changed the history of the whole palace: in 1829, the American diplomat Washington Irving, and in 1832, the Welsh scholar Owen Jones. Irving's writings, *The Tales of the Alhambra*, is still in print and sold all over Granada today. Jones's masterwork, *Plans, Sections, Elevations, and Details of the Alhambra*, a book to which he gave his life and his fortune, was scientific, accurate, and magnificent. Published in the years 1842–45, it contains reproductions of most of the Alhambra's ornamental tile and plaster work. Even to produce the books, Jones had to work a revolution in the art of color printing, until then poorly developed. The books are unprecedented in the history of design, and they gave the Alhambra to the world irrevocably.

At the heart of the gift given were faithful renderings of a sacred art unknown in the West: the art of ceramic tiles with complex geometric designs. In the Alhambra, such tiles cover wall after wall. In our years in Granada, these tiles have been our companions and our teachers. In them we find an example of how the beauty of another culture may be a mentor to understanding and a map that leads onward to the most surprising joy.

I can remember, when in college, seeing for the first time a photo of one of the tiled walls of the Alhambra. Though I had the most complete ignorance about their nature, I was spellbound by the fierce, lovely complexity of form and wondered what on earth could be the basis of it. But it was not until we moved to the Albayzín that I had the time, because of our many visits to the monument, to study in peace the tile work. They offered an undiscovered country. I had long hoped to visit and learn there, though it was a place so beautiful I did not know if I could return with my story.

So let us begin. It is a story that begins two millennia ago, though we can tell it in a few pages. Just as our garden had an ancestor in a garden of the sixth century BC, so do the tiles of the Alhambra have an ancestry in southern Italy, in the same century, in the teachings of Pythagoras, a figure so important that almost nothing is known about him. We know he was born on a Greek island, traveled through the Near East, and settled in southern Italy. There, he did something rare: he wrote nothing but lived so as to exercise an extraordinary influence on mathematics and philosophy. Many tales are told about him, including two wonderful declarations: that he could be in two places at once, and that rivers spoke with him.

What is important for us is that Pythagoras thought that the world offered a beautiful order, and to learn that order, we had to study number and proportion. If we did so, then we had a chance to come into possession of a key to learning our place on earth, and the real purposes of life. This core idea, that numbers have both a practical

and a spiritual use, goes along with another idea of Pythagoras: that
the soul is immortal and may dwell in another world with forms
of goodness that are permanent. Recall that Homer consigns the
soul after death to Hades, a dismal world of regret and lamentation,
which Tiresias the prophet calls "a joyless place" and which even
Achilles trashes unforgettably, saying that he "would rather be above
ground still and laboring for some poor portionless man, than be
lord over all the lifeless dead." Compared to such a destination, the
notion of Pythagoras held a lustrous promise.

Though his central idea has undergone strange adventures
through the centuries, it is simple: that beyond doctrine, belief, and
ritual, beyond habit and appearance, there exists a durable world,
an objective reality we can understand. One of the primary means
to such understanding is number. That is to say, numbers are not
only essential to our life on earth, they also are our introduction to
another world of understanding, one based on an order deep within
us and natural to our experience. So, for example, we have in our
lives the sun, the moon, the stars, each of them with its own movement through our day and night. Yet this movement is not random,
but harmonious and comprehensible, and susceptible to description
with numerical formulas. Similarly, with the playing of music. For
instance, musical order created by vibrating strings turns out to be
related directly to numbers. This discovery, attributed by tradition
to Pythagoras, provided a foundation for the making of musical harmony. It works like this: if you take a string of given length and pluck
it, the sound produced is called a unison, or fundamental pitch. Now,
if you divide the string into two equal parts and pluck it, you hear a
higher note: exactly one octave higher. If you divide the string into
two parts, in a ratio of 2:3, the sound produced is called a perfect

fifth; if the ratio is 3:4, then the sound produced is called a perfect fourth. So these orderly sets of sounds are precisely related to ratios among the first four whole numbers.

Music and number have a natural, powerful relation. In the legend of Pythagoras, this relation led to one of his most durable ideas, that of the *música mundana,* or the Music of the Spheres. The whole notion of numerical harmony is extended into the sky. Just as the movement of a certain length of a string produces a given musical tone, so the movement of the each of the planets produces, according to its distance from earth, a extraordinary musical tone. And taken together, the movement of the planets makes a music so beautiful that it is present everywhere and always, and so powerful that it governs the rhythms of nature. It is a harmony within life, the very music of creation. It is said to be the music heard by Moses when he took up the tablets on Mount Sinai. It is said to be the music we hear as we die, a prelude to our entry into a world beyond time. We may, as we live, hear this music ourselves, and make a life in concord with it, but we may do so only by uncommon learning.

Plato, Euclid, and many of the astronomers and scientists of classical antiquity incorporated these ideas and added a host of others in the flowering of mathematics that began in classical Greece and continued through the Hellenic period, building a significant body of knowledge that lay in manuscripts and practices throughout the Mediterranean, but especially in the libraries of Alexandria and the Middle East. With the sacking of Rome in 410 and the beginning of the Middle Ages in Europe, these writings fell into disuse, and their collection and study would wait until the eighth century, after Islam had carried its faith throughout the Mediterranean. As it formed stable governments and centers of study, its scholars took up the scientific and philosophical heritage of antiquity and enriched it with their own labors and discoveries. The center of these efforts, in Baghdad during the reign of Haroun Al-Rashid, was called the House of Wisdom.

Among these workers were an anonymous and brilliant group of writers known as the Brethren of Purity, whom we have met when we visited the translation school of Alphonso the Wise. The Brethren, in their labors, helpfully decided to summarize all knowledge in a single book. The book has fifty-two chapters, and the first three take up, respectively, number, geometry, and astronomy. As to the necessity of number in our efforts to find the truth of things, the Brethren say boldly: "the science of numbers is the root of the other sciences, the fount of wisdom, the starting point of all knowledge, and the origin of all concepts." In geometry, according to the clear propositions of the group, we can relate number and form and create figures that exist in our minds, which gives us a way to begin to understand a durable, intelligible world beyond our senses. In this way, they claim, we can begin to build for ourselves a life in concord with a freely offered and permanent order within the world. As to astronomy, the Brethren, who revered Pythagoras, wrote of the wondrous harmonies of the Music of the Spheres, which by their account resounded according to measure and melody, ringing now like struck brass, then playing like some celestial lute. This is the music that is perfect, which we might imitate on earth, so as to be able to hear and remember in our own music the very order that informs all the visible world. In this way, sensual experience leads naturally and inevitably to stability and luminosity of mind.

There are other fascinations in the writings of the Brethren, not least their intense focus on the heavens as they relate to the ascent of our souls toward the divine. They wrote of the several spheres of the heavens, corresponding to the seven visible planets. And, as though they were giving patient instruction to Dante when, more than three hundred years later, the poet worked out his plan for the *Paradiso*, they detailed the way the soul must pass through each of the spheres to reach its destined fulfillment.

These ideas we have sketched—from Pythagoras through Plato and the scientists and translators of newly emergent Islam, culminating in the summaries of the Brethren of Purity—these ideas form the context we need in order to understand the beauty and meaning of the tiles that grace the walls of the Alhambra. The craftsmen who made them were working in a culture in which many of the distinctions we take as given—between science and art, sense and spirit, quantity and quality—were not rigidly established. And so we have in the tile work of the Alhambra, and the tile work throughout the Middle East, an example of an art based on geometry. It is an elaborately sensual creation with spiritual meaning and a work of precise quantities that we are meant to use, as we gaze, to refine the quality of our perception.

We have been voyaging through the centuries, just to do a simple thing: to stand together before a wall of tiles and say of what we see in them. Before we do so, we have to talk a bit more about number: specifically how, in the current of reasoning we have been following, the first few whole numbers relate to the earth, to the heavens, and to the sacred. We need to try to see the force field of associations bound up with these numbers. We need to see, beyond quantity, what they mean when we relate them to our experience on earth. To take up this subject means to venture into domains of thinking and experience that some might call mystical. But it is, in fact, a plain and practical endeavor, neither remote nor fanciful. It is based upon the simple proposition that to approach the sacred, we do not need religious institutions, a system of belief, doctrines, training, ritual, dogma, theology, or faith. What we need is love, study, and understanding. What we are trying to understand are the workings of beauty in tile work meant as a delight to the eye and as an embodiment of the sacred.

We need to start with the idea that numbers mean something, that the first few whole numbers have profound associations with our daily life and spiritual experience. These associations give us the grounding we need to look at the tiles.

To begin with the number one: it is the number of unity and refers to the divine, to what is original, complete, perfect, undivided, and whole. It includes all life and both the material and spiritual world; it holds both our origin and our destiny. It corresponds, in other words, to the fundamental conception of sacred power in Judaism, Christianity, and Islam. In geometry, the symbol of unity is the circle, which from an invisible center traces out the perfect form from which all others can be derived. From the circle, craftsmen were able, with a kind of ecstatic improvisation, to work out the myriad shapes and patterns found in the walls of tile in the Alhambra and throughout northern Africa and the Middle East. What is more, the conception of beauty historically has, in many cultures, been bound closely with the very notion of unity embodied in the circle. When we encounter beauty, it is at its best radiantly inclusive, showing the connections among things, the resemblance and joinery of things, bringing together gracefully what seems separate—man and woman, mind and body, earth and heaven, human and divine.

Next, the number three: this number which, long after the composition of the Old Testament and the life of Jesus, became so central in Christian theology. It calls to mind the three celestial bodies most bound up with human life, the sun, the earth, and the moon. It contains as well the way the essentials of our lives are naturally understood in groups of three terms: say, lover, beloved, and love itself; the knower, the known, and knowledge itself; the perceiver, the perceived, and perception itself; and of course birth, life, and death. What is more, the number three, in the mysticism of the religions of the *convivencia*, marks our threefold motion: we descend from a divine and original world; we become part of a material and sensible world; and then, with work and knowledge and love, we rise again to a perfect world whence we came. In geometry, when a circle is twice reflected and extended outside itself, then as the reflection is completed, we have the first polygon, the triangle, which is the very first way we have to enclose space within lines.

From this figure, many other forms in Islamic tile work are derived. If we take two triangles together, we get a central symbol of Mediterranean spirituality, the six-pointed star, which refers to the very motions of descent, incarnation, and ascent described, the simple pattern of a personal journey.

The number four summons for us the elemental division of every year into four parts, since by the motion of the earth the sun seems to move south and north along the ecliptic. Twice during the year, at the vernal and autumnal equinox, the day and night are of equal length, and at the winter and summer solstice, we have our longest night and longest day. This fourfold division of the year gives us the traditional way to mark the seasons and refers as well to the ancient quartet of earth, air, fire, and water, as well as to cold, heat, wet, and dry, and to the four cardinal points of the compass. Four was also a key number for the Pythagoreans, who associated it with justice, perfection, and the nature of the soul. The square is easily inscribed within a circle, by locating four equidistant points. Also, if we continue in our reflection and extension of circles, so that the originating circle is itself encircled, a square emerges.

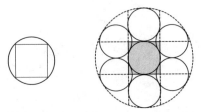

The number five is especially bound up with each of us because we have five senses to connect us with the world. In the mysticism of the Middle Ages, as it was found in the Middle East and in Spain, our five senses do not show us a real world, but introduce the world. That is, our five senses may be developed into a further set of five capacities, more subtle and powerful, so that we may learn to see things whole and true and act with more insight and prescience. With full development of such capacities, a man or woman will have a direct, creative, and conscious connection with a divine order that shows itself on earth. In geometry, we invoke the number five with the pentagon, which we can inscribe within a circle using only a compass and straightedge. The pentagon has remarkable qualities, since if we connect its vertices, we create a beautiful set of pentagonal stars. The ratio of the side of a pentagon to the diagonal of a pentagon (that is, to each of the sides of the star) gives us the golden ratio, identified with beauty throughout history. The golden ratio is found not only in the human body and in beautiful human creations, but also everywhere in the natural world—in nautilus shells, in sunflowers, in pine cones, even in the play of light. So are patterns of growth and movement in nature related directly to geometrical ratios and the integration of mind as we seek to understand our place and purpose in the world.

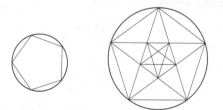

What we are sketching here are cumulative, vital associations with the first few whole numbers. They are essential to understanding the tiles of the Alhambra, since the design of the tiles holds a meaningful pattern, and what it may mean is bound up with numbers. A sense of the meaning of numbers, along with rules of numerical order, ratio, and harmony, were used to create the patterns of the tiles.

Let us move on to the fine prospects afforded by six, seven, eight, and twelve.

As to six, it is an essential quantity in geometrical design because of its connection with the circle and its perfections. If we, from a point, inscribe a circle, and reflect that circle outward, we find that six circles, only and always six, will fit around the circumference. If you connect the center points of the surround of circles, you draw a hexagon that mirrors and encloses the first. If you draw lines to connect the vertices of the hexagons, you get the six-pointed star that is a symbol of perfection in the religions of the *convivencia*. Of course, in all three religions, God created the world in six days, and rather than take this in a brute, literal sense, we might see it a statement about the way form is conceived in the mind and expressed in the world. So the center point of a circle, from where a circle is created, corresponds both to origin and to completion, both the invisible source of things and the still point—call it the day of rest—after form is brought forth.

To state this again: the center point gives rise to the first circle, then to six reflected circles, which gives us the hexagon. The hexagon holds the six-pointed star, which portrays by tradition our journey from our origins, to earth, followed by our ascent once more, after our life and learning here.

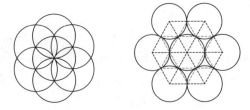

The center point and the inevitable hexagon, together, bring us to seven, especially rich in associations. It is three plus four, and so incorporates by reference the three stages of the journey, and, as well, the number that refers to the earth, its seasons, its cardinal points, and its essential components. What is more, it represents the ancient idea of the seven heavenly spheres and, as we saw, the six days of creation and one of rest. Seven is also one-quarter of the lunar cycle, which is the basis for the rhythm of work and rest worldwide. If we multiply three and four, we have twelve, another emblematic number in the faiths of the *convivencia*, showing up in the twelve disciples of Jesus, the twelve "pure ones" of Shiite Islam, and of course in the traditional division of the sky into the twelve signs of the zodiac. Even today, we live with these concentrated references, in the modern division of the day into twice twelve hours. One more harmony; if we add the numbers from one to seven, we have twenty-eight, the number of days of the complete lunar cycle. To bring things back for a moment to the Albayzín, it is the number of *aljibes* that brought fresh water to the barrio; it's as though the Albayzín wanted to make a gesture of affection and recognition to the night sky.

One last set of associations, this time for the number eight. Eight is the double of four, which is associated with the earth. When it is expressed in the octagonal star (a square rotated one-eighth turn upon another square), it is a beautiful image of the turning earth and of the movement of life. Within the octagonal star is a perfect octagon, which throughout Christendom is the shape used for the baptismal font. It signifies spiritual rebirth, since Jesus rose from the dead on the eighth day of the Passion. In the Sermon on the Mount, Jesus speaks of the eight beatitudes. In the Kabbalah, eight is the number of transcendence. Eight, as the next number after emblematic seven (the heavenly spheres and the week of Creation), represents the domain of fixed stars: an especially rich association, given the plentitude of stars in the tile work we will shortly have before us. It is the step beyond the created world, to the re-creation of ourselves in a domain of light, the step from the life created for us to a life in creation. To put it another way: eight is the number of matter becoming spirit. Because of this, eight in many cultures is an auspicious number. In the Koran, there are eight forms of paradise, and eight angels carry the divine throne. It is worth mentioning that this linkage of eight to spiritual practice is worldwide: witness Buddhism with its eightfold way. Even in China, Taoism has eight immortals, and there are eight pillars of heaven. Closer to home, and directly relevant to the Alhambra, the octagon is the preeminent symbol of the Sufis, said to hold the wisdom at the source and confluence of Islam, Judaism, and Christianity.

Now, having in mind all this heritage, let us walk into the Alhambra, and into the throne room in the Tower of Comares. Above us, we see a ceiling of inlaid pieces of wood, over one thousand eight hundred of them, in seven circles marked by myriad stars. From the four corners of the room, four bright channels run, marking the course of the four rivers of paradise. They run to the center of the concentric stars at the highest point in the ceiling, the source of creation and its final destination. Around us are walls of iridescent tiles, each wall with its own design. Let us choose one to study and look into the world of number and form and see where we are led by the play of mind made available by an art meant to offer us a kind of treasure map for meditation.

It is just beside the entrance of to the throne room, a modestly sized panel. Let's look at it carefully together.

The tiles fit together seamlessly. It looks as if the wall is in movement, which is an effect found throughout the Alhambra. The solid wall pulses with the energy of form. At the heart of this panel is an golden octagonal star, bounded by white lines, which create another octagonal star, which in turn unfolds into a larger, green octagonal figure. This beautiful design is surrounded in turn by eight golden figures, each with five points, and in form like human forms with arms outstretched, as if they were dancing. Then, as we look at the tiles, we find the central octagonal star reproduces itself, as eight deep blue octagonal stars, arranged symmetrically around the golden figures. If we refocus and try to see the center section of the design as a whole, we notice that the white line surrounding them makes a perfect octagon. After a moment, we can hold both the center octagonal star and the surrounding octagon in focus, so as to see both the centerpoint and its frame.

This is a good time to pause. For just with this one initial exercise, we have had to experiment with our vision, to change our perspective on the design, to see what is figure and what is ground. This figure-ground switching, commonly found in optical illusions, here is deliberately urged upon us, since crucial elements of the design remain concealed unless we refocus our attention to select another set of elements. But this skill of switching, whereby we question and change our assumptions about what we perceive, is of course an indispensable skill in perception of whatever kind, in whatever

study. Here, before a wall of tiles in the Alhambra, we are given a
chance to practice this art. So the tiles are a kind of athletic field of
perception, where we might exercise in order to strengthen this very
capacity of mind.

To return to the tiles: we next see that, beyond the enclosing
octagon, the pattern flowers out along the interlocking white bands.
It flowers both horizontally and toward the corners. This flowering
occurs with various five- and six-pointed polygons, none of them
regular pentagons or hexagons. Until suddenly, in the corners, we
see the central pattern suddenly re-created (the golden octagonal star,
unfolding into an octagonal figure, etc.). Surrounding the golden
octagonal stars and figures in each corner, we see the same set of blue
octagonal stars, and the same outline in white lines of the perfect
enclosing octagon. One key pattern, then, is in the center and in all
four corners. And there is a stunning sensation of movement, since
the central pattern, as re-created in the corners, is incomplete. It is as
if the whole design were alive and expanding before our eyes, moving
beyond the borders of the design.

Here again is the role of this tile work as conductor of the mind:
we see that the movement of the design is based on a harmonious and
natural change of one form into another. Now, all of us change in the
course of life, and the tiles speak to the notion that we might transform ourselves according to a radiant pattern alive within the world,
and within us. Rather than change being chaotic and unwelcome,
the tiles would suggest that there exists a natural path of change that
might be traditional and available, by which we might proceed with
clarity, precision, and integrity.

To put it another way: it is as if we are to learn that a clear and
beautiful pattern in our own lives, once understood, can then, as our

perception is extended, be found clear and resurgent in the world. It is a portrait of the way our lives might be part of an enveloping life, the way the world might offer a common and beautiful unity. Our minds, as we study these tiles, develop because we are being continuously sensitized to patterns of clairvoyant power. All of us live by patterns, in the way we think and the way we work. To see a pattern in each of our lives is to understand our place in that pattern, and, by extension, to know what to expect in the world from a given configuration of events.

To return once more to the tiles: if we look to each side of the central figure, we see the two strange forms: four octagonal stars (two green and two black) that look as if they are emerging from a white-bordered blue octagonal star; and at the corners of the figure, four green polygons with five vertices each. Once again the impression is that of inevitable emergence, of movement, of a harmonious channeling of energies.

And in the overall design, we can try to follow any one line, and track its various uses as it moves through the overall design. It is like driving a race car, since any one line swerves and veers, banks and curves, reverses course and rockets off in a new direction. It's exhilarating; it's just like walking in the Albayzín, and I have been tempted to post a satellite shot of the barrio on my wall, just to see if any of the patterns in the tiles are found in the network of streets that define our barrio. In following the lines in this wall of tile before us, we stop and note the forms they define: here a star, there an octagon, further on an emblematic figure of a man or woman standing, arms outstretched, in exaltation. In all this tracking, what is obvious becomes actively part of our experience, for there is no isolated line, there is no end point to the movement of the pattern; any one line can play its part in a whole variety of forms. We see before us what we say we have known all along: the necessary, organic connection of all things. It is driven home not in the pale form of a mere idea, but as a richly sensual experience of meditation as we look into the tiles. It is the idea made real, lovely, and irresistible.

Let's return, after this journey around one wall of tiles, to the numbers that govern this design. First, it is dominated by eight, the number that is a portrait of earth as both material and transcendent, as matter in movement, yet turning in concord with a harmonious and perfect order. Transcendence, in some way, has to begin with the effort to bring a stable, harmonious order to the mind, to create a center point of peace that can sustain us and safeguard us as we live through the storm of events that comprise our days. The numerical theme here is a dense concentration of eightfold symmetries—a variety of stars and octagons, into which are woven the eight human figures. This very pattern, resurgent in the corners of the wall, suggests again how an order we find within may then be found in life itself. In other words, it is suggested that we can earn a capacity of mind that permits us to find within the world a more durable, transcendent order. Surely these tiles are meant to portray just such a deepening of experience, at core an experience of a merciful order in the mind that is at the same time a living order in the world.

The figures at the sides of the wall hold the numbers four, five, six, and eight: an internal blue octagonal star, surrounded by four emergent stars, making five centers altogether (the central star and the four emergent stars). The number five, we recall, refers to our senses and their progressive development as we try to refine our capacities of mind and perception. And it refers, as well, to the organic growth in the natural world. So once again, we have a geometric figure that portrays what can be our unity with the green and growing world, as we learn to join our life to all life.

If we stand back and review our meditation upon the patterns of just this one wall of tiles, what might we carry away with us? To understand the design, we must use care and patience, change perspective by switching figure and ground, learn how to see emergent patterns, focus on how one pattern fits with another, and comprehend how the whole is connected. And all of this, bound up with whole numbers which have the most resonant, productive associations with spiritual history, with the workings of the earth, and the order of our minds. What if these tiles are meant to teach? What if here, before us, is art that has the power to help us test our perceptions, to learn to sense patterns in the world itself, to be able to follow the harmonious unfolding of events, to recognize how one form of understanding leads to another, to sense our connection to the whole? What I claim here is that the tiles of the Alhambra are not just beautiful. They have a *useful* beauty. They are a gift offered to us so that we may learn by means of the dynamic exercise they give our perceptions. We are given a chance to form capacities of mind that make a harmonious and sentient change in the way we live. That is, we begin to see how patterns in life can show the workings of a more fundamental, inclusive order, an order in the world and within us. To begin to see ourselves as part of a comprehensive order connected with beauty is to have, beyond faith, a hope of integrity brought to us by a design both generous and sacred. We are in the presence of an art of stars. Whatever the delight they give with their beauty, whatever the admiration they excite with their play of arabesque, they speak to us of knowledge we need to thrive.

I offer these ideas in the full awareness that some readers will think I have gone round the bend, and that such reasoning provides not an effective suggestion so much as a heady dose of flimflam and blarney. I can only recommend to any such reader an extended stay with these walls of tiles, so that you may see for yourself what they offer you.

Either these tiles are a sacred art with a mathematical and cosmological basis, or they are merely décor. Either they are a beautiful proposition of number and pattern, an instructive offering to the mind, a music of numbers, a hopeful declaration about life and spirituality in the culture where they were created—or they are just another exercise in ornament. I have tried, over many visits, to see why they have exercised so powerful a hold on the imagination of so many over the centuries. And why they are so sophisticated: for example, modern mathematicians who work in an exotic field called plane crystallographic group theory have noted seventeen possible two-dimensional symmetry groups. Every single one of them are found in one or another place in the Alhambra. Workers in another rarified field in mathematics, called quasi-crystalline designs, have identified a certain pattern called a Penrose diagram, named after a cosmologist from Oxford. These same designs show up in Islamic tile work as far back as the thirteenth century.

We watch them with exaltation. Here, before us, is a work of understanding, designed with genius, that asks only our attention and study. Different walls of tile have distinct patterns, all with their own detail and import. In some designs in other rooms of the Alhambra, we see the same figures are produced in different forms and at a different scale. This is a principle known to us in the modern discovery of fractals, which are patterns in nature produced at dramatically different scales, which we see everywhere, from clouds to coastlines. It is another instance of the uncanny way these designs anticipate modern discoveries.

Experience must confirm and enliven what is mere concept. To offer such experience is part of the essential value of the Alhambra tiles. If there is a common theme in studies of the mind, it is that we fail to see what is most obvious. We see what we assume and cannot see what is right in front of us. As Jesus put it in the *Nag Hammadi Gospels*, in this exchange:

> And the disciples asked: *When will the Kingdom of Heaven come?*
>
> And Jesus said: *The Kingdom . . . is spread out upon the earth, but men do not see it.*

Standing before these walls of tiles, in visit after visit, we were seeking to answer the simplest of questions: Where, now, do we live? Our move to Granada had led us into the houses and gardens of our neighbors, who taught us how to live in the Albayzín. We studied the history of our garden, then of our barrio, then the glories and surprises of Al-Andalus. And this work led us across the Darro, to ascend to the Alhambra, and there to stand in the palace of the Nasrids and look at, and into, the trustworthy beauty of the ceramic tile work found everywhere in the castle.

Those lustrous designs became part of the design of our days; they made ideas material, made them into life. It is a most hopeful art, a portrayal of harmony deep in the world, of the meaning of numbers and the formation of order, of connection and clarity and the unity of faith and people. We think of it, even today, often, and always in praise of the anonymous and brilliant craftsmen whose light still shines in Granada and in the world.

The Lucid Work of Love
and Helpfulness

a S IF WITH some strange gravity, the art of Islamic tile work draws us into a unity. If we can accept that this tile work is a medieval art rooted in the sacred, then it is reasonable to ask how might it be related to the spiritual practice of the people of the time. Of course we know the basic tenets of Islam, Judaism, and Christianity. But beyond that, is there, within the practice of those faiths, a calling to a unity, a *convivencia* of the soul, that summons us with the claim that we might look to the origin and core of religion? To answer this question, we might start with an old woman playing a tambourine in Córdoba in the twelfth century. Her music will lead us to the world of the Sufis.

The tambourine is in the hands of a woman named Fatima, and she is 95 years old. She lives in a hut made of reeds. She has a deep and useful understanding of the world. She teaches students she selects. Among them is a young man whose name is Ibn El-Arabi. It is he who has built Fatima's house for her. And it is he who will one day be known as one of the great mystics, writers, and teachers of the world.

Ibn El-Arabi was born in 1165, in Murcia, a town in the south-east corner of the Iberian peninsula. He would live in Seville and study throughout southern Spain. Later, in his travels to seek learning, and as a teacher, he would have time in Morocco, in Tunisia, in the cities of Mecca and Cairo, in the city of Konya in present-day Turkey, finally to settle in Damascus. Some two hundred fifty-one books of his survive, some of them revealed to him in dreams, some of them written in an hour, and many of them set down as if he were "taking dictation from God." The English mystic and romantic poet William Blake, centuries later, would use the same phrase for his visionary writings.

Within Islam he is known as "the Greatest Shaikh," and in the West by the wonderful name "Doctor Maximus." I can hardly think of a life story that holds more wild variety. When young, Ibn El-Arabi met Averroes, who was a friend of his father. The philosopher was renowned, the budding mystic a mere teenager. They immediately fell into one of those conversations that had questions like this one, asked by Averroes: "What solution have you found as a result of mystical illumination and divine inspiration? Does it correspond with what it arrived at by speculative thought?" It's just the kind of question we ask of teenagers these days. Ibn El-Arabi, who despite his tender years sought out such conversations, replied: "Yes and no. Between the yes and the no the spirits take their flight from matter . . ." And so on. One would have liked to be present for an afternoon of musing with those two gentlemen.

But even Averroes was mild company compared with some of his other acquaintances. Take this encounter, for example, from Ibn El-Arabi's own account:

*On another occasion, I was in a boat in a port of Tunis. I
had a pain in my stomach, but the people were sleeping so
I went to the side of the boat and looked out over the sea.
Suddenly I saw by the light of the moon, which was full that
night, someone coming towards me on the surface of the
water. Finally he came up to me and stood with me . . . After
talking to me awhile, he greeted me and went off, making
for a lighthouse on top of a hill over two miles distant from
us. This distance he covered in two or three steps . . .*

This water-walking, moonlit visitor turns out to be a character
named Khidr, who in Mediterranean accounts is a mysterious and
immortal guide who wanders the earth, giving physical and spiritual
help to those who are worthy of such help. He is identified with the
Biblical figure of Elias and the storied figure of St. George.

So it went with Ibn El-Arabi, whose life was full of encounters
with teachers, visible and invisible, and whose accounts of his deal-
ings with the divine fill hundreds of matter-of-fact pages. His poems
may be received directly into the minds of other people in faraway
places; he communicates telepathically with saints of his own day.
He was capable, according to one of his students, of getting in touch
with any of the saints and prophets of any period in history. He did
this by calling them back to earth, where they assumed a form like
that they had in life; by encountering them in dreams; or by absenting
himself from his own body so that he could venture off to see them. It
would be a nice adventure some afternoon, I say, if one had the need
and the means of travel.

The fame of this Andalusian poet and theologian shone throughout the world of the Mediterranean. Kings, sultans, emirs, all

competed to have him grace their courts. When he was in Konya, in
Anatolia, as a tribute to him the king built a sumptuous palace, on
the idea that the famous teacher would move in and make a home in
Konya. Not long afterward, a beggar approached Ibn El-Arabi, asking him for alms. But Ibn Arabi had nothing of his own to give away
at that moment. So he made the beggar a gift of his new palace.

In Mecca, he came across a brilliant young girl, and his description of her survives:

> *a slender child who captivated all who looked upon her,*
> *whose presence gave luster to gatherings, who amazed all she*
> *was with and ravished the senses of all who beheld her. Her*
> *name was Nizam (Harmony) and her surname Ain as-Shams*
> *(Eye of the Sun). She was religious, learned, ascetic, a sage*
> *among the sages of the Holy Places.*

Nizam was the inspiration of another poem of his, called "The
Interpreter of Desires." It takes up a theme that he will return to
in other writings: that we come to the truth through our love for
Divine Beauty as revealed on earth, and that the most perfect revelation of beauty is in a woman. Now, this attitude scandalized
some of the more dogmatic clergy in Cairo, and he was accused
there and in Aleppo of having, in his verse, an indecent and blas-
phemous revel in sensuality. The verdict of the offended clergy had
the exalted moral sensibility we associate with fundamentalists
everywhere: they decreed that Ibn El-Arabi should be killed. But he
wisely took refuge from Cairo in Mecca. Later in Aleppo, he wrote
a full interpretation of his earlier work, demonstrating in exhaustive detail how each of the lines lead us to perceive divine content in
earthly reality, and by means of love find our way to what endures.

His interpretation was called "The Treasures of Lovers"; so did he escape by use of his pen being killed for use of his pen. He was not about to stand down and let the bigots have their way. And he could fight against them, since he kept company with kings and sultans, as well as with the leading religious lights of the time. He said directly to the King of Aleppo:

> *know that when worldly desires get the better of men's*
> *souls and scholars seek positions at the courts of kings, they*
> *forsake the true way and resort to far-fetched interpretations*
> *of the Law to satisfy the whims of their masters who require*
> *legal support for their selfish purposes . . .*

One reads this and thinks that Ibn El-Arabi might have been executed on the spot for speaking the truth about so many clerics. We recognize the type he refers to, from history and from the present time—those who pervert religion to build their own power. But such was Ibn El-Arabi's authority that the king replied:

> *You have often voiced your disapproval of the oppression*
> *and wrongs which occur in this kingdom of mine, and I*
> *agree with you that these things are indeed reprehensible;*
> *but know, Sir, that each of these things is done by the au-*
> *thority of a jurist who draws up the decree which justifies it,*
> *may God curse them . . .*

This is but one example of Ibn El-Arabi's courage, where he did the rare, indispensable thing: bearing truth to the heart of power. Over eight hundred years later, it is still the dream of many of us that such an exchange might occur between such a person and the ruler of a country.

In his later years, Ibn El-Arabi settled, again at the invitation of a king, in Damascus, where he wrote summary treatises on his teaching, more cycles of mystical poetry; where he carried on his teaching; and where he died in a characteristic way. One day he was in his doorway, and a group of pious clerics and followers were passing, and Ibn El-Arabi called out: "Your God is under my foot!" Offended in public and righteous in their fury, the clerics confronted the teacher, loudly accused him of sacrilege, and assaulted him together. He died soon after the beating. When his body was undressed for burial, in his shoe was found a coin, and thus his last declaration became clear: a simple observation about the greed of the clerics, who worshiped money and the material world, rather than God.

Can the life and teachings of Ibn El-Arabi help us understand the tiles in the Alhambra, with their unreservedly beautiful teaching of unity? And can they help us to understand the uncanny current of mysticism that runs through the centuries of Al-Andalus? They can, because of one of the books written by Ibn El-Arabi, and because he was a Sufi.

The book is *The Sufis of Andalusia*, and it recounts the travels and companions of Ibn El-Arabi during the first half of his life. Throughout Andalusia he finds companions on the path of learning, and we should meet some of them and learn about their lives.

How did they live? They were capmakers, tailors, potters, cobblers; caulkers of ships and gatherers of chamomile; weavers, a slave girl, a doctor; rich or poor, literate or not. All of them had work, lived outwardly normal lives, but with a select few, like the young Ibn El-Arabi, they shared other capacities. One Abu Abdallah was on a trip through the desert with a group in need of water, but only bitter, salty water could be found. Abdallah made it sweet water through his touch. He could also, in such journeys, contract the earth so that extraordinary distances could be covered in the single step. The gatherer of chamomile, an illiterate named Al-Rundi, was a solitary who spent long years in the mountains and along the coast. Sometimes, when he stood on mountains at prayer, a column of light from the sky illuminated him, as in the transfiguration of Jesus. Al-Rundi could collect grass and, if need be, strike it with his finger to set in on fire; and this, of course, to be able to light the lamps of the house. Another companion, by the name of Abu Imran, was a man of considerable riches, who renounced them all. He was granted a special knowledge that permitted him to be anywhere on earth, according to his wishes. Once he was captured on trumped-up charges and taken away in chains to Fez and locked in a room. In the morning, the guards found only the chains; Abu Imran was safely and comfortably in the house of a friend. There are yet more companions: a slave girl, who when not in forced labor would walk in the mountains and had the capacity to converse with rocks and trees. The doctor, who lived in Córdoba and cared for the desperately ill. When Ibn El-Arabi asked him how he could live among such people, he replied that to him the sick had the odor of musk.

To come full circle, let us relate what Ibn El-Arabi tells us of the old woman Fatima. She was a weaver who was married for twenty years to a man who contracted leprosy. She cared for him until he died. Later, too crippled to make her living, she lived on the scraps of food left by her door. It was in this period of her life that Ibn El-Arabi built her a hut of reeds. Though full of years, she was so lovely that Ibn El-Arabi confessed to being shy around her. As well he might have been, for she could change the world with her prayers, meet with the jinn, and perform miracles, including practical ones: once

she was out of fuel to light her lamps, and she changed the water in
a bucket into oil by dunking her hand into it.

Such were the friends and teachers of Ibn El-Arabi in medieval
Andalusia. They combine the ordinary and the preternatural. They
work and pray alongside their neighbors, yet they have potent,
uncommon spirits. They are of earth yet are entrusted with extraordinary powers: they can see into the minds of other people, travel
through the air, heal the sick, see into the future, engage in telepathy.
Their lives are often simple and helpful, and their miracles, for the
most part, are hidden; they are natural, practical efforts. Who were
these people, and what is Sufism?

This is a question whose answer is held by the reader. But we
can say something in general about the Sufis, and about Ibn El-Arabi
and his teaching, for his teaching bears a direct and irresistible relation to what we learn when we study the tile work of the Alhambra.
As the tiles bring together a host of forms into a finely connected,
beautiful unity, so does Ibn El-Arabi bring together the faiths of the
convivencia by means of a teaching called the Unity of Revelation.
It is a simple idea: that the revelation of the divine, such as those of
Abraham, Jesus, or Mohammad, is always and everywhere the same.
From the revelation of any important teacher, a religious institution
may develop, as in the case of Judaism, Christianity, and Islam, and
these institutions are different according to the history, culture, and
language of the society in which they are found. In the case of the
founders of religions, the revelation is that of a public teacher. In all
other cases, such revelation—the same revelation—may be earned
privately by anyone with the interest and the capacity.

It is important to note that this central teaching of Ibn El-Arabi
does not invalidate the religious customs and theologies of Islam,

Judaism, and Christianity. It maintains, instead, that such practices and ideas can be conceived of as the place we begin, so as to work our way to the inner content of faith, the proof, end point, and validation of faith: the experience of the divine, as we live, here on earth.

What might be the teaching that dedicates itself to helping a person find a way to just such an experience? This is just what Sufism claims to possess, a knowledge of the inner content of religion expressed in a teaching with a heritage of centuries. In some times and places, this work of teaching was especially strong and vital, and the eight centuries of Al-Andalus produced distinguished teachers, stunning mystical poetry, and splendid craftsmanship. And it produced Ibn El-Arabi, who along with Jalaludin Rumi, the Sufi poet of Anatolia, is one of the central figures in the religious life of the Mediterranean and the world.

Yet the Sufis did not build institutions, and they did not teach anyone who happened to claim interest. They taught, and teach, only those who have the capacity to learn. For such people, studies are individually prescribed. All the same, it is useful to try to sketch the general form of such a teaching, insofar as it can be addressed in language and from the outside. First, since at its core is an experience of revelation (rather than a notion, text, or set of rituals), the Sufis have no institution; they have no dogma, fixed theology, inflexible rules, holy scriptures, system of reward and punishments, clerics, or claims of a right to punish others for their beliefs. In place of all this, they have a teaching, and the teaching is carried out by any way that works; say, by stories, proverbs, conversation, the making of art or the design of a wall of tiles, an essay or an ecstatic utterance. It is even carried out by means of specially crafted jokes, which teach us something about the way our minds work.

The aim of the teaching is to transform the self, by means of love, so as to know a living reality present on earth in its full beauty and permanence. In such a transformation, love and knowledge come together, and a person can thereafter be of the most timely, secret, and fabulous help to others, and to life itself.

If the aim is self-transformation, then a student should have an idea of whether his mind, or her mind, is contaminated by pride, greed, or self-esteem. And so one straightforward approach of Sufi teaching is to provide the means to assess the state of one's mind.

But rather than offer summary statements, it makes sense to offer some real examples of this teaching, so let's begin with the jokes. How about this one, from the collection of stories about the legendary Nasrudin:

> *The king sent a private mission around the countryside*
> *to find a modest man who could be appointed as a judge.*
> *Nasrudin got wind of it.*
>
> *When the delegation, posing as travelers, called on him, they*
> *found that he had a fishing net draped over his shoulders.*
>
> *"Why, pray," one of the them asked, "do you wear that net?"*
>
> *"Merely to remind myself of my humble origins, for I was*
> *once a fisherman."*
>
> *Nasrudin was appointed judge on the strength of this noble*
> *sentiment.*
>
> *Visiting his court one day, one of the officials who had first*
> *seen him asked, "What happened to your net, Nasrudin?"*
>
> *"There is no need of a net, surely," he replied, "once the fish*
> *has been caught."*

Many of the jokes in this tradition are like this, always ready to point out hypocrisy or manipulation, always ready to show events and people for what they are, rather than how they are imagined to be, and, especially, how they imagine themselves to be.

The history of Sufi proverbs and short declarations is the most surprising and useful that I have ever come across. These sayings are easily retained in the mind. Their range is remarkable. They delight us but also make us think by, for example, recommending virtues, like gratitude, that we take for granted, as in:

Call yourself unlucky only if you take up coffin making and people stop dying.

Or they refer with bemusement to something permanent in us, to a potential to do work which is at once practical and transcendent:

If you do not want to be dismissed, do not take over a post that will not always be yours.

Light is often a metaphor in this tradition: both the light of the earth, and another, animating light that sustains us beyond all explanations:

There is a light deposited in hearts that is nourished by the light coming from the treasuries of invisible realms.

And all such labors are meant to find what is essential in us, to turn back from our common idiocies, so that we may be ready for a living reality. It's as if the world answers us to exactly the extent that we are prepared. When we are ready to understand, and only then, may our perceptions deepen and progress, and that reality show itself on earth:

How can the laws of nature be ruptured for you, so that
miracles result, while you, for your part, have yet to rupture
your bad habits?

But in the meantime, as we are learning, we can understand
only with correct preparation and with the right timing and company. Without such advantages, we may focus only on ourselves, on
reward and expectation, on our own gain. This need for another way
of work is the subject of a beautiful declaration of an eighth-century
Sufi, a woman named Rabia:

I will not serve God like a laborer, in expectation of my wages.

And if we do not learn, then what we seem to be, what we make of
ourselves in this life, with all its adornments, customs, and demands,
will take us over, until there is little left of us:

If you do not shave the beard, it will not be long before it is
pretending to be your head.

This is a short tour of Sufi proverbs and is meant to give the mer-
est savor of the rich materials on offer in the writings of this accomplished group.

Let's finish this sampling by quoting one of the most famous stories of the Sufis, one that turns up throughout Western culture, so
that it has become a shorthand way to refer to a problem in thinking, and its solution. It is the story of the elephant in the dark, here
quoted in the version published by the extraordinary Sufi scholar and
writer Idries Shah.

THE BLIND ONES AND THE MATTER
OF THE ELEPHANT

Beyond Ghor there was city. All its inhabitants were blind. A king with his entourage arrived nearby; he brought his army and camped in the desert. He had a mighty elephant, which he used in attack and to increase the people's awe.

The populace became anxious to see the elephant, and some sightless from among this blind community ran like fools to find it.

As they did not even know the form or shape of the elephant, they groped sightlessly, gathering information by touching some part of it.

Each thought he knew something, because he could feel a part.

When they returned to their fellow citizens, eager groups clustered around them. Each of these was anxious, misguidedly, to learn the truth from those who were themselves astray.

They were asked about the form, the shape of the elephant, and listened to all they were told.

The man whose hand had reached an ear was asked about the elephant's nature. He said: "It is a large, rough thing, wide and broad, like a rug."

And the one who had felt the trunk said: "It is mighty and firm, like a pillar."

*Each had felt one part out of many. Each had perceived
it wrongly. No mind knew all: Knowledge is not the companion of the blind. All imagined something, something
incorrect.*

*The created is not informed about divinity. There is no Way
in this science by means of the ordinary intellect.*

This beautiful story, taken from a twelfth-century version by the
Afghan poet Hakim Sanai, one finds in all kinds of forums today: in
newspapers, in university studies, in books about the brain. It portrays the way we deal with the parts of a problem, rather than seeing it as an integrated whole, for what it really is. And the story has
whole other ranges of meaning, like most of the stories in the Sufi
tradition.

Once a person has completed the studies prescribed as being most
useful to her, then she may go forth into a life that may be apparently
unchanged but is fundamentally transformed. Any so-called school
she might have attended as part of her learning is then disbanded:
"The workshop is dismantled when the work is done."

One central aim of Sufi work, then, as taught by Ibn El-Arabi,
Idries Shah, and other men and women through the centuries, is to
lead a student to meet herself, or himself, as in the saying: "He who
knows himself knows his God." Or as said one of Ibn El-Arabi's
teachers, a man who was accompanied by an angel: "Reckon with
yourself before you are brought to the Reckoning."

In all this, the Sufis insist, throughout the centuries, on the dis-
tinction between the literal and the figurative, between container and
content, appearance and reality. It is a spiritual practice that sees

literal-mindedness as a mortal failing akin to idolatry. Closely allied is their idea of virtue: rather than being the end point of spiritual development, the development of personal virtues such as honesty, generosity, or humility is seen as the bare, modest beginning, the essential baby steps. Virtues are not valuable in themselves, and they are a mortal handicap when they become a basis for pride. Instead, they are instrumental, a means of traveling to the next stage of knowledge.

The same is true with beauty: it is not thought to be reality, but the beginning of reality, an experience meant as a pathway we follow to prepare ourselves for a much more powerful experience.

THIS BRIEF EXCURSION among the writings of the Sufis and their Andalusian champion Ibn El-Arabi takes us back to the walls of tiles in the Alhambra. For the work of the Sufis and the work of the tile design are at once practical and transcendental. They bring beauty into our days but open for us a way to another life that is, in the ancient phrase, "Undone from self but alive to love." That is, we are called to a life in which treasures of understanding are offered to our hands the moment we can be entrusted with them. We live in a world today when such possibilities are discredited when they are not ridiculed, or just wholly dismissed out of hand. Love is sentiment now, and not a resurgence of soul that remakes a life.

But like Al-Andalus, the beauty and power of the ceramic tiles is being rediscovered. And so is the work of the Sufis. It makes one think that even in the darkness of our times, any of us might have a chance to discover that a secret and powerful labor of helpfulness and goodwill goes on all around us. It is a labor that speaks to us of light as a preternatural offering to life. It is a teaching that holds transfiguration to be a natural heritage of the mind.

On Flamenco, Poetry,
Genius, and Murder

O UR DAYS IN the Albayzín had many parts: our grapevine and books; the centuries of design intelligence within
the layout of the streets; the play of light along the narrow lanes; the incorrigible good nature of our neighbors; Gabriella's
superb preschool in the barrio; the Arab bakery; the wonderful
newsstands in Plaza Nueva, which even sell on occasion the books
of Gabriel García Márquez and Dante; the persimmons and pomegranates and figs from our trees; and the tomatoes, basil, and rosemary from our vegetable garden. We even went so far as to cure our
own olives. Our first year's effort came out tasting like mildewed
cardboard mush that would have disgraced a toxic waste dump. The
second year's batch was memorably delicious. It made us feel as if we
might still be capable of learning.

Gradually, over the months and years, the parts of our experience
gathered force and began to make a whole beauty, one with a strange
spectrum of effects. It was more than the hot spring Andalusian light
on the honeysuckle vine, or the waft of orange blossoms through

the rooms of the house, or the soaring of the swifts every morning
in their fantastical acrobatics. Such delights held the sensuality of
the Albayzín at a high pitch. Beyond the sensuality, the history and
poetry natural to the place, and the role of Granada as a magnetic
center of events with the most far-reaching consequences, played
upon our minds and became centermost in our musing. It was as if
the neighborhood brought body and mind together, as if the each day
formed a lens, and we could see before us a strange fortune. We were
being drawn irrevocably into life in the Albayzín, and the joy of it
was beyond anything I could have conjured. I simply had never been
in a place of such tough, enveloping beauty, and I began to think that
the Albayzín had some hidden power, that against all the odds it had
been able to deflect the darkness and terror seething in the history
of Granada, that it had suffered near devastation, but through some
genius for survival, some singular life force, it had risen again with its
hidden traditions and raucous energies.

We came to understand, in part, how such a thriving might be
possible because of flamenco. It is the classic music of Granada and
of Andalusia, and we had a lively interest in the art, though we in fact
knew little of it. Less than little: to call us rank beginners would be
to lavish praise upon us. But we devoutly wanted to hear some good
flamenco, so we embarked upon our research using the time-honored
method of asking questions in bars. One gentlemen, in the district
of the Realejo, just near the *centro*, told us that at a certain theater
that very night we might hear some *flamenco puro*. We straightaway
bought tickets and sat down in a cavernous performance hall that
was sparsely inhabited. Upon the stage was nothing but two chairs
and microphones. Now and then a thickset man would come and
go, repositioning the chairs, testing the microphones—obviously a

technician. He was the very image of someone who, in the United States, would drive a big truck. He walked ponderously to and fro, as the time for the performance came and went. The stage was empty. The lights in the performance hall were brightly lit. We wondered what was going on. The same man appeared again, sat down on one of the chairs, and looked into the distance. We thought perhaps technical difficulties had overcome him, and the show as well.

Then the lights went down suddenly, and we realized the thickset gentleman had nothing to do with trucks. He began to sing. I remember the fine hair on Lucy's arm standing on end, and my own shock at his unreserved, fierce, resonant voice. He sang one song, then another, each of them with scorching virtuosity, an independent, cut-loose ferocity. He was present with us but in a world of his own, made of his voice. We had never heard anything like it in our lives. We gripped tightly our chairs. The singer would hold a note until he had ripped it to pieces. There were prolonged and aggressive battles with single lines in the song. Sometimes a verse would be repeated until it was a rough, hypnotic induction, with singer and audience bound together in trance. The intonation was harsh, then melodious, sometimes a cry, sometimes a growl or snarl. There were notes of purest exaltation and of convulsive bitterness. I thought: a man soaring into a religious vision . . . then, two minutes later, no, a man slaughtered by anguish. Now and again I had the most absurd reflections, such as: Isn't there supposed to be a dancer? A swarthy woman in a fluffy dress? What was going on? But such curiosities were blown straight out of my head by the unabated force of the songs. After four or five numbers, another man walked out with a guitar, took the remaining chair, and began to play for the next song. They performed together the rest of the evening. Their coordination was lively, subtle, precise, and beautiful. Some invisible communication, rich and life-giving, passed continuously between them. We tried to follow where they led us, and it was a rough territory of love and death, which could only be traversed with a music of deep remembrance and release. Then they were done and stood to acknowledge the audience and to salute one another, and they were gone, as if whisked away into shadows only they could see.

Lucy and I had walked into the concert hall as one couple and left as another, transformed by the raw force of an art we hardly knew existed. It was as if a blasting cap had gone off in us, and the encounter with flamenco led us back to the Albayzín, which turned out to have a most lively flamenco tradition of its own. Though we did not know it at the time, flamenco would come to mark our months and years in Granada, to answer our questions, reshape our minds, and introduce us to an art whose survival was just like the survival of the Albayzín: the music, like the place, just could not be killed.

We sought out *flamenco puro* whenever we could. The commercial flamenco in Granada is like commercial adaptation everywhere: the current of life has been extinguished. But the authentic tradition holds its strength, and we had exultant evenings in Granada as the music wove itself into our lives. Every now and then, late in the night, listening to one of Andalusia's prodigiously gifted singers, in the dark room the hair would rise on the back of our necks, and we would be caught up in some uncanny transport of mind, a riptide and release of emotion. A whisper would go around the room . . . "*¡El duende, es el duende!*" There is no way to talk about flamenco without talking about *duende*. This word, which has no equivalent in English, is bound up with music and poetry, with physical passion and incendiary soul, and, most of all, with Andalusia. It is so complex and marvelous a quality that early in the twentieth century, only one person was willing to take a crack at an extended definition. Of course he is from Granada, and of course he is the poet Federico García Lorca.

In 1933, in Argentina, Lorca presented a lecture called "The Theory and Play of the Duende," a title that must have baffled the audience, since *duende*, in the dictionary, means "an elf or mischievous goblin" or "a mysterious and ineffable charm." Lorca, of course, had a different idea. He wanted to use the notion of *duende* to reorganize the aesthetics of the Western world. Perhaps of the whole world. To read the lecture is like riding a rocket of concepts; you have to hang on tight. But it is writing based on Lorca's immersion in flamenco and his rich concord with the art. And it has all the poet's dark, natural ebullience.

So let's ride: Lorca wants to address the creation of art and the art of creation, principally in music, poetry, and dance. We have in our history, he says, counted on two sources of support and revelation: either an angel or a muse. The angel, messenger of heaven, is a guide and a gift-giver, a defender and savior, prophet and bearer of proclamation. He visits from another world, comes to dazzle the man or woman at work, and delivers a grace so trustworthy that the worker becomes the natural agent of an irresistible power. The art needed comes forth fully illuminated, in its beauties, with the savor of a divine visitation.

The muse is the ancient and traditional guide of the worker in the arts, and she appears to those with a readiness of mind and spirit, after long labor. She has an implacable and demanding beauty. Lorca tells us he has seen her twice, which qualifies him for a report and a critique. The muse can suggest, provoke, and inspire irrevocably. She fires the intelligence with a radiant and penetrating spirit. The risk is that she may dominate and devour the artist. But there is another grave risk, according to Lorca. The real risk is that such intelligence will restrict and distort poetry and lock poems in a style that is no more than "aristocratic finery."

Having given us the angel and muse, Lorca turns to his real subject, the third great source of creation, the *duende*, which he finds throughout history but identifies with Spain and with Andalusia. Unlike the angel and muse, who come from without, *duende* lives within, a primordial force bound with blood and death and earth. Reject the angel, he recommends, and give the muse a boot out the door. And come to life in the struggle with *duende*, a struggle that will leave a wound that will never heal, a wound that opens onto creation itself. It frees a force of earth that surges in the blood, shakes us to the core, and acts upon us like wind on sand, like a storm on the sea. It is both incandescent sorrow and communion with God. It leads its possessor beyond form to the source of form, and beyond style and artifice to a suffering that bears us to clarity. And to a state of life where our senses become a work of the earth, where creation and action are the same. Late in his fierce essay, turning to the presence in poetry of *duende*, Lorca gives us this tender paragraph:

> *The magical virtue of poetry is to be always infused with duende, so to baptize in dark water all those who behold it, since with duende it is easier to love and to understand, we are sure to be loved, to be understood, and it is just this struggle for expression and communication that sometimes takes on a fatal character.*

This is expression that folds together life and death, and it is the art of flamenco at its best. Lorca would say: poetry at its best, and any other art.

To this world we went, with sometimes weeks in between our excursions, so that we could recover our senses. Like raw, traditional blues in the United States, it's an acquired taste. And like the blues, it runs deep into life and seems to color even our dreams. Our first, baffled encounter had instructed us rightly: the singing is primary, then the guitar. Andalusia has a deep bench of flamenco guitarists. They should be considered one of the principal assets in the national treasury of Spain and one of the most precious holdings of Europe. And there are dancers, after all, though more rarely, who can send a bolt of electricity through the audience. And most performances have musicians who accompany the singing with their hands, in the sonorous rhythm called *palmas*. Also, the *caja*, a box on the floor, that is the percussion instrument of flamenco. All in all, it's such a rare and distant country that it is useful to have a map.

It turns out to be a map of human experience, in raw and forthright song. Each song is a poem. Love and death are the double suns around which many of the songs revolve. Yet flamenco turns out, as well, to hold in its art the whole prodigious complexity of Spanish history. So far from being an exclusively gypsy art, the gypsies fell heir to the whole musical heritage of Al-Andalus, to which they brought their genius for assimilation, as well as their resolute independence and strong ties to the Andalusian earth. And so flamenco comes in a bewildering and exultant variety of forms, since a poem that is sung might be derived from Arabic or Jewish sources, from gypsy ceremonies, or from the folklore of any of the host of cultures that found a home in Iberia: from Christian rites, Indian music, or even Celtic traditions.

There is even flamenco that takes in musical contributions from Latin America—like the *milongas* from Argentina, or the *guajiras* from Cuba—and so enriches the songs with the savor of the New World.

There is flamenco that comes directly from work, work songs that hold the rhythm and ardor of labor, its effort and loneliness. The *trilleras*, for instance, originated among grinders of wheat; the *tarantas* are work songs of the miners; the *martinetes*, music and poetry from the dark shop of the blacksmith, that use the sound of hammers striking an anvil; the *caleseras*, songs of the labor and solitude of the drivers of carts in the country, with the rhythm of horse's hooves and the mystery of long mountain roads. There is even a genre of songs from jail cells, the *carceleras*, sung in lament, or to carry a message to loved ones in freedom. To this day, there is a flamenco workshop in the Albolote prison in Granada.

There are song traditions tied directly to cities, as if they had grown from the alleyways, the plazas and caves, then were refined over decades and centuries until finally they came to embody a place in song. The *malagueñas* hail from Málaga, as a descendant of the great fandangos, and the *granainas* and *media granainas* are forms redolent of Granada itself, with pronounced Moorish rhythm and storytelling. The *rondiñas* celebrate the mystical city of Ronda, a city with a history of Sufi scholars and a surround of strange and beautiful mountains. The *murcianas* hail from Murcia, birthplace of the great poet, mystic, and theologian Ibn El-Arabi. The lively *sevillanas*, with their inspiriting and contagious rhythm, are part of the history and savor of the great Andalusian city of Seville, where Ibn El-Arabi studied. We do not know if the great twelfth-century poet set down any verses that even today flare here and there as flamenco in Andalusia. But this is Spain, and you never know.

There is a whole genre of flamenco, the *nanas*, that consists of lullabies, which is just as it should be, for what parent can deny the surge of hope and thankfulness that visits us when we hold a baby. It's a moment honored by song in just about every culture.

A cinnamon angel
Watches over your crib
His head toward the sun
His feet toward the moon.

Off to sleep goes
My rose among roses
Sleep, little girl,
As late night closes

My baby carnation,
Opening rosebud
Sleep, my life,
I'll sing you a lullaby . . .
Sleep, little star of the morning

I quote these lovely verses to show how full a spectrum of experience flamenco may explore. As in traditional American blues, we have songs of the most tender communion, songs of longing and cherishing, and then the next moment, songs of black rancor, acid bitterness, or loss so anguished we feel mauled slowly to death. Many of us come in the course of our lives to such extremes because we love, and because so often the cultures and countries we make fail the ideals we bring to them. Flamenco gives verse and voice to the core of such common experience because there is nothing it will not take on: it is a music of celebration because it faces down the darkness.

Take, for instance, these three verses from different *soleares,*
songs of solitude:

The world I live in
Is lost to hope
No need to bury me
I am buried alive.

I saw her black eyes
Now all the world
Is black to me.

Your street is not just your street
It is any street.
Any road. Anywhere.

And this quatrain about hard luck:

Misfortune falls upon me
What can be done?
Saints whom I painted
Demons become.

Lorca sees the centermost of flamenco in the great *siguiriyas,* primordial songs of cut-loose emotional power. The singer holds death
close. The distinguished flamenco guitarist and writer D.E. Pohren
tells us this form is not so much sung: it is unleashed upon the audience. And just as Lorca gave us his far-rambling essay, full of meta-
phors like fireworks on the nature of *duende,* so we have from him an
emblematic speech on the *cante jondo*—deep song—which he takes
to be the source and central form of flamenco singing. It is February
of 1922; it is Lorca's debut as a lecturer, and he will focus on musical

history and on the *siguiriyas*. He has, with the revered Spanish composer Manual Falla, organized a festival in Granada—the *Concurso de Cante Jondo* (Contest of Deep Song), and the months preceding the festival are marked by Lorca's talk, given at the usual Spanish ten in the evening, to the accompaniment of guitar. We should let the poet speak for himself. A set of quotes will bring us fully into his presence.

> . . . *cante jondo is like the trill of birds, the song of a chanti-*
> *cleer, the natural music of the woods and fountain . . . It is*
> *a most rare example of primitive song, the oldest in Europe,*
> *bearing in its sound the shuddering, raw emotion of the first*
> *Eastern races.*

And who are these original poets and musicians? Lorca goes on to recognize them explicitly: he says that some of the oldest songs, the virtual stem of the great *siguiriyas*, "preserve their Arabic and Moorish affiliation." And later research has proved him right. D.E. Pohren, when he constructed his genealogy—a whole family tree of flamenco singing, guitar, and dancing—noted how a whole set of branches showed strong Arabic influence, among them many of the work songs and songs associated with cities that were some of the strongholds of Al-Andalus. And in his *Encyclopedia of Flamenco*, he notes other Moorish influences, in forms such as the *zambra*, which clearly has roots in Muslim music and dance. There are other remarkable sources, which Lorca did not—perhaps dared not—mention. Some flamenco genres, especially the *saetas*, have Jewish origins. In one of those transcendent ironies found throughout Andalusia, they are songs devoted to Jesus and Mary, and their modern versions are sung principally in the precessions of Semana

Santa, the famous celebrations of the Holy Week immediately preceding Easter. Such a musical form, of course, has made no sense
for half a millennium but is perfectly sensible when we think of the
centuries of the *convivencia*.

But let us carry on with Lorca's speech. Here are some passages:

> *The gypsy siguiriya begins with a terrible cry . . . It is the*
> *cry of dead generations, a penetrating elegy for lost cen-*
> *turies, a plaintive evocation of love in a place of uncanny*
> *moons and wind.*

> *It is not a matter of coincident sources, it did not reveal itself*
> *in one decisive moment, but is formed by an accumulation*
> *of historical and secular events here on our peninsula.*

And what are these sources? Whence comes the *cante jondo*?
Following the research of Falla, Lorca tells us of three main formative influences:

> *. . . the adoption by the Spanish church of liturgical chanting,*
> *the invasion of the Saracens, and the arrival in Spain of numer-*
> *ous bands of gypsies . . . resulting in a song purely Andalusian.*

Lorca goes on to quote Falla on the strange technical properties of
cante jondo, which Falla derives, in part, from the Byzantine liturgy:

> *. . . some Andalusian songs from a period well before the*
> *adoption of the Byzantine liturgy by the Spanish church are*
> *closely allied to music known today in Morocco, Algiers,*
> *and Tunis, music that is called, movingly to any Granadan*
> *with a heart, "the music of the Moors of Granada."*

It is already an extraordinary lecture, and Lorca is just getting warmed up. He wants not only to speak in praise of *cante jondo*. He wants all of Granada to join him:

. . . we must cry out in defense of these pure and truthful songs.

Lorca wants to lead his audience to an art that lives outside official channels, an art with unquenchable life, indispensable to life. In the months surrounding his lecture, he had, on foot, wandered throughout the province of Granada in the company of his childhood friend—Manolo Angeles Ortiz. Together they visited villages and farms, bars and campfires, listening, waiting, searching for the masters of *cante jondo*, listening to songs in small plazas in the twilight. Manolo Angeles was full of grief, having just lost his wife, who had died a year after giving birth to a daughter, Lorca's goddaughter. On country roads, he and Lorca sang to one another:

It is deep, truly deep, deeper than any well, deeper than the seas of the world, deeper even than the hearts of those that create it presently and the voices of those who sing it, because it is almost infinite. It comes from a faraway people, crossing beyond the cemetery of the years . . . it comes from the first tear and the first kiss.

It is the song of night . . . it has nothing but night, deep night shot through with stars.

All of these exclamations proceeded from Lorca's long study of Spanish popular music, the music that could not be extinguished by political power, that survived in the daily life of Andalusians. The poet was a gifted musician and knew hundreds of folksongs by heart. He could sit down at the piano and play and sing for hours. In *cante*

jondo, he found more than music. He found a poetry with the savor
of earth, a unity with earth both physical and spiritual.

> *All the poems of* cante jondo *show a magnificent pantheism,*
> *in dialog with the very earth, air, moon, and seas, with humble*
> *violets or rosemary or a bird. The things of the world come*
> *into their own and take form energetically in the lyrics.*

Lorca, in the months preceding his lecture, had written a first
draft of his first major work of verse, called, as we might expect,
Poem of the Deep Song. In it he sought to be just such a singer, to
compose songs in verse of rare vehemence and strange authority, so
as to connect us to Andalusian land and history and to a current of
beauty that carries away those who love the region and its people.
After a search for the earliest roots of the lyrics that he had, with
Falla, studied so intensively, he thought he knew where to look for
the poetic sensibility he found there.

> *Just as in the* siguiriya *and its derivatives we find ancient ele-*
> *ments from the East, so in many lyrics of the* cante jondo *we*
> *find an affinity with the most ancient songs of the East:*
>
> *When our songs come to the extreme pitch of suffering and*
> *love, they match the expressive verse of magnificent Arabic*
> *and Persian poets.*

And who does Lorca single out among those poets of the east?
None other than Hafiz and Omar Khayyam, two of the great Sufi
poets of Persia. It is remarkable to contemplate, this impassioned
bond proposed by Lorca between some of the greatest mystical
poetry in history and the life-giving beauty of *cante jondo.* It is as if
Lorca was reaching back into just the history Spain had turned away

from so violently and urging us to examine it once more, urging us to consider what comes of a hard but beautiful unity of cultures, to consider the improbable power of poetry to survive through centuries, even if it must take refuge in taverns and by campfires.

Lorca and Falla worked in company of other aficionados in Granada, all through late 1921 and the winter and spring of 1922 to prepare the *Concurso*. One week before it was to begin, Lorca, having given his first lecture, now gave his first poetry reading, accompanied by a young guitarist named Andrés Segovia. Thus in that one night in one small room in Granada, the audience had two of the most extraordinary artists in modern Spanish history.

Lorca read poems from his unpublished *Poem of the Deep Song*, and the force of his joy in the form left his audience enraptured. A local reviewer in the newspaper *Defensor de Granada* said: "This dreamy young man who is so in love with the beautiful and the sublime will soon be a glory." Lorca was 23 years old and electric with promise.

The *Concurso* on June 13 and 14 of 1922 was held in the Alhambra and attracted an extraordinary four thousand people to an open courtyard alongside the palace. Performers came from all over Andalusia, and the two winners were the 72-year-old Diego Bermúdez, who had walked eighty miles to sing, and Manuel Ortega, an 11-year-old who would go on to become one of the great *cante jondo* singers of the century. The second night of the contest, there was a downpour. Hardly anyone left. The *Concurso*, first of its kind in Andalusia, was an explosive success noted all over Spain, and in Paris and London as well. It was a brilliant moment in Granada.

During that time, we have a sense of Lorca's coming into his own. He was irrepressible and bold. He would visit gypsy camps to read his poems in homage to the *cante jondo*, and the Lorca biographer Leslie Stainton tells us of one such visit:

> *When he read* Poem of Deep Song *to one group of gypsies, they were so dazzled by his impassioned performance that afterward they swarmed around him, kissing and hugging him as though he were one of their own.*

Lorca took just such risks, trying out his work on strangers and friends. He was a phenomenon, a young man of exotic energy, working up a world of his own. Everywhere he would go in the ensuing years, he found his way to a company of friends with deep gifts of their own. The list is long, dazzling, and we can only touch on a few names: Manuel de Falla, Salvador Dali, Luis Buñuel, Luis Cernuda, Rafael Alberti, Vicente Aleixandre, Juan Ramón Jiménez, Pablo Neruda, the professor and politician Ferdinand de los Rios, the great actress Margarita Xirgu, the philologist Ramon Menéndez Pidal. It is as if Lorca lived in a force field of great minds. Three of them, Neruda, Aleixandre, and Jimenez, would win the Nobel Prize in Literature.

When we read the descriptions of Lorca, what moves us is the incandescent life of the man: poet, musician, essayist, playwright, actor, director, producer; incorrigible creator of whimsical, tragic drawings, puppeteer, folksinger, storyteller; and a sensitive, devoted friend. He gave electrifying readings of his verse and experimented with language and form with a restless ebullience. With the production of his play *Mariana Pineda* in 1927 and the publication of the book of poems *Gypsy Ballads* in 1928, he became a celebrated figure in Spain. More plays followed, and more travel: New York and then Havana, where the sensuous lifestyle and beautiful companionship gave him what he called later "the happiest days of his life."

We read of this and remember another element of Lorca's character: his almost complete lack of pretension. For all his life, he was never Don Señor anything, to anyone. He was just Federico.

In 1931, with the coming to power of the Spanish Republic, Lorca had a chance come momentously his way: to go throughout the Spanish countryside, bringing the life of Spanish classical theater to small villages. The original idea had come from Madrid University, and it was part of the effort of the Republic to reform education nationwide. The idea was to take the plays of Cervantes, Lope de Vega, and Calderón de la Barca to plazas and theaters and to perform free of charge, using the best young talent, carrying a portable stage that could be swiftly assembled with basic sets and lighting, and taking everyone with them: not just the players, but the carpenters and electricians, drivers and stage managers. This university theater was known as *La Barraca* (a country barn or storehouse), since its members hoped to have such a simple structure in Madrid for plays year-round. They never got their permanent venue, but they did elect Lorca their artistic director. He auditioned students, gathered talent, advised on the set and props, arranged music, and brought in help from among the whole community of the arts. And in midsummer 1932, Lorca and the students set out in a caravan: a bus, a couple of vans, a few cars. Reading about it, it is hard to imagine a more utopian initiative: as a public service, to see that brilliant Spanish plays, with vitality and joy, brought something of the whole spectrum of Spanish theatrical imagination to people who had almost no chance of such an experience. Despite the attacks of the ultra-right-wing press of the day and some outright attempts to sabotage the troupe, *La Barraca* was a rambunctious success, with rapt audiences and celebration among the critics. The most moving story is from the first tour, in the plaza of the tiny village of Almazán, where during the presentation of Calderon's *Life Is a Dream*, it began to rain. The players carried on. The audience, mostly peasants, stayed on with them, deeply moved by the play, following every turn of events onstage, clapping and laughing at one or another episode. It is a moment with an uncanny similarity to the second night of the Contest of Deep Song at the Alhambra. Twice in his short life, García Lorca had brought to the people of Spain an art so beautiful that people would sit in the rain to watch, to listen, to understand.

The year of 1933 was fateful for Lorca, for Spain, and for Europe. In Germany, Hitler was appointed chancellor, the Reichstag was set on fire, the Third Reich was proclaimed, and the Gestapo was formed. In Spain, Jose Antonio Primo de Rivera established the Falangists, the Spanish fascist party, and elections in Spain brought the right wing back to power after two years of Republican government that, based on the country's new Constitution, had embraced universal suffrage, separation of church and state, the right to divorce, freedom of worship, heavy investment in education, and other progressive themes. To the extent these hopes had been embodied in law, the new government set about repealing them, or dismantling the effort to enforce the laws. Since Spain lacked a neutral, independent, and efficient civil service—a centerpiece of effective government—the national leaders and legislature could begin, delay, or undo national programs. In 1933, this whipsaw worked again. Lorca, always a man of his time, was drawn into political declarations, and in May, he was the first to sign a protest against the "fascist barbarism" of Hitler, as the Führer consolidated power in Germany with laws targeted against Jews and widespread book burnings. Yet Lorca kept up his writing, and in the spring of that same year, his play *Blood Wedding* opened under his direction in Madrid and took the city by storm. Not only was it received with joy by the audience, who went so far as to interrupt the play twice to salute Lorca personally with their applause, but the critics, one after another, lauded the depth of the work and the beauty of its language. There were immediate plans to move the production across the sea to Buenos Aires; venues were found, dates were set, and Lorca set off for Argentina. *Blood Wedding* opened in Buenos Aires to widespread public acclamation. A few months later, another play of his, *The Shoemaker's Prodigious Wife*, opened to more acclaim. Lorca's life there was hyperactive, a wild variety of theatrical responsibilities, lectures, readings, parties, and interviews. He became, for months, the central phenomenon of the city. The great Chilean poet and future Nobel Prize winner Pablo Neruda, who formed his friendship with Lorca during that visit, called it "the greatest triumph ever achieved by a writer of our race." Remembering those times years later in his autobiography, Neruda said that Lorca was

> *an effervescent child, the young channel of a powerful river.*
> *He squandered his imagination, he spoke with enlighten-*
> *ment . . . he cracked walls with his laughter, he improvised*
> *the impossible, in his hands a prank became a work of art.*
> *I have never seen such magnetism and constructiveness in a*
> *human being.*

Lorca had become, at age 35, one of the most celebrated writers in the Hispanic world. In Spain, he had a rare sense of the complex splendor of his country's heritage, a sense derived from his homeland in Granada, his study of Arab and Persian poetry, and his immersion in flamenco. Upon his return to Spain in early 1934, he took up with vigor all his projects. He handed out versions of the poems in his unpublished book *Diwan of the Tamerit*, meant in tribute to the Arab poets in Granada before the coming of Ferdinand and Isabel. He finished his play "Yerma" and wrote the unforgettable elegy "Lament for Ignacio Sánchez Mejías," after that Andalusian bull-fighter—a friend of Lorca and aficionado of flamenco—was gored to death by a bull that summer. He kept up some oversight of *La Barraca*, which performed in Seville and still toured the country to excellent critical reviews, though it was under attack in the right-wing press as a band of promiscuous youths who perverted the peasants with, among other terrible defects, their "obedience to the dictates of Jewish Marxism." However absurd these taunts were, they took their toll, and the funds available for *La Barraca* began to dwindle.

In 1935, he moved forward with a host of projects. At one point early in the year, he had three plays in Madrid showing at once: *Yerma*, the imported Buenos Aires production of *Blood Wedding*, and a revival of *The Shoemaker's Prodigious Wife*. It was also the year of the first performance of *Doña Rosita the Spinster*, which is set in our very own Albayzín. Lorca was incorrigibly a man of Granada, and within Granada, of the Albayzín. Not only did he write about the barrio, he visited there often and loved the *carmenes*. He knew the way their beauty could transform daily life, felt the simmering of paradise in the gardens there, with the radiant presence of the Alhambra on the promontory just above. He wrote to a friend, "I love Granada but only to live there on another plane, in a *carmen*. The rest is nonsense. In a *carmen*, close to what one loves and feels. White walls, flowering myrtle, and fountain."

As is the case so often in Lorca's work, the dream of love in a place of beauty turns into a nightmare of grief and betrayal. Though *Doña Rosita the Spinster* is full of flowers, they come to signify not the trustworthy unfolding of mind and senses, an intimation of paradise, but instead the withering away of the life of a beautiful young woman. Doña Rosita is caged by the social and religious conventions of the time and by the rigor of her own self-deception. It was a common theme of Lorca's: the way, even among the most promising and powerful beauties, human dishonesty, treachery, and self-delusion can corrupt love, so that the living die within before dying in the body. Doña Rosita's fiancé is called to Argentina to work with his father on the land. She waits for him to return, to take up the only life in the society of the day open to her: as a Catholic wife. The years pass; Rosita works on her wedding clothes, a nightdress, sheets. More years pass as she awaits the man who called her his "nightingale on the mountain," who pledged to return to her "in a boat all of gold" with "sails of jubilation." His arrival, he has told her, will be marked by the "bright dove of my faith." He promises "by the diamonds of God" to return to her.

He does not return. He observes the convention of letter writing, and he marries someone else, a rich woman he courted in Argentina. Rosita is left with nothing, since women, by the Catholic and cultural standards of late-nineteenth-century Granada, had no other options left. The *carmen* is sold to pay debts incurred to pay for flowers in the garden. Rosita, her aunt, and a housekeeper leave the house at night, in the rain, glad that no one will see their destitution and shame. It is the Albayzín of futility and social oppression, and it strikes a theme common in Lorca's plays: women destroyed by the society of their times and paralyzed within a delusion encouraged by that society. Rosita has so many virtues: she is brave, loyal, devoted, and holds virtuously to the one chance given her. But she is imprisoned in a definition of virtue that limits her chances at life and at love. It might be called lethal virtue.

The analogy, of course, is with the way Lorca, as a homosexual, had to live in a society that forbid him an honest life and the love he sought. Catholic Spain was violently contemptuous of same-sex love. Those rare periods in his life when we see Lorca happy are in places such as distant and sensual Havana, where it seems the poet was more at liberty to love as he chose. In Spain, whatever his liaisons in any other country, he was passionate about the young and handsome Rafael Rodriquez Rapún, and one of the few open conversations Lorca had with anyone about his sexuality was in Barcelona, when he thought Rapún might have left him for a gypsy woman. He failed to appear at a rehearsal of *Blood Wedding*. The director of the play found him, shattered, alone in a café. He told the director, Rivas Cherif, that "My flesh, my blood, my entire body and soul have been betrayed." Saying that he had been attracted to men since childhood, he tells Cherif that he has "never known a woman." And when challenged by the heterosexual Cherif, Lorca cries out for liberty: "Normality is neither your way of knowing only women, nor mine. What's normal is love without limits." Lorca says he seeks "a new morality, a morality of complete freedom." A society that values love as defined by Catholic tradition of dominant males, with procreation the primary duty of females, he turns away from: "With my way, there is no misrepresentation. Both partners remain as they are, without bartering. No one gives orders; no one dominates; there is no submission. There is no assigning of roles . . . There is only abandon and mutual enjoyment."

It was a conversation concealed by Rivas Cherif for more than twenty years. But Lorca's poetry cries out against tyranny of every kind, whether it be the suffocation of women in gender roles or a brutish morality bound to power and social control. Lorca warns us of the suffering fated for any society that denies its own history and our common need for the freedom to learn, to love, and to live by bonds of respect, honesty, and goodwill.

Granada, by Lorca's reckoning, had known its share of tyranny. And yet Granada and the Albayzín, with their deep art and Moorish glamor, their flamenco and their brilliant history of Arabic and Jewish poetry, were the places Lorca loved most on earth. In his poetry and letters and in his conversation, he identified himself, his poetry, and his sense of beauty with Granada. Yet this was the city of the triumph of Ferdinand and Isabel, their conscripted Catholic church, and the power of the Inquisition. What must Lorca have thought of all this? In the years of 1935 and 1936, he said clearly what he thought. In a famous, and at the time infamous, newspaper interview with *El Sol*, in Madrid, on June 10, 1936, he spoke of the fall of Granada to Ferdinand and Isabel as:

> . . . *a disastrous event, even though they say just the opposite in schools. An admirable civilization was lost, and a poetry, astronomy, architecture, and sensitivity unique in the world—all were lost, to give way to an impoverished, cowed city . . .*

It was a brave, accurate, and desperate statement, this bitter criticism of popular opinion and assumption. Yet it was true to his work and his experience. Lorca was Granada's most celebrated native son. His family had deep roots there, and Lorca had many cherished friends and colleagues in the city. In the newspapers there, his words and actions, and even his travels, were closely followed. And yet, among some in the city, he was known as *"el maricón con la pajarita"*—"the fag with the bow tie."

In the months before the interview, Spain had been in torment. The narrow victory of the Popular Front, a coalition of leftist parties, had in February of 1936 given them, because of the way the votes translated into parliamentary seats, a strong majority of 267 to 132 in the Cortes—the sole governing legislative body in Spain. This in turn strengthened the power of Primo de Rivera's Falange, which gained support throughout the country, increasing in membership and organizing violent confrontations where possible. The country began to slide toward the agony of civil war, with the population urged in melodramatic and inflammatory terms to choose between communism and fascism, as if those were the only two ways forward. In the meantime, Lorca continued to write and told a friend he had another five books of poetry now ready for publication—an astonishing total. He gave a reading to the Madrid Worker's Club and joined organizations that fought against dictatorships in the Americas and in Portugal. His ideals were equality and personal freedom, informed by the blessed power and consolations of art. He would say in his last interview:

> *I am totally Spanish, and it would be impossible for me to live outside my geographical boundaries . . . I am a brother to all men, and I detest the person who sacrifices himself to an abstract, nationalist ideal just because he loves his country with a blindfold over his eyes . . . I express Spain in my work and feel her in the very marrow of my bones; but first and foremost I am a cosmopolitan and a brother to all.*

As the months of 1936 unrolled, there were anarchist and communist strikes, resurgent violence and provocations on the right and left, and ominous rumors of a military uprising against the

Republic, which after all was the elected government of the Spanish people. Lorca was depressed, confused, erratic, moody. And even all these years later, we have, in July of 1936, the sense of a fuse being lit and burning down to one fateful decision after another, burning down to darkness.

Lorca had promised Margarita Xirgu that he would go to Mexico for the staging of his plays. Early in July, Lorca had a ticket in his pocket and made plans to say goodbye to his family in Granada. On July 11, 1936, he dined with Pablo Neruda and other friends at Neruda's flat. A rightist there, Augustín de Foxá, told him flatly not to go to Granada. Luis Buñuel was there. He, as well, urged Lorca not to go to Granada. On July 13, Lorca boarded the train for Granada. All three newspapers in the city announced his arrival. The presumption was that he was still bound for Mexico. On July 14, he was with his family in the family compound he loved, the *Huerta de San Vicente*, just west of Granada. In the next few days, he was already back in his cherished Albayzín, in a *carmen*, reading a new play to his friends. The Civil War began on July 17 with the fascist rebel announcement from Morocco by General Franco. Seville fell to the fascists almost immediately, and the military in Granada declared for the rebels and took control of the city on July 20; took control, that is, except for the Albayzín, which held out for three days. There were widespread arrests in the city, beatings, torture, and summary executions. The executions took place every day directly behind the Alhambra. Granada was coiling with violence. The mayor of the city, Lorca's brother-in-law, was arrested.

Two and a half weeks passed. The repression intensified, and the summer turned to blood sport. On August 7, the city's chief architect arrived at the Huerta. His name was Alfredo Rodriquez Orgaz, and he was a hunted man. Lorca's father, a prosperous landowner sympathetic to the Republic, offered him passage to safety behind Republican lines. Lorca could easily have accompanied him. He would have been guided by farm workers loyal to his family. Orgaz escaped that night. Lorca chose not to go.

On August 9, a group of conservative local landowners came to the Huerta in search of the brothers of the caretaker of the Lorca family property, a man named Gabriel Perea. The brothers were wanted on trumped-up charges. Gabriel was tied to a tree and whipped. Lorca went to intervene and was knocked to the ground. The intruder knew the poet, kicked him, and called out: "It's the little fag . . ." And they told him he was under house arrest.

Lorca was now terrified. He telephoned the young poet Luis Rosales, whom he had seen often in Madrid. Luis had joined the Falangists, more out of convenience than conviction. And he had two older brothers who were key players in the fascist cabal who now ruled Granada. The whole family admired Lorca, including the father, Miguel, a prosperous merchant whose stores were in the heart of the city. Luis came straight to the Huerta to help decide how to keep Lorca safe. Luis suggested immediate flight to the Republican zone. It would have been straightforward. Luis himself had arranged for the escape of other men from the city. Lorca refused. Luis suggested refuge in the *carmen* of Manuel de Falla, a devout Catholic, the most celebrated composer in Spain and an international figure. It was hard to imagine anyone violating Falla's house. And the composer had felt a close bond with Lorca, since their work together on the *Concurso de Cante Jondo* fifteen years earlier. Lorca was unwilling to ask such a favor of Falla. Instead, he chose for refuge the Rosaleses' house, in the center of Granada, a few blocks away from the command center of the fascist military that now controlled the city. And there he went, the same night.

The next day, August 10, Lorca settled in nervously at the house of the Rosaleses. Every day, he read notices in *Ideal*, a local newspaper, of more executions behind the Alhambra. He took time to study in the library, finding a medieval Spanish poet who enchanted him and whose verses he read aloud to the family. He thought of a poem to be composed with Luis, in honor of all those fallen in the Civil War. On August 15, men arrived at the Huerta with a warrant for his arrest. They forced from the poet's family his place of refuge. It was only a matter of hours before they would come for him. The Rosaleses immediately suggested, again, refuge with Manuel Falla. It seemed Lorca was considering it.

On the morning of August 16, a fascist firing squad executed Lorca's brother-in-law, whose only crime was being mayor of the city. Lorca was informed immediately. That afternoon, police and military forces swarmed around the Rosaleses' house, occupying the block, watching from rooftops, taking up positions in the Plaza de la Trinidad. Esperanza Rosales, the matriarch of the family, refused to surrender him. She was told that Lorca was to be arrested "for what he had written." After further confrontation, two of the Rosales brothers, Miguel and Luis, walked outside with the poet and went with him to the civil government building. There, Lorca was locked up. But Miguel assured Lorca nothing would happen to him.

José Rosales, one of the leading fascists in Granada, now arrived back in the city from his military duties in the Vega. He was furious that Lorca had been taken. He entered by force into the office of the military governor, Commandant Valdés Guzman, to confront him. Valdés had a written accusation against Lorca, full of idiotic and

fraudulent charges, among them that Lorca was in contact with the
Russians via a secret radio transmitter at the *Huerta de San Vincente*.
So far as is known, only one fact in the accusation was true: that
Lorca was homosexual. Rosales, determined to free Lorca, went to
see him in his cell and assured him he would be back in the morning
to take him to safety. With the help of a lawyer who was the head
of the Granada Falange, Rosales wrote a statement explaining why
they thought Lorca should be protected and why they had sheltered
him in their own house. For they knew, now, that they were themselves in danger. The statement was distributed among rebel command posts, and the next morning, August 17, Jose Rosales had in
his hands an order from the military command for Lorca's release.
He went straight back to Guzman. Guzman told him that Lorca had
already been taken away. But he had not. He was still in his cell that
morning, and the whole day of the 17. On that same day, if not the
day before, Lorca's mother went to see Emilia Llanos, who lived at
the base of the Albayzín. She begged Emilia to intercede with Manuel
de Falla so that Lorca could be set free. Emilia set off at once to the
Fallas' *carmen*, but on the ascent was told by someone in the street
that Lorca had already been killed. In despair, she abandoned her
effort to see Falla.

At around three in the morning of August 18, Lorca was taken
away in the company of a schoolteacher, Galindo González, who
had a wooden leg. They were driven up above the city, just outside of the village of Viznar. There, they were taken into a building converted from a summer center for children into a military
prison. First they were told they were to be assigned to work building roads. Then they were told they were to be killed. Shortly thereafter, Lorca, the schoolteacher, and two bullfighters arrested in the

Albayzín were taken along a road toward Aynadamar, the source of water for the Albayzín, whose name in Arabic means "the Fountain of Tears." There, at about 4:45 AM, just at first light, Lorca, the schoolteacher, and the matadors were shot to death. One of the executioners said that Lorca got special treatment: "two bullets in the ass for being a queer."

On that same morning of August 18, Manuel de Falla, who knew that Lorca had been arrested, bestirred himself at last and went to the government building in Granada to help the poet. He was a few hours too late.

Not even Sophocles could have set down a design of such fateful malevolence. If Lorca had gone to Mexico as he had planned, if he had listened to his friends and not boarded the train to Granada, if he had escaped to the Republican zone with Orgaz, if he had escaped with the help of Luis Rosales, if he had taken refuge with Falla, if the Rosaleses could have protected him as they thought they could, if the military order for his release would have been honored, if Jose Rosales would have confirmed that Lorca was still in his cell, if someone had not lied to Emilia Llanos in the street, if Manuel de Falla had intervened a day earlier, if the rebels in Granada had not despised Lorca . . . if, if, if . . .

The work of García Lorca was banned in Spain for a generation.

His death was one of hundreds of thousands, and it has come to stand for the irreparable loss to Spain and to the world, of so many, with such molten hatred, in a gaudy saturnalia of violence, as civil war gave way to the rebel takeover of the country.

The Secret in the Labyrinth

*N*OTHING IS MORE common in the Albayzín than to come upon visitors lost in the labyrinth of streets. The maps given out are wretchedly bad, showing not so much the layout of the streets but a series of mysterious clues as to where they might be found. The only way to learn the streets is to live there. We gave directions just about every day; often, we accompanied the inquirers, since anywhere they were going in the Albayzín would have on offer a host of eccentric beauties. And we could go in hope of being lost ourselves.

Just about every day, we walked in the barrio to buy bread or wine, to meet friends in a café, to find our way to flamenco, to dine outdoors on beautiful terraces or in plazas full of warm stone and spirited company. And every day, as we tried to learn enough to make sense of our neighborhood, as we worked in the garden or sat out late at night in the golden light of the Alhambra, we knew well enough what grew in us: thankfulness. There is a secret in the labyrinth of the Albayzín, in the history of the fortress and the city to which the Albayzín gave birth: the Alhambra and Granada. To come upon it was, for me, the most improbable result of our sojourn

in the centuries of history here, and our embrace of the life here. The
secret lives in the lustrous survival of the place. If the Albayzín means
anything, it means that beauty may banish violence, grace bear us
beyond hatred, and understanding conduct us to deliverance. What
is delivered is simple: a life with children and safety, with flowers and
common pleasures, good company, poetry, and trust, with time to
talk and study, to work and to love. I do not know what more any
of us can ask.

To say that such a life is within reach, today, in the repellent
darkness of our own times, is thought to be sentimental. To think an
easygoing, workaday, peaceable, open-minded life in the company of
those we love might be available anywhere is said to be naive and simple minded. Yet if it is possible in the Albayzín, it is possible anywhere
on earth. The barrio survived centuries of depredation and neglect to
come round once more to its present resurgent splendor. In just the
same way, the great Jewish and Arab poets of Al-Andalus, after more
than a half a millennium of absolute neglect, now live in our hands.
We can know them, know their names, their joys and fateful songs,
and they are just as much a part of the heritage of Spain as Cervantes
or Lope de Vega. The onetime vizier of the ruler of Granada, Ismail
Ibn Neghrela, waited over nine hundred years for his poems to be read
at all: they were discovered in a crate in the early twentieth century
and not published until 1934. Yet now they are ranked among the
most powerful Hebrew verse of the period, in all their wild variety,
from the erotic to the satirical and proverbial. As for García Lorca, if
anyone wants proof that execution, book bans, and censorship cannot kill a man or his work, then I invite you to walk down the streets
of Granada today. You will not go twenty feet without seeing the
portrait of Lorca. It is on posters, on the side of buses, and shown in

bookstores and theaters. His plays are often performed, his poetry is widely read, his letters and interviews are known and quoted. His drawings adorn postcards and book covers. His work is made into ballets and flamenco shows. The airport and two parks are named after him. He loved Granada so much, and now, eighty years after his death, we can see how much the city loves him.

We have so many memories of the Albayzín that, wherever we are in the world, they visit us. It's a place for learning and for loving. It has an idyllic charge. Lucy and I gave ourselves to the place, and to one other.

I remember the day Lucy visited the Albayzín blacksmith and came home with a birthday present for me: a weathervane that she had designed, which from its central axis offered to the bright air of the Albayzín the crescent moon of Islam, the star of David, and a Christian cross. It stands above our house, in honor of the past and in hope for the future.

If we are to have a future, it will be in a place where beauty can be tasted every day, where the best of the past illuminates a way forward, where we can count on the care of all our children.

I remember playing soccer with 3-year-old Gabriella in the twilight of Plaza Bib Rambla, where she managed to kick the ball directly through the door of the lingerie shop. It scored a direct hit on the pantie rack, caromed over to the camisoles, and settled in among the filmy gowns. I thought we had committed a rather grave offense. I stood blushing in the street. Gabriella walked boldly into the store and was greeted with a smiling welcome, soothing talk, and soft laughter. Then her hand was filled with caramels and she was ceremoniously given back the rather soiled ball and helped to the door, that her twilight play might carry on.

I remember waking early in our house, one morning after a late-night party in our home with a score of families from the neighborhood. In Gabriella's room I found two small children asleep, snuggled up with our daughter. I did not know their names. But I knew that later in the morning, their parents would come by the door, to bear their little ones home with smiles and easygoing sweetness. It was the way we trusted one another.

I remember crossing Plaza Nueva, at the base of the Albayzín, with Lucy and me trailing, as usual, our rocketing daughter. We passed by a priest so old that I thought he might be headed to an appointment with a taxidermist. But he stopped us and proved very lively indeed, talking to us animatedly through a nest of wrinkles and gesturing to Gabriella. When she came back to gaze up at him, he reached into his black robes and took out five orange balloons and held them out to her small hands. She was all smiles. So was he. I was ready to convert to Catholicism on the spot, Inquisition or no Inquisition.

I remember being in the taxi cab headed back to Plaza Nueva, with Gabriella asleep in my arms and a shopping bag heavy with books at my feet. The taxi driver was a laconic, heavyset man who looked as if he had not moved from his driver's seat in several months. He pulled up to the plaza and, seeing my predicament in the rearview mirror, flung open his door and leapt from the cab with the fine form and energy of an Olympic athlete. Striding around the cab, he opened the door and reached in to take Gabriella in his arms with infinite gentleness and whispered to her as I got out with the books and was able to hold her again. I had no doubt that he would have abandoned his taxi and carried her home.

Every morning we walked among flowers and shadows to Gabriella's school, Arlequin. And on Saturday mornings, we went together down through the Albayzín to her ballet class, taught by a woman with musical Russian-accented Spanish. On the move through the cool slanting light, we talked and improvised as usual, and wondered at the streets where we walked together. Then all at once Gabriella said:

> *The color of the Angel Gabriel's wings is blue-green, with gold and yellow. There are angels of clouds, of stars, of heart, of light, and the angel Gabriel, and the angel of love.*
>
> Dios *is made of clouds and light and stars and wisdom.*
>
> *The house of* Dios *is hard to find, and no one of the angels knows how to get there, except for the angel of love. But the angel of love showed the angel Gabriel the road halfway there, and so the angel Gabriel, too, knows how to start on the way to the house of Dios. We go there. What we do there is have a tea party, and in the tea is wisdom.*
>
> *When you drink the tea, then it means that you can start to grow wings. When you're little you can only grow little wings. The wings I have I can use only to fly to ballet and to Arlequin. But when you get taller, you get to grow bigger wings so you can go farther, but to grow bigger wings you have to keep going to the house of* Dios *to drink the tea of wisdom.*

We came to her ballet studio, and she was silent. It was the sudden declaration of one 4-year-old girl in the morning light, and I heard in her words her own savoring of the life offered gently every day by the neighborhood we had come to love. She had wanted to say for herself where she had been led by the beauties of the Albayzín.

I remember a day several months after the work had been completed on our *carmen*. It was about one in the afternoon, and there was a knock on the door. When I opened it, there stood Mario, one of the *albañiles* who had worked there so many months. In his hands was a two-gallon jug of olive oil from the fruit of his own trees, pressed that morning as a gift for our family. The oil was the most beautiful green I had ever seen; it concentrated within itself all the spring and summer of Granada. It lasted us for over a year. It was the best olive oil we had ever tasted. It is the best we will ever taste.

If anyone wants to be rocked by currents of beauty and infamy, Granada is the place. Every year, over three million people visit the Alhambra. Once a gypsy lodging, animal corral, and ammunition dump, it has been resuscitated into the most admired monument in Spain, a place of providential grace and blessing. The Alhambra presents to the world the art and culture of Al-Andalus, which survived a program of extermination and contemptuous neglect. García Lorca has survived his own murder in rambunctious good form. And the Albayzín, after five centuries marked by piecemeal demolition, arson, military invasion, and pillage, is now one of the best places in the world to live. It is one of the best places there will ever be to live. It has been perfected by catastrophe. The streets hold the spirit of *cante jondo*: let history come with death and ruin, and deep song will rise in time with a beauty that cannot be killed. In just this way, the Albayzín rises every day into the sunlight of Andalusia.

Wherever I walk in the world, I turn a corner, and that is the sunlight I feel on my face.

The End

RECOMMENDED READING
AND LISTENING

*t*HERE IS A wilderness of books about the Albayzín, Al-Andalus, Islamic tile work, the Sufis, and the literature of the period. For those who want a path forward, this brief list, chosen from hundreds of books, will give you a useful beginning. For those who want to carry on with a long expedition, see the complete bibliography.

ON THE ALBAYZÍN

The best single source is in Spanish, a three-volume work:

El Albayzín en la historia, El Albayzín en la leyenda, las tradiciones y la literatura, and *El Albayzín y sus monumentos.* All three are by Miguel J. Carrascola Salas. The books are comprehensive, affectionate, and learned.

Albayzín, solar de reyes, by Gabriel Pozo Felguera, is a superb one-volume summary that ranges over the centuries of this iconic barrio.

ON AL-ANDALUS

The Legacy of Islamic Spain, edited by Salma Khadra Jayyusi. Incomparable. A series of wonderfully intelligent essays on the whole sweep of history in Medieval Spain. A breakthrough in historical writing.

The Arts of Intimacy, by Maria Rosa Menocal, Jerilynn Dodds, and Abigail Krasner Balbale. A collaboration of three of the world's leading scholars of Al-Andalus. Brilliant, meditative, deeply learned. With clear explanations of the beautiful art, architecture, culture, and literature of the period, and a searching investigation of the history. The book has superbly selected color illustrations and an invaluable bibliography with the authors' commentary. A major achievement in writing about the period.

God's Crucible: Islam and the Making of Europe, 570–1215, by David Levering Lewis. An elegantly written, recent, magisterial look at medieval Europe, which allows us, as no other book I know, to understand Al-Andalus in the context of European history.

A Vanished World, by Chris Lowney. A thoughtful examination of the period by an independent scholar. Useful, witty, capacious, and a superb travel companion.

ON ISLAMIC TILE WORK

Islamic Patterns: An Analytical and Cosmological Approach, by Keith Critchlow. For an erudite examination of the sacred art of Islamic design and tile work, this is the book. A searching, patient journey into practical and mystical geometry.

Islamic Geometric Patterns, by Eric Broug. The very best book for those who want to take compass and straightedge in hand and make for themselves some of the complex, lovely patterns of the tiles. Unmistakable, essential fun.

ON THE SUFIS

The Sufis, by Idries Shah. The seminal work of the times on the subject. This book, and many others by the same author, are available in English, Spanish, and other languages. They offer an authentic portal into the Sufi tradition. In them, a beautiful and useful tradition of storytelling is clarified, revived, and strengthened, and the stories offered have a generous spectrum of meaning. A complete list of the works of this author can be easily obtained online at, for example, www.idriesshahfoundation.org

The Book of Wisdom, by Ibn 'Ata Illah. This beautiful translation by Victor Danner of a twelfth-century Cairene mystic is full of phrases and ideas that stay in the mind and provide material for sustained musing and helpful conversation.

ON LITERATURE

The Dream of the Poem, edited and translated by Peter Cole. A recent, revelatory compendium of the Jewish poets of Al-Andalus. Essential for an understanding of the poetic landscape of the times, and an introduction to poets whose work is coming into prominence only now, in our times, principally because of the gifts of Professor Cole.

The Literature of Al-Andalus, edited by Maria Rosa Menocal. A selection of essays on the writers of Al-Andalus, their forms, their influence, their experiments. Such a helpful book—musing, knowledgeable, clear.

MUSIC

La música de pneuma: las tres culturas de la música medieval española by Paniagua, Eduardo. A rapturous look at the music of all three faiths of Al-Andalus on CD.

Magna antologia del cante flamenco is an anthology of flamenco of the last many decades and includes many spine-tingling classics that are otherwise difficult to access. Ten CDs. It is produced by Hispavox and compiled and presented by José Blas Vega. A rare, powerful surge of beautiful song.

ACKNOWLEDGMENTS

*t*HIS BOOK WAS written with the help of my family and the scholars, writers, friends, and readers who looked at many drafts of the book over the years. I could never have moved to Spain without my wife Lucy Blake. With her derring-do, resourcefulness, and high spirits, Lucy made our residency possible and our life a delectation. She is a superb writer and an acute critic, and I hope this text holds some of her insight and intelligence. Our daughter, Gabriella, showed me the Albayzín with the fresh lights of her young mind. Her company was, and is, an unreserved joy, and my notebook of her ideas and declarations is one of my most treasured possessions.

Javier Martínez de Velasco, a gifted scholar and resident in the Albayzín, read the whole book with care and erudite attention and saved me from many errors and infelicities. My dear friend Elizabeth Dilly, lover of language and devotee of good books, read this whole text, as well, and I happily incorporated her corrections and suggestions. Bob Blake reviewed the whole manuscript and gave me his sage and worldly comments, which were invaluable to me.

As this manuscript took final form, Jack Shoemaker, my editor at Counterpoint Press, offered his wise counsel and helped me to make the book decisively more clear, open, and forthcoming. To have so learned and generous an editor is the good fortune every writer dreams of.

Any remaining difficulties or inaccuracies in the book are wholly my own responsibility, and a reader with comments of vitriol or animosity is hereby encouraged to vent his bile upon the author only.

All translations from the Spanish are my own, unless otherwise noted. The drawings in the chapter on Islamic tiles are my own, with the exception of the two drawings with seven circles, one with a square drawn around the center circle and the other with a hexagon drawn to connect the vertices of the six circles surrounding the center circle. These two drawings are by Keith Critchlow.

This book could not have been written without access to a great library, and my use of the libraries of Stanford University was possible because of the generosity and goodwill of Professor Gerald Crabtree. At the Green Library at Stanford, the staff at the reference desk was consistently helpful. Christopher Matson, in particular, helped me track down references to Saint John of God and the surgical tools of Abulcasis, among many other obscurities. When I needed to order obscure books not available in the library, Christine Kelly and her colleagues at the legendary Sundance Bookstore were of inestimable help to me.

I would like, as well, to name and thank some of the principal scholars who informed my thinking and illuminated my days: Maria Rosa Menocal, her colleagues Jerilynn Dodds and Abigale Bilbale, Thomas Glick, Salman Khadra Jayyusi, Idries Shah, L.P. Harvey, Keith Critchlow, Barbara and Stanley Stein, Luce López-Baralt, Willis Barnstone, Peggy Liss, David Lettering Lewis, Chris Lowney, Peter Cole, Paul Preston, and D.E. Pohren. There are many others; bless them all.

I am a mere layman and have had the good fortune to meet very few indeed of these scholars. Some of them are no longer with us. But their books live in my hands, and I will be in their debt always.

NOTES

*t*HESE NOTES HOLD a wide range of references, since this
book had of necessity to condense readings of secondary and
primary sources within a few pages, a few paragraphs, or even
a sentence or two. The idea was not to write a new scholarly work,
but to bring together in one book, from hither and yon, hundreds of
the ideas, facts, and ruminations of the very wide-ranging and superb
scholarship of the last several decades. This work has transformed
our understanding of Al-Andalus, and much of my text is meant in
homage to the work of the many scholars who have brought us this
new understanding.

This book relates how one family made sense of where they lived.
To make such an effort, as we come to love a place and people, is the
natural inclination of many families. At the same time, as a family
story, this text necessarily left aside much of the hedging, qualification, nuance, and argument—sometimes ferocious argument—that
is sometimes present in the scholarship I consulted. The aim here
was to paint a picture in broad strokes, to cover a lot of ground, and
to provide a point of entry for those readers who want to explore
more thoroughly the details of, say, the arts of medicine or poetry in
Al-Andalus, or the Inquisition, or the macroeconomics of Spain in

the centuries after Ferdinand and Isabel. For those who want to learn more about the background and context of the history and ideas I have written about, these notes are meant to help. The combination of the notes and bibliography give a more complete sense of the depth, richness, and variety of scholarly work that provides the foundation for the propositions and conjectures in this book, and they will also lead the reader to contrary views. For any reader who wants yet more detail and ease of reference, I will maintain and enrich these notes with links to images, references, and online resources, all in the website that accompanies this book.

ONE AFTERNOON IN GRANADA

2 **"A crimson ribbon your lips . . .":** Bloch, *The Song of Songs*, 4:3. This translation by Ariel and Chana Bloch is beautiful.

"An enclosed garden . . .": ibid., 4:12,13.

"Let us go early to the vineyards . . .": ibid., 7:13.

Solomon's temple itself: *1 Kings*: 18, 20, 42, 49.

the only artifact: This object is in the Israel Museum of Jerusalem.

3 **Some scholars:** No one really knows what fruit was eaten in the Garden of Eden, but the idea that it was an apple was dreamed up by Cyprianus Gallus, a theologian working in Gaul in the fifth century. The pomegranate and the fig are the most likely candidates, since both trees grow in Palestine. The pomegranate, in particular, was a valued and powerful symbol, not only serving as iconic decoration of Solomon's temple, but woven into the hem of the robes of religious leaders. Even the crown of Solomon was said to have the shape of a pomegranate.

This hypnotic Sura: *The Holy Quran*, Sura LV: 62–72.

4 **In the Hadith:** See, for example, El-Naggar, *Treasures of the Sunnah*, pp. 89–91, referring to the collection of Hadith compiled by the fifteenth-century Cairene scholar Imam as-Suyuti. Intelligently selected and useful selections of Hadith may be found in Shah, Idries, *Caravan of Dreams*, pp. 16–25, and in Shah, Tahir, *The Middle East Bedside Book*, pp. 54–60, 256–267.

Such signs are called, in Arabic, *ayat*: Seyyed Hossein, *An Introduction to Islamic Cosmological Doctrines*, pp. 6 (note 9), 258. It is important to understand that these signs are said to occur in the natural world as well as within us. They are the visible signs in the phenomenal world of a permanent and beautiful reality. For a more complete exposition of an Islamic view of the cosmos, and of *ayat*, see Nasr, *Religion and the Order of Nature*, pp. 60–61, 136, 143.

To the buying of a pomegranate: Jalaladin Rumi, the *Mathnawi*, Book 1, verses 717–719.

5   "His name was John of God": There is much biographical information on John of God. See, for example, Butler, *Lives of the Saints: March*, pp. 69–74. It should be noted that John of God is not only the founder of the Hospitaller Order, but he is also, bless him, the patron saint of booksellers. In Granada, a relatively unvisited but surpassingly lovely place is the hospital of John of God. It's one of those places that uses beauty, as well as medical arts, to heal. For photos and a description of the hospital, see Larios, *El hospital y la basilica de San Juan de Dios*.

THE *CARMEN* OF OUR SERENDIPITY

15   A house and garden respectful of the traditions of Andalusia: For those readers who would like to look into these traditions, see Pinar Savos, *Antiguos carmenes de Granada*, pp. 81–87. See also the fine and instructive paintings in *El Albayzín, inspiration de pintores*, pp. 82–90 and passim. The book offers a colorful sense of the neighborhood, which is as much like a painting as any I know. Another book of paintings is Segura Bueno, *Granada al natural*. See pp. 71–82 for images of the Albayzín, its plazas, gardens, and the interior of some *carmenes*.

THE TIME TRAVELS OF A GARDEN

27   The first recognizable such garden: Dicky, *The Hispano-Arab Garden, The Legacy of Islamic Spain*, p. 1016. For a look at Cyrus the Great's sixth-century BC garden at Pasargadae, see Hobhouse, *Gardens of Persia*, p. 14. For a diagram of quadripartite gardens in Samarra from the ninth century BC, see Hobhouse, ibid., p. 74.

Islamic Paradise Garden: For examples from Granada, see Lehrman, *Earthly Paradise*, pp. 87–107. For a discussion of the paradise garden, see Dickie, "The Hispano-Arab Garden: Notes Toward a Typology," p. 1016. For further examples that highlight the tradition from Persia, see Hantelmann,

Gardens of Delight, pp. 38–39 for gardens in Spain; and for enticing residential gardens in Morocco, see pp. 137, 148, 157.

the adventurer Xenophon: For a summary of the usage of *paradeisos*, see the references in Liddell and Scott, *A Greek-English Lexicon*. Xenophon used the word in his *Anabasis*, *Cyropedia*, and *Hellenica*.

the blessed association of paradise and gardens: widely known, of course. For a fine summary and discussion, see Moynihan, *Paradise as a Garden*, pp. 1–12.

Eden itself is not a garden at all: Genesis, 2:8

30   gardens hold beauties: For an insightful commentary on the meaning and metaphysics of Islamic gardens, see Harrison, *Gardens*, pp. 196–197. And it is useful to think of the way these gardens are associated with the development of insight, the search for truth, and the work of transcendence. There are a number of spiritual texts conceived directly in relation with these beautiful enclosed spaces. Take, for instance, *The Walled Garden of Truth* by the twelfth-century teacher Hakim Sanai. Or the *Garden of Mystery*, a fourteenth-century Persian poem by the mystic Mahmud Shabistari. Both of these texts offer insights into the beauties and practice of Sufism, a powerful influence throughout the Mediterranean and especially in Al-Andalus.

33   There are ornate fountains: See, for example, Jashemski, *The Gardens of Pompeii: Herculaneum and the Villas Destroyed by Vesuvius*, pp. 58, 60–61, 70, 77, 102, 108–109, 112, 304–305, 307, and 309, and on p. 329, a reconstruction of a Roman garden in the Getty Museum in Los Angeles. Another good source for images of the gardens in Pompeii is Farrar, *Ancient Roman Gardens*, the color plates that begin after p. 142.

34   Battening down to make their historical mark: For those who long to know more about the Visigoths in Spain, and their kings in purple slippers and ermine robes, see, for example, O'Callaghan, *A History of Medieval Spain*, 44–51. Also Makki, "The Political History of Al-Andalus," pp. 5–6, and Snow, *The Root and the Flower*, pp. 36–42.

In the year 711: This resonant and legendary event is discussed in a wide variety of texts. See, for example, Snow, ibid., p. 42. For a more complete and a beautifully written account, see Lewis, *God's Crucible*, pp. 118–132.

35   "O citizens of Al-Andalus . . .": quoted in Reina, *Abu Madyan, El amigo de Dios*, p. 85.

36   the first Islamic dynasty: Hodgson, *The Venture of Islam*, pp. 217–219. Also Lapidus, *A History of Islamic Societies*, pp. 56–67.

37   For in Rusafa: Ruggles, *Gardens, Landscapes, and Vision*, pp. 42–45.

38 the fig, the apple, the pear: See, for example, Trillo San Jose, *Agua, tierra y hombres en Al-Andalus*, pp. 43–48. Also Glick, *Islamic and Christian Spain in the Early Middle Ages*, pp. 70–75.

Historians have even looked at the pollens: Amor, "Aplicación de modernas técnicas de la ciencia paleobotanica a la restauración de los antiguos jardines, mediante la recogida de muestras de tierra," pp. 215–219, and Ruidor Carol, "Plantes employeés dans les jardins historique de l'Islam," pp. 221–233.

39 These estates, called *Munyas*: Ruggles, ibid., pp. 45–48. See also Dickie, "The Hispano-Arab Garden: Notes Toward a Typology," pp. 1027–1029.

like the *muwashaha*, or the *zajal*: For a very useful essay for those who want to understand this inventive poetry, see Monroe, "*Zajal* and *Muwashshaha*: Hispano-Arabic Poetry and the Romance Tradition," pp. 403–413. For a comprehensive and brilliant survey of what is known about the *muwashaha*, and a history of the scholarship, see Rosen, "The *Muwashshah*," passim.

40 "Juice is extracted . . ." Schultz-Dornburg, *Sonnenstand*. "The Calendar of Córdoba," trans. John Brogdan, intro.

41 The Madinat al-Zahra: See, for example, Dodds, "The Arts of Al-Andalus," pp. 603–605. And Ruggles, ibid., 87–109. Also Triana, "Madinat az-Zahra," pp. 233–244. Better yet, go to see the ruins just outside of Córdoba. The *Junta de Andalucia* publishes a fine guide, replete with drawings, maps, renderings, facts, and careful speculations. See Vallejo Triano, *Madinat al-Zahra: guia oficial del conjunto arqueológico*, passim.

43 the gentleman and scholar Ismail Ibn Naghrela: Ruggles, ibid., pp. 63–64. Note that Naghrela is known also by his Hebrew name of Shmuel HaNagid.

44 Ibn al-Khatib: quoted in Dickie, "The Hispano-Arab Garden: Notes Toward a Typology," p. 1026.

Andrea Navagiero: quoted in Dickie, "Granada: A Case Study of Arab Urbanism in Muslim Spain," p. 104. We should note that we as a civilization owe this man a great debt, for it is he who brought the sonnet from Italy to Spain. This life-giving information passed from Navagiero to the poet Juan Bascon, in 1526, as the two of them walked along the banks of the Darro. See Barnstone, *The Spanish Sonnet*, pp. 3–4

45 "Outside the city . . .": quoted in Dickie, ibid., p. 105.

WHERE WALKING IS LIKE FLYING

55   **What would we find?:** See the color plates for a come-hither offering. If one
is interested to trace the evolution of the Albayzín, there is an enlightening
source: Castilla Brazales, *En busca de la Granada andalusí*. The book
has original and beautiful drawings of the Albayzín, and of noteworthy
buildings in the Albayzín. See especially the drawings of *La puerta de los
Tableros*, pp. 100–101; *El Maristan*, pp. 108–109; *La Mezquita Mayor del
Albayzín*, pp. 196–197; and the *Baño del Albayzín*, pp. 278–279. Another
source with reproductions of plans of the barrio as it evolved since 1494 is
Calatrava, *Los planos de Granada*; pp. 34–58 have the earliest renderings,
then the book carries on to 1919. Also, Castello Nicás, *La renovación
urbana en el Albaicín*, has a good early history, supplemented with photos,
pp. 23–64.

57   **Let's start with the geography:** For a complete exposition with excellent
maps, Bosque Maurel, Joaquín y Amparo Ferrer Rodríquez, "Geografía de
antiguo reino de Granada," *Historia del Reino de Granada*, pp. 17–36.

58   **They are called *los Iberos*:** Carrascosa Salas, *El Albayzín en la historia*, pp.
27–33. Also Pozo Felguera, *Albayzín solar de reyes*, pp. 17–19.

   an excavation: on the corner of *Cuesta Maria de la Miel* and *Camino Nuevo
de San Nicolas*.

60   **At least they had dishes:** Have a look at them in Cano Piedra, *La ceramica
en Granada*, pp. 34–36.

   ***mampostería*:** If you want to see one, Carrascosa Salas, ibid., has a Zirid
example, p. 50.

61   **The Ibero-Roman city:** Carrascosa Salas, ibid., pp. 34–68. Pozo Felguera,
ibid., pp. 18–22. For a much longer treatment of the whole province of
Granada, see Gonzalez Román, Cristóbal, "La Antiguedad," pp. 69–103.

62   **to historical notice:** Carracosa Salas, ibid., pp. 67-69.

63   **Council of Elvira:** There has been a scholarly argument about whether
this council, or synod, was held in Elvira or in the settlement that would
centuries later be called the Albayzín. I opt for the Albayzín, rather than
the much more exposed Elvira, which was prosperous but vulnerable. For a
historical exposition supporting this view, see Dale, *The Synod of Elvira and
Christian Life in the Fourth Century*, pp. 10–11. On the background of the
council, see Hess, *The Early Development of Canon Law and the Council of
rdica*, pp. 40–42. The translations here at taken from *Council of Elvira,
ca. 306*, Catholic University of America. n.d., Web, April 2004.

72   **In 743 a group of Syrians:** Pozo Felguera, ibid., p. 23.

So began the reign of the Ziris: Carrascosa Salas, ibid., pp. 85–91.

Almorabitin: Carrascosa Salas, ibid., p. 89. Also Castilla Brazales, *En busca de la Granada andalusí*, pp. 47–49. And Pozo Felguera, ibid., p. 174.

Aljibes: On these wonderful sites, by far the most detailed description and background is Castilla Brazales, ibid., pp. 46, 54, 69, 76, 80, 82, 123–125, 132, 155–157, 163–166.

73   "The water is most healthful . . .": quoted in Carrascosa Salas, ibid., pp. 89–90. For a more complete account of the remarkable and durable project that brought water from Aynadamar to the Albayzín, see the introduction by Carmen Trillo San Jose to Garrido Atienza, *Las aguas del Albaicin y Alcazaba*, pp. XXXIV–LXXI. With illustrations and the original 1902 text of Garrido Atienza.

the name of Badis: Pozo Felguera, ibid., pp. 26–27. And Carrascosa Salas, ibid., pp. 91–92. On the beautiful names of the neighborhoods and plazas, see Carrascosa Salas, ibid. p. 91. Also Dickie, "Granada: A Case Study of Arab Urbanism in Muslim Spain," pp. 90–91.

74   There were farmers, laborers, muleteers; millers: Carrascosa Salas, ibid., pp. 121–123. A more extensive summary is in Pozo Felguera, ibid. pp. 43–48. For a sketch of the commercial organization of the Albayzín and Granada, see Dickie, ibid., 96–98.

75   Where did they live?: One of the best ways to answer this question is to visit a well-preserved house in the Albayzín at 16 Calle de Horno de Oro. In the Carmen de Aben Humaya, near Calle San Nicolas, they may let you see the interior, a beautifully preserved and restored ancient house with a painted wood ceiling. For a detailed description of this *carmen*, see Castilla Brazales, ibid., pp. 126–131. Other examples in the Albayzín are the building at the Escuela de Estudios Arabes at the Casa de Chapiz, and restorations at 2 Calle de Yaguas; 1 Plaza de Aliatar; and 14 Plaza San Miguel Bajo. For a description of both the houses and *carmenes* in their classic form, see Pozo Felguera, ibid., pp. 101–104.

76   What did they eat?: I give here only the briefest account of this delicious culinary art. For a range of mouth-watering examples, see the recipes in Fernández Bustos, *Herencia de la cocina andalusí*, pp. 101–141. In the same volume, for descriptions of the cuisine as it evolved through Al-Andalus, see pp. 25–65. If you are in the kitchen and longing to cook, there are more recipes for food and fresh beverages in Elexpury, *Al-Andalus, magia y seducción culinarias,* pp. 61–76. More further enticing accounts also Pozo Felguera, ibid., 125–130. And Carrascosa Salas, ibid., pp. 125–128.

They dressed in loose clothes: For some images, see Pozo Felguera, ibid., p. 39. Also for a description and two images, see Carrascosa Salas, ibid., pp. 121–123.

77 **There were setbacks:** For a summary of both the achievements and the fanaticism of the Alhomads, see Menocal, Dodds and Barbale, *The Arts of Intimacy,* pp. 128–129. For specific information on Granada, Pozo Felguera, ibid., pp. 31–32.

78 **Almohad minaret:** Castilla Brazales, ibid., pp. 120–121. For a photograph and description, see Carrascosa Salas, *El Albayzín y su patrimonio,* p. 44.

the first of the Nasrid kings: For the political history, see Makki, "The Political History of Al-Andalus," pp. 77–84. To get a more pictorial sense of their influence and accomplishments, see Menocal, *The Arts of Intimacy,* pp. 247–260. For a shorter treatment, Carrascola Salas's *El Albayzín en la historia,* p. 94.

79 **"At the foot of the mountains . . .":** Munzer, p. 84.

"All the slope . . .": quoted in Dickie, ibid., p.105.

80 **"the houses were delightful . . .":** quoted in Dickie, ibid., p. 101.

Flowering trees found their way into the names of things: For a range of these evocative names, see Dickie, ibid., p. 90. Also Carrascosa Salas, ibid., pp. 91–93.

81 **Late in the fifteenth century:** For a fine summary of the complex run-up and bitter power politics of the marriage of Ferdinand and Isabella, see Liss, *Isabel the Queen,* pp. 57–116.

Boabdil: See, for example, his partnership with Ferdinand in that king's siege of Málaga, in Harvey, *Islamic Spain 1250 to 1500,* pp. 300–301.

82 **Granada was starved into submission:** This is a story that has been told innumerable times. See, for example, the authoritative Harvey, ibid., pp. 307–314.

The Articles of Capitulation: This text and summary of this pivotal document is from Harvey, ibid., pp. 315–321.

84 **an Edict of Expulsion:** For the text, Edict of Expulsion, Web, http://www.sephardicstudies.org/decree.html.

Effectively transferred the preponderance of Jewish wealth to Christian hands: I write this as someone with long business experience, buying and selling in a variety of markets. It is remarkable and painful to read of these forced and violent transfers of wealth earned by long labor. Anyone who has ever been in business will know what you get in a forced and urgent liquidation of assets. And such destruction of Jewish families led often enough to their enslavement or death. See Liss, ibid., pp. 310–312. Also Snow, *Spain, the Root and the Flower*, pp.147–149. Also Reston, *The Dogs of God*, pp. 262–266. Almost all commentators point out that the Crown got an important share, which they used for rewards to their allies, for debt payments, or simply for royal enrichment.

85   Hernando Talavera: Liss, ibid., pp. 259–263. Harvey, ibid., p. 329. Castro, *The Spaniards*, p. 250.

Cardenal Ximenes de Cisneros: Liss, ibid., pp. 358–361 and pp. 368–370. Barrios Alguilera, *Granada Morisca, la convivencia negada*, pp. 72–74. On the consequential and prophetic negotiation with Portugal, see Harvey, *Muslims in Spain*, pp. 16–21. In the same volume, for details on the provocative and aggressive actions of Cisneros, see pp. 28–33.

88   It amounted to more than five thousand volumes: Bosmajian, *Burning Books*, p. 64. To get an accurate account of the grotesque details, see Baez, *Historia universal de la destrucción de libros*, pp. 126–129.

Ferdinand and Isabella issued another edict: For the background and explanation of this contemptuous declaration, Harvey, ibid., pp. 56–58.

89   a further series of proclamations: Carrascosa Salas, ibid., pp. 105–112.

90   This attempt to eradicate a whole culture: To get a sense of the issues, the back and forth, the bribes and intimidation and sorrow of these times, see Nuñez Muley, *A Memorandum for the President of the Royal Audiencia and Chancery Court of the City and Kingdom of Granada*, passim.

91   By the end of 1568: For an account of the period leading to the war, see Harvey, *Muslims in Spain 1500–1614*, pp. 209–217.

92   There were repellent massacres: For an account of the slaughter of four hundred Muslim women and children who were prisoners of Ferdinand and Isabel's army, see Marmol, *Historia de la rebelion y castigo de los mariscos del reino de Granada*, p. 220. Where Muslim villagers found Spanish troops looting their houses, they burned the houses down with the soldiers inside, Harvey, ibid., p. 228.

they tore it to pieces: Carrascola Salas, ibid., pp.129–130. For a description of the various studies of what was left, Barrios Aguilera, "Albaicín morisco," pp. 35–41.

Contemporary accounts record the scene: For a precisely observed and mortifying account of this expulsion, see Marmol, ibid., pp. 183–184.

93   In 1571: Carrascola Salas, ibid., p. 129.

94   **But then in 1595:** For a summary of this fantastical episode, see Harvey, ibid., pp. 265–290. For a translation of some lead tablets in the same volume, see pp. 382–400. For a superb and detailed treatment in a religious and historical context, see Harris, *From Muslim to Christian Granada*, pp.108–152.

96   **By 1620:** Pozo Felguera, ibid., p. 71.

      "A radical depopulation": Barrios Aguilera, ibid., p.33.

97   **"the rents from the property":** Barrios Aguilera, ibid., p. 36.

      In the Albayzín: Carrascola Salas, ibid., pp. 158–162. Also Pozo Felguera, ibid., pp. 72–73.

98   **"Many are the curious old . . .":** Tenison, *Castile and Andalucia,* p. 98

      "almost all of this opulent barrio . . .": quoted in Carrascola Salas, ibid., p. 167. To get an idea of how much of the barrio was turning back to fields and gardens, there is a postcard from 1900 that is reproduced in Barrios Rozúa, *El Albaicín: paraíso cerrado, conflicto urbano,* p. 103.

      The Maristan: An extended description and background of this extraordinary institution—a hospital and refuge for those with mental disorders—is in Castilla Brazales, *En busca de la Granada andalusí,* pp. 103–109. There is a lovely sketch of the building.

99   **The first *carmenes* in the Albayzín:** Tito Rojo, "Los cármenes del Albaicín, entre la tradición y el invento," pp. 58–65. For a pictorial summary of their evolution, see pp. 69–70. See also an account of the history Pozo Felguera, ibid., pp. 103–108.

100   **"The streets are narrow . . ."** García Lorca, *Granada, paraíso cerrado y otras páginas granadinas,* pp. 231–234.

102   **García Lorca spent time:** Gibson, *En Granada, su Granada*, pp. 114–116.

      The poverty, crime, hunger, and hopelessness: An indispensable summary of the background and details of this time, and the relations between clergy and barrio, is in Barrios Rozúa, "Iconoclastia y resacralización del espacio urbano en el Albaicín," pp. 71–86. For an account of the churches burned or sacked, with photos, see Pozo Felguera, ibid., pp. 79–89.

103   **Through 1936:** Barrios Rozúa, ibid., pp. 87–88.

104   **Nobody likes to see history run the same tape over and over:** Barrios Rozua, ibid., pp. 88–92.

105   **"We must redeem the Albayzín from Godless Marxism . . .":** quoted in Barrios Rozúa, ibid., p. 91.

"The glory of Spain coincides . . .": This paragraph is taken from speech of Generalissimo Franco given in 1942. The text, and other excerpts from his speeches, are widely available. See, for example, Intercentres, *La nueva España de General Franco.* "Imperio y religión," Web.

106 The population: Pozo Felguera, ibid., p. 148.

"In fact, the Albayzín has arrived . . .": quoted in Carrascola Salas, ibid., p. 204.

AL-ANDALUS: NOTES ON A HIDDEN, LUSTROUS, INDISPENSABLE ERA

111 A medieval chronicle: These writings sometimes have named authors and are sometimes anonymous. They are intensely political and are full of wondrous and portentous language, with a full dosage of the messianic and the biblical. Some of the principal writers were Hernando de Pulgar, Gutierre de Palma, Diego de Valera, Anton de Montoro, and Iñigo de Mendoza. For a discussion of the way certain chronicles were meant to serve directly and deliberately as propaganda for Isabel in particular, early in her reign, and the close relation of the chronicles to other texts, see Guardiola-Griffiths, *Legitimizing the Queen: Propaganda and Ideology in the Reign of Isabel I of Castile,* pp. 45–46, 71–73, 95.

112 St. James the Moorslayer: For a summary with images of this crusading, emblematic figure, see Menocal, Dodds, and Balbale, *The Arts of Intimacy,* pp. 100–101.

the narrative core: For a much more comprehensive account of the fevered and phantasmagorical story I have condensed here, see Liss, *Isabel the Queen,* pp. 168–176, with accompanying notes, which give us the type and tenor of the many chronicles and other texts that contributed to the story as a whole.

114 Even through the twentieth century: The great polemic, of course, was between Americo Castro, who introduced the notion of *convivencia* to describe the decisive interactions of Christians, Jews, and Muslims in medieval Spain, and his adversary Claudio Sancho-Alboroz, who broadly rejected such ideas. Sancho-Alboroz even proposed that the backwardness of Spain was somehow due to Semitic influence, an idea that would be startling if it were not so transparently a part of the toxic idea of "blood purity." Though Castro's ideas have been criticized, refined, and corrected, his contribution was determinative and brilliant. For a useful, technical discussion of some of this controversy, see Glick, *Islamic and Christian Spain in the Early Middle Ages,* pp. 340–348.

115 **Jose Maria Aznar:** This piece of braggadocio is available on the Web on
     YouTube. See Aznar, Speech at Georgetown, September 21, 2004.

116 **What books do they translate?:** They translate the very widest range. For
     many of the books and a fascinated portrait of the process, see Burnett,
     "The Translating Activity in Medieval Spain," pp. 1042–1048. Also
     Menocal, Dodds, and Barbale, *The Arts of Intimacy*, pp. 232–235. And the
     indispensable Glick, *Islamic and Christian Spain in the Early Middle Ages*,
     pp. 327–336. It is wonderful to read about this laborious and consequential
     work, the very portrait and model of the *convivencia* at its best.

118 **a crucial part of the foundation of the Renaissance:** The reliance of late
     medieval and Renaissance Europe on scientific and mathematical texts
     translated in Spain is now firmly established. See, for example, al-Khalili,
     The House of Wisdom, pp. 190–203, 229–231.

120 **"People of a Book.":** For the basics of this principle, see Armstrong,
     A History of God, pp. 159–160.

121 **An architectural *convivencia*:** Menocal, Dodds, and Barbale, ibid.,
     pp. 12–13. For a description and drawings of the form, see Burkhardt,
     Moorish Culture in Spain, pp. 13–14.

123 **The medieval synagogue of Samuel Halevi:** Menocal, Dodds, and Barbale,
     ibid., pp. 241–246, with illustrations.

124 **Cristo de la Luz:** Menocal, Dodds, and Barbale, ibid., pp. 113–117.

125 **Abd al-Rahman III:** As the best known of the rulers of Al-Andalus,
     information on his rule is widely available. For a whole range of readings,
     see the following: Makki, "The Political History of Al-Andalus." pp. 35–38;
     Menocal, Dodds, and Barbale, *The Arts of Intimacy*, pp. 22–25; Cabrera,
     "La pacificación de Al-Andalus," pp. 27–32; Lewis, *God's Crucible*,
     pp. 319–327.

     Hasdai Shaprut: another legendary figure, very well-known. For a richer
     suite of information, see the following: Pinilla, "Figuras relevantes de la
     Corte," pp. 66–67; Bueno, *Los Júdios de Sefarad*, pp. 39–49; Scheindlin,
     "The Jews in Muslim Spain," p. 190; Lewis, *God's Crucible*, pp. 330–332.

126 **Ismail ibn Neghrela:** Scheindlin, "The Jews in Muslim Spain," pp. 190–194.
     Shmuel HaNagid, *Selected Poems of Shmuel HaNagid*, Peter Cole, trans.
     pp. xiii–xx.

127 **Earth to man:** *Selected Poems of Shmuel HaNagid*, ibid., p. 121.

     Luxuries ease: *Selected Poems of Shmuel HaNagid*, ibid., p. 131.

     I'd give everything: *Selected Poems of Shmuel HaNagid*, ibid., p. 15.

128 **Solomon Ibn Gabirol:** For a illuminated and illuminating look at the work and life of this man, see *Solomon Ibn Gabirol*, Peter Cole, trans., pp. 3–39. The discovery that the great Christian/Muslim philosopher Avicebron was the Jewish Gabirol is told on pp. 13–14. Peter Cole has brought the Jewish poetry of Al-Andalus to the world. For a fine essay on Gabirol that sets his work in the context of Jewish theology and literature, see Tanenbaum, *The Contemplative Soul*, pp. 57–83.

130 *florilegio:* The poems that follow here are a small sampling from the treasure house of the poetry of Al-Andalus. May the reader find her way into that house and stay a long while. See Recommended Reading for some sources.

"Is it the darks of your eyes . . .": Jayyusi, "Andalusi Poetry: The Golden Period," p. 333.

"She's played adulteress . . .": Jayyusi, ibid., p. 338.

"But what is strange . . .": Jayyusi, ibid., p. 340.

131 **"Do you belong . . .":** Jayyusi, ibid., p. 342.

"Blest be the one who . . .": Jayyusi, ibid., p. 342.

"Your love is firm . . .": Jayyusi, "Nature Poetry in Al-Andalus and the Rise of Ibn Khafaja," p. 383.

"He almost drank my soul . . .": Jayyusi, ibid., p. 385.

"Its covering is composed . . .": Jayyusi, ibid., p. 376.

132 **"The silence of gardens . . .":** Jayyusi, ibid., p. 371.

"It blocked every which way . . .": Jayyusi, ibid., p. 391.

133 **a deep study of Arabic prosody:** Scheindlin, "The Jews in Muslim Spain," p. 193. In more detail, Scheindlin, "Hebrew Poetry in Medieval Iberia," pp. 39–45. For a more complete idea of the literary context, Menocal, Dodds, and Barbale, *The Arts of Intimacy*, pp. 144–153.

"By God and God's faithful—": this poetry and many of the verses that follow are taken from the work of Peter Cole, who has selected, edited, and translated work from the whole range of poetry in Hebrew written in Al-Andalus. There are no words to convey the importance of what Professor Cole has accomplished: He has given to the world, in English, for the first time, some of the most powerful, insightful, and beautiful poetry of the whole Middle Ages. This first quote is from his *Selected Poems of Shmuel HaNagid*, ibid., p. 6.

134 "You who seek my peace . . .": *Selected Poems of Solomon Ibn Gabirol*, Peter Cole, trans., p. 57.

"We woke . . .": Cole, *The Dream of the Poem*, p. 122.

"Why is that dove . . .": Cole, ibid., p. 127.

135 "The heavenly spheres . . .": Cole, ibid., p. 174.

"Man in his love . . .": Cole, ibid., p. 197.

"As long as a man seeks . . .": Cole, ibid., p. 223.

136 "The day you left . . .": Cole, ibid., p. 258.

137 Ibn Tufayl: For a fine and searching account of his work, see Burgel, "Ibn Tufayl and his *Hayy Ibn Yaqzan*: A Turning Point in Arabic Philosophical Writing," pp. 830–839.

138 "It became clear to him . . .": Tufail, *The Journey of the Soul*, p. 16.

139 "he realized that . . .": Tufail, ibid., p.28.

140 "he would select . . .": Tufail, ibid., p. 42.

"he imitated . . .": Tufail, ibid., p. 43.

141 "When he spun rapidly . . .": Tufail, ibid., p. 43.

"Immersed in this state . . .": Tufail, ibid., p. 45.

142 He will be called Averroes in the West: For background and context on Averroes, see Urvoy, "Ibn Rushd," passim. For his views on the intellect and psychological material, see al-'Alawi, "The Philosophy of Ibn Rushd," pp. 804–825. For an overall sense of how his thought relates to evolving philosophy in the West, see Colish, *Medieval Foundations of the Western Intellectual Tradition 400–1400*, pp. 144–148.

146 Science and mathematics: I am of course condensing and selecting from a whole spectrum of materials. To get a more expansive sense of the scientific work of the period, a scholarly and exceptionally useful survey is in Glick, *Islamic and Christian Spain in the Early Middle Ages*, pp. 293–336. For many details on mathematics, astronomy, geometry, and instrumentation, see Samso, "The Exact Sciences in al-Andalus," pp. 952–964. For advances in mechanics, botany, agriculture, pharmacology, see Vernet, "Natural and Technical Sciences in al-Andalus," pp. 938–945. For a fascinating review of maritime, geographical, and navigational expertise, see Hamdani, "An Islamic Background to the Voyages of Discovery," pp. 273–280. For an account in the context of Europe in the Middle Ages, see Lewis, ibid., pp. 367–370. For a look at the science of Al-Andalus in its position as the undisputed leader of European science, see Vernet, "The Legacy of Islam in Spain," pp. 108–182.

For a complete account in Spanish, see Vernet, *Lo que Europa debe al Islam de España*, pp. 197–379. To have a look at some astrolabes and globes, see Dodds, *Al-Andalus: The Art of Islamic Spain*, pp. 376–383.

150 **Dioscorides:** Vernet, "Natural and Technical Sciences in al-Andalus," p. 938. Also Glick, ibid., p. 306.

151 **In agriculture:** on the organization of irrigated agriculture in Al-Andalus, Trillo San José, *Agua, tierra y hombres en Al-Andalus*, pp. 42–69. For clear explanation with helpful drawings of the *noria* and *qanat* and other technologies, see Trillo San Jose, *Agua y paisaje en Granada,* pp. 50–64. For an account of agronomy and a sense of the richness of agricultural writing, as well as plant lists and the work of al-Tighnari, see Garcia Sanchez, "Agriculture in Muslim Spain," passim. For a summary look, see Glick, *Islamic and Christian Spain in the Early Middle Ages*, pp. 79–81. And in the same volume, for municipal agricultural technique and crops in specific regions in Al-Andalus, pp. 68–79.

153 **"The month when . . .":** Schultz-Dornberg, *Sonnenstand. Medieval Hermitages Along the Route to Santiago de Compostela*, "The Calendar of Cordoba," intro.

156 **"We must not hesitate . . .":** quoted in al-Khalili, *The House of Wisdom*, p. 132.

157 **Abulcasis:** For one portrait of Abulcasis, see Morgan, *Lost History*, pp. 198–205. Further comments are in Vernet, *Lo que debe al Islam de España*, pp. 247–249.

161 **by the vigor of its survival:** For material on Ziryab, see Wright, "Music in Islamic Spain." *The Legacy of Islamic Spain*, pp. 556–560. Also Glick, ibid., 228–229. For more context and the relation of music to literary arts, see Menocal, *The Arabic Role in Medieval Literary History*, pp. 28–33 and pp. 99–103. More very helpful commentary with many additional historical details is in Reynolds, "Music," pp. 64–67. To have a look at the instruments themselves, see the illustrations in *Musica y poesia al sur de Al-Andalus*, pp. 73–93. In the same volume, a general summary is on pp. 35–39, followed by a description of the instruments. The text is in Spanish, French, and English. For examples of the music itself as it has been recovered and interpreted, a number of CDs are available. See Paniagua, *La música de pneuma: las tres culturas de la música medieval española*, as well as Paniagua's other collections.

"The Arabo-Andalusian musical legacy . . .": Reynolds, "Music." p. 60.

162 *qiyan:* Menocal, Dodds, and Barbale, ibid., pp.105–106. Also Menocal, *The Arabic Role in Medieval Literary History*, pp. 27–28. Also Reynolds, ibid., pp. 63–64.

164 **the troubadours:** To read about this extraordinary poetry, as it relates to
Al-Andalus, the most illuminating text I know of is Menocal, *The Arabic
Role in Medieval Literary History*, pp. 27–33, 71–90, 103–111, 118–120.
For a sampling of verse written by women in this same tradition, see Bogin,
The Women Troubadours, pp. 80–159.

the *Cantigas* de Santa Maria: There is online a complete text and
translation of all of the *Cantigas*, including the original text of the poems,
an English translation, notes on the manuscripts, classification of miracles,
a bibliography, and search capacity. Surpassingly useful. See the Oxford
Cantigas de Santa Maria database. For a discussion of Alphonso's personal
role, see Snow, "Alfonso as Troubadour: The Fact and the Fiction," passim.

168 **the musicians who performed these songs:** For background on the *Cantigas*
as sponsored by Alfonso the Wise, the famous Christian king of Al-Andalus,
as well as images from original mss., see Menocal, Dodds, and Barbale, *The
Arts of Intimacy*, pp. 222–228.

170 **the Spanish Kama Sutra:** The book is Lopez-Baralt, *Un Kama Sutra español*.
The original work of the anonymous author is pp. 347–388. The book sets
this extraordinary essay in the context of Western theology and literature
and specifically in the context of Spanish literature and erotic writing, such
as it was. A scholarly, admirable, enlightening read.

171 **Beginning with Saint Paul:** For a clear, comprehensive summary of early
Christian writing and attitudes toward sexuality, see Lopez-Baralt, ibid.,
pp. 101–133.

177 **Ibn Hazm:** The Arberry translation is the standard, Ibn Hazm, *The Ring
of the Dove*. For a description of his notion of the transcendent dimension
of love, and the iridescent joys of sexual union, see Ormsby, "Ibn Hazm,"
pp. 245–246. For an intelligent look at the possible links between Ibn
Hazm's ideas and the tradition of courtly love, see Giffen, "Ibn Hazm
and the Tawq al-Hamama," pp. 435–437.

178 **the *Zohar*:** A standard modern text is Matt, *The Zohar*. For explanation
and commentary, see the shorter, earlier version of a small selection of the
text, see Matt, *Zohar: The Book of Enlightenment*. For writing on Kabbalah
as part of the essence of Judaism, see Lancaster, *The Essence of Kabbalah*,
pp. 27–32.

179 **the Sufis:** The seminal work on these men and women is Shah, *The Sufis*.
Material about them hardly fits in an endnote, but much more material and
a host of references will be found in the chapter here entitled "A Lucid Work
of Love and Helpfulness." The influence of the Sufis in the development
of Al–Andalus is demonstrable and crucial, yet it is just beginning to be
understood.

Granada itself owes its origins to the Sufis: Harvey, *Islamic Spain 1250 to 1500*, pp. 29–37.

180 **two directly related Sufi texts:** For an account of the superb scholarship that brought these sources to light, see Lopez-Baralt, "The Legacy of Islam in Spanish Literature," pp. 530–532. al-Nuri's book is from the ninth century.

Saint John of the Cross: Lopez-Baralt, ibid., p. 530, recounts how the legendary scholar Miguel Asin Palacios traced key symbols in the mystical poetry of Saint John of the Cross to Sufi writings, especially those of Ibn Abbad of Ronda. As to the poetry of Saint John of the Cross, a beautiful translation, with commentary and biographical information, is in Barnstone, *The Poetics of Ecstasy*, pp. 153–190.

181 **a source for Dante:** The book is Asin Palacios, *La escatología musulmana en la Divina Comedia*. In 1982, a fourth edition was issued in Spain. On this subject, it is worth looking into illustrated texts of about the *miraj*. A fine one is *The Miraculous Journey of Mahomet*, reproduced from a manuscript in the Bibliotheque Nationale in Paris. Looking at the book, anyone would think of Dante.

Dante scholarship has come round to the idea: See the enlightening summary in Martínez Gásquez, "Translations of the Qur'an and other Islamic Texts before Dante (Twelfth and Thirteenth Centuries)," pp. 79–92.

Color: This subject is treated in depth by Bolens, "The Use of Plants for Dyeing and Clothing," pp. 1008–1012. For the details on Byssus, p. 1008. For a comprehensive look at the use of color in the art and culture of Islam, have a look at Bloom and Blair, *And Diverse Are Their Hues*, passim. A magnificent book.

183 **A spectrum of facts:** These selected accounts are gathered from a wide variety of sources among the recent writings on Al-Andalus. They are a small sampling of the many examples of interfaith community in Al-Andalus. For my own selection of books helpful for understanding this era, see the Recommended Reading list. As to some of the volumes that relate the examples I cite, see, for example, the rich detail in Lowney, *A Vanished World*, pp. 106, 202–208, 221–223. For an account of the *convivencia* in the context of Jewish history, see Gambel, "Jews, Christians, and Muslims in Medieval Iberia: *Convivencia* through the Eyes of Sephardic Jews," pp. 15–22. For an account of conversions and interfaith marriages, see Fletcher, *Moorish Spain*, pp. 36–40; and in the same book, notes about interfaith wine-bibbing and an important rabbinical advisor to al-Mutamid, pp. 94 and 108. More information on interfaith marriages is in Snow, *Spain, the Root and the Flower*, pp. 111–112. For interfaith relations in the caliphate, and among the community of slaves, Guichard, "The Social History of Muslim Spain," pp. 690–693. On dynastic interfaith marriages

and their arrangement by means of ambassadors who were poets, see Boase, "Arab Influences on European Love-Poetry," pp. 465–466. For an account of the religious, judicial, and commercial evolution in Al-Andalus, with all its contradictions and difficulties, see Glick, *Islamic and Christian Spain in the Early Middle Ages*, pp. 187–202. For some overall historical context, see Lewis, *God's Crucible*, pp. 202–207.

185 **the Blessed Ramon Llull:** To get a sense of the variety of his works and read a fine, sensitive, scholarly introduction to them, see *The Selected Works of Ramon Llull*, translated by Anthony Bonner. See also the fine exposition of Llull's oeuvre in Stone, "Ramon Llull," pp. 345–356.

187 **"While the wise man . . .":** *The Selected Works of Ramon Llull*, ibid., p. 303.

188 **The *convivencia* was a dangerous experiment:** The reader should be aware that there is still a debate about the nature, value, and details of the *convivencia*; that is, how the experiment of the three faiths living together actually played out on the ground. Though more is learned each year, the argument about the details and the significance can take on real venom, with all the complications of ideological or political motives a part of the exchange. For this writer, these debates are a tiresome and troublesome waste of life, a kind of conceptual tar pit. I do not think that the historians of the period I quote in this book have an ideological or political agenda. I certainly do not. That being said, the notion that Jews and Arabs, together with Christians, did something magnificent in Iberia, to the benefit of Europe and the world, is to some scholars and readers somehow inconsequential, or even offensive. I certainly do not wish to give offense, though I may do so, despite my efforts to focus on the facts, as I have selected and gathered them. I am, simple-mindedly enough, just trying to tell the story of one family living in Andalusia. I am saying what it meant to us. And to set forth that meaning, it is important to ask, among many other questions: What was accomplished in Al-Andalus? And why did it matter?

191 **the origins of the Inquisition:** The literature of the Inquisition now fills whole archives, since this legendary institution kept such good records. I am drawing upon a variety of recent studies here, and the reader looking for all the useful and sordid complexity of Inquisitorial history and development, and its place in Spanish life, may find it as follows: For more on the scene in Toledo and details of the auto-da-fé, see the authoritative Kamen, *The Spanish Inquisition*, pp. 205–213. In the same volume is a excellent chapter on Inquisitorial operations, pp. 174–192. And see also Kamen's review of trials and punishments, pp. 193–213. Kamen has a superb review of the political background, pp. 28–65. For a condensed and brilliant study in Spanish of the Inquisition, look to Pérez de Colosia, "La Inquisición: estructura y actuación," passim. For an examination of Inquisitorial trials,

tortures, and punishments, and their relation to modern totalitarianism, see Perez, *The Spanish Inquisition*, pp. 133–175. In the same volume, for a concise review of the administrative organization, see pp. 101–132. And for the comparison to Stalinist trials and other forms of state terror, see his conclusion, pp. 222–225. For an examination of the Inquisition in relation to the modern world, including torture practiced by the United States of America during the administration of Richard Cheney and George W. Bush, see Murphy, *God's Jury*, pp. 223–251. On the relation of the Inquisition to the Spanish pope, the sybarite and murderer Rodrigo Borgia, see Reston, *The Dogs of God*, 279–290. A reader wanting an account in English of a torture as it occurred, duly noted down, as well as a portrayal of an auto-da-fé, see Cowans, *Early Modern Spain: A Documentary History*, pp. 51–57. For two full descriptions of autos-da-fé, see Constable, *Medieval Iberia: Readings From Christian, Jewish, and Muslim sources*, pp. 330–342.

204 **the ideal occasion for what-if history:** For a look at this genre of historical writing, there is a fascinating compendium of texts in Cowen, *What If*. I am not aware of a what-if essay having been written of the course of Spanish history after 1492, but it would be a most instructive and beneficial exercise, and I pray someone will take it on.

206 **to shape the destiny of Spain:** Part of this durability is due to the genius of Ferdinand and Isabel for propaganda, noted, for example, in the preface of the scholar Peggy Liss in her biography of Isabel, *Isabel the Queen*, p. xiii. She is quoting the Spanish scholar José Manuel Nieto. As to the durability of Ferdinand and Isabel's policies, take, for example, the decree of 1492 to expel the Jews from Spain, the so-called Alhambra Decree: It was not formally revoked until 1968. Recently, the government of Spain has begun, over five centuries after the expulsion, a program to welcome back to Spain Sephardic descendants who are currently members of the Jewish community. The program has attracted interest, criticism, and bewilderment.

208 **a centerpiece for their financial policy:** This is a fascinating macroeconomic story of the national decline of the most prosperous and advanced commercial and scientific culture in Europe. I am, just as in other sections of this book, condensing a wide range of material, as well as drawing on readings in macroeconomics in my own work in the investment community. The most comprehensive treatment, incomparable in its scope of reference and in the riches of scholarly detail, are the three volumes by Stanley J. and Barbara H. Stein: *Silver, Trade, and War*, *Apogee of Empire*, and *Edge of Crisis*. This achievement brings into focus the minutiae of the decline, the massive national corruption, and its disastrous cumulative effect. On the use of silver to support the empire, pay for military operations, and secure debt, see *Silver, Trade, and War*, pp. 40–56. In the same volume, to review the decisive commercial concessions of the Treaty of Westphalia, see pp. 57–67. For the resultant flow of capital to fund the industrialization of Western

Europe, and Spanish collusion in corruption that enriched other countries, see pp. 77–89. For a concise portrait of the failure of Spain to establish a competitive textile manufacturing of woolen goods for domestic and colonial supply, see *Apogee of Empire*, pp. 210–218. In the same volume, on Spain's structural economic defects and the inability of the country to invigorate the peninsular economy, see pp. 221–222. On the persistence of a rentier economy in Spain and the failure to develop manufacturing even in the late 1700s, see pp. 354–355. In the *Edge of Crisis*, to read about the dependence of Spain, as late as 1800, on the silver production and minting in Mexico, see pp. 163–174. For the makeup of Madrid's budget deficits during this period, see pp. 214–217. For debt financing of military operations in this later period, see pp. 284–286. For the government use of the vast wealth of the church in Spain and the New World, see pp. 296–297. On the conjunction of war and debt leading Spain to crisis, see pp. 476–477. On the role that geography, poor roads, and above all, indirect and regressive taxation played in the painfully slow process of market integration in Spain, see Grafe, *Distant Tyranny*, pp. 244–245.

211   **"In 1557, for example . . .":** Stein, *Silver, Trade, and War*, p. 46.

      default on his own people three times: Graphs and discussion of these defaults can be found in Reinhart and Rogoff, *This Time Is Different*, pp. 70–71 and 88–89.

212   **"Despite the esteem . . .":** Lewis, *God's Crucible*, p. 327.

      The commerce of Al-Andalus: Once again, this section draws upon a whole range of scholars. Preeminent among them is Olivia Remie Constable, in her *Trade and Traders in Muslim Spain*. For a summary and general conditions and evolution of trade, see pp. 4–12. For a discussion of ports and trading activity, see pp. 17–19. For the fame of the shipyards and markets of Andalusian cities, see pp. 23–27. For the centrality of the *dirham* of Al-Andalus in North Africa, see p. 35. For trade with the Christian north, see p. 47. On the fascinating tradition of merchant-scholars, see pp. 54–55. On the transition from Jewish and Muslim traders to Christian traders, especially the Genoese, see pp. 62–67. For a general description of the vigor and variety of this trade, see Constable's article, "Muslim Merchants in Andalusi International Trade," p. 759.

213   **merchant-scholars:** See the enlivening material in Constable, ibid., pp. 54–55, 80–85.

      practical knowledge pressed into action: For details on mills, textiles, paper, cork-soled shoes, ceramics, glass, clocks, and leathers, see Glick, *Islamic and Christian Spain in the Early Middle Ages*, pp. 275–292. For some of the same goods and a sampling of agricultural exports, see Constable, ibid., pp. 169–203. For technology of dyeing, see Bolens, "The Use of Plants for

Dyeing and Clothing," pp. 1008–1012. For more specifics on the silk and furniture industries, see Constable, ibid., pp. 173–181.

214 **"... so many streets and lanes ...":** This quote is from Bermudéz de Pedraza, and the full paragraph and a further description of the markets of Granada in Al-Andalus may be found in Dickie, "Granada: A Case Study of Arab Urbanism in Muslim Spain," p. 95–97.

these markets throve: For an illuminating description of the commerce of the period in the context of Medieval Europe, see Lewis, ibid., pp. 206–208, 279–280, 335. See also a discussion of national income, monetary circulation, population, taxation, and overall economic vigor in Chalmeta, "An Approximate Picture of the Economy of Al-Andalus," pp. 746–756.

Spanish words connected with market regulation: A set of these words, along with their Arabic roots, is in Messner, "Arabic Words in Ibero-Romance Languages," p. 454.

216 **a dramatic shift in attitudes toward work:** For example, Constable, ibid., p. 67, notes how early this attitude took root, writing that "in the twelfth and thirteenth centuries no Castilian of social standing would have considered a commercial profession." There are long and valuable discussions of this change in Castro, *The Spaniards,* pp. 245, 317–321. He writes, for instance, on p. 319, "No other European country so stigmatized manual labor." In the same volume, on the disdain for commercial and intellectual activity, see p. 159. On the debasement of economic affairs, see p. 364.

217 **the animals ate Iberia alive:** To learn about the Mesta, see Lowney, A Vanished World, pp. 113–144. On the rise of wool to dominate the export economy of Spain, see Constable, ibid., pp. 227–229. On the peninsular reach of grazing herds and the participation of military orders in the south with extensive landholdings, see Fletcher, Moorish Spain, p. 147. On Ferdinand and Isabella's dependence on revenues from the Mesta to finance their military adventures and other crown expenses, and the concentration of land among the nobles and military orders, see Liss, Isabel the Queen, pp. 276–277. On the long-term ecological damage of such transhumant pastoralism, with its cumulative destruction of the once-verdant landscape of Andalusia and Castile, see Glick, Islamic and Christian Spain in the Early Middle Ages, pp. 105–109. For a brilliant analysis of this phenomenon in a wider Mediterranean context, see Eisenberg, The Ecology of Eden, pp. 211–212.

irrigated agriculture: An excellent source is the pioneering and careful work of Carmen Trillo San José. To gain a pictorial sense of the transition from dry agriculture to the irrigated systems of Al-Andalus, see her *Agua, tierra y hombres en Al-Andalus,* pp. 171–176. Illustrations of how irrigated land was owned and managed, along with some statistical figures on ownership, are on pp. 161–170. On the pertinent Islamic customs and the family organization of agricultural lands, see pp. 157–159. On coming of irrigation to dryland agriculture and the subsequent division of irrigated land among a multitude of small holders, see pp. 35–59. As to Granada itself, see Carmen Trillo San Jose, *Agua y paisaje en Granada*. For her analysis of the sociopolitical dimension of irrigated agriculture and discussions of polyculture, see pp. 83–101. For a treatment in English of the agricultural variety of Al-Andalus, the so-called Arab "green revolution" in Iberia, see Glick, ibid., pp. 70–75.

218 **"The ordered landscape . . ."**: Glick, ibid., p. 105.

219 **the *latifundia***: For a historical discussion of their essentially feudal nature, see E.V.K. Fitzgerald, "Latifundia," pp. 204–205. For more details on the system of the *latifundia* as it evolved and the failure of agrarian reform in the early nineteenth century, see Harrison, *An Economic History of Modern Spain*, pp. 25–26. For statistics on the dominance of the *latifundia*, the harsh labor conditions, and the relation to rural anarchism, see pp. 105–108. Since a theme of this book is the remarkable durability and influence of some of the important initiatives of Fernando and Isabel, it is instructive to consider the crucial role the *latifundistas* played in the military rebellion of 1936 that began the Spanish Civil War, and their active participation in the campaign of extermination that followed. See Preston, *The Spanish Holocaust*, pp. 20, 30, 32–33, 55, 57, 67, 70, 125, 135, 141, 148, for a sampling. The book is replete with examples of the close and murderous cooperation between large landowners, the rebels, and the fascist party.

". . . came to possess almost half the arable land in Spain." Castro, *The Spaniards*, p. 245.

220 **Education declined in quality in Spain:** See, for example, Crow, *Spain: The Root and the Flower,* pp. 234–235. On the banning and burning of books by the Inquisition, the most concise account is Perez, *The Spanish Inquisition*, pp. 177–195.

221 **in a wholehearted effort to find the eminent Spaniards in science:** Take, for instance, the *Smithsonian Timeline of Science*, which catalogs and illustrates the scientific progress of humankind. In the period from 1492 to 1900, I found only two Spaniards: the sixteenth century physician Michael Servetus, who spent almost all of his professional life outside of Spain and was a Protestant, and Diego Aguilera, who in 1793 flew a glider.

book-burning: Perez, ibid., pp. 180–182. See also Baez, *Historia universal de la destrucción de libros*, pp. 125–129. Baez notes, as well, that books, for example, of Ibn Hazm were burned in Seville in Al-Andalus. And in Al-Andalus, the books of the Sufis were sometimes burned by Islamic fundamentalists. It was not only Christians who burned books.

222 "These people also used certain characters . . ." for Diego Landa's description of his incineration of Mayan culture, see Landa, *Yucatan Before and After the Conquest*, p. 82.

224 "Indeed, the notion of *re*–conquest . . .": Glick, ibid., p. 34.

"The European Conquest of the Americas . . .": Harvey, *Muslims in Spain, 1500 to 1614*, pp. 291–292.

226 ". . . the shadow of Spain . . .": Stein and Stein, *Silver, Trade, and War*, pp. 3–4.

227 "Spain's decline had multiple facets": Stein and Stein, ibid., p. 103.

228 "What had been inherited . . .": Stein and Stein, ibid., p. 159.

A country of seigneurial privilege: For a wealth of detail on the stratification of Spanish society during this complex period, see Stein and Stein, ibid., pp. 93–94, 104–105, 144, 158, 262–263, 266. On flow of silver to the other countries of Europe, see pp. 7–8, 17–18, 23, 25, 27, 48, 50, 52, 77. On the reduction of Spain to a commodity economy, see pp. 9, 34. On the enrichment of the rest of Europe, as it developed market, trading, and financial expertise, see pp. 16, 35, 55–56, 59, 63–64, 71, 101, 149–150, 266. On the ferocious demand of the military on the state treasury, see, for example, pp. 41,43, 45–46, 53. For a look at how the process played out over time, see the summary statements in Nadall, *El fracaso de devolución industrial en España*, pp. 226–228. For another look at a later period, with respect to landholdings, see Harrison, *An Economic History of Modern Spain*, pp. 5–6. In the same book, for details of the failures of the 1800s, see the chapter "An Industrial Revolution Manqué," pp. 43–65. For another dimension of the scholarly work of the period, see a few of the tables, for example, p. 14, in *El legado económico del antiguo régimen en España*. What is fascinating is that all the figures begin in 1500, as though Al-Andalus did not exist at all. So even though the earnings shown for inhabitants of Holland and England surge past and ultimately double those of Spain in the period 1500–1820, the figures still do not take into account that Spain, on every commercial, financial, and technical front, had an enormous head start on every other country in Europe.

230 There will be bitter attacks: Anyone who has discussed these matters in educated company in Spain will know how deep and furious conversation can become, even in the present day, once anyone begins to address the history of Al-Andalus, the subsequent decline of Spain, or the civil war that began in 1936. It is as though fact is napalm, and the most straightforward statement can be taken as explosive attack on the national character of all of Spain. But this book does not in any way intend or imply any such attack. Though our subject is, in part, the history of the Albayzín, Al-Andalus, and Spain after Ferdinand and Isabel, the economic and sociopolitical evolution

covered in this book is relevant to any society, and similar evolution can
occur, and has occurred, in any society. I simply do not think that violent
conversation is a good use of life, and I will not accept the notion that the
presentation of facts obtained by honest effort makes any person vile and
contemptible.

231 **exterminating angels:** The reader will be aware that this view of mine is
at variance, to put it as mildly as possible, with that of many esteemed
historians who see Ferdinand and Isabel as admirable figures in history,
whose greatness brought empire and honor to Spain. I encourage
wholeheartedly the encounter with the work of such historians, so that the
different views can be brought into focus. Two excellent contemporary
examples are Thomas, *Rivers of Gold: The Rise of the Spanish Empire From
Columbus to Magellan*. And in Spanish, Ladero Quesada, *La España de los
Reyes Católicas*. Both these books offer detailed, scholarly, and laudatory
engagements with the Catholic Monarchs.

232 **". . . the suffering of women in the prison . . .":** Preston, *The Spanish
Holocaust*, p. 511. Lest anyone think I am noting a rare abuse by Franco
and his cohorts, let me emphasize that the humiliation, rape, and murder
of women by Franco's military was standard practice throughout Spain
during the Civil War, and in its aftermath. See, for example, Preston, ibid.,
pp. 149, 156, 158–9, 160, 166, 204–205, 313, 333–4, 448, 478.

233 **The yoke and arrows:** In the rhetoric of the military rebels and their
allies in the Catholic Church, their political initiative was linked directly
to Ferdinand and Isabel. See, for example, the written declaration of the
fascist Onésimo Redondo, Preston, ibid., p. 46, in which he identifies the
Spanish working class with the Arabs and praises Isabel for her militant fight
against "the Moorish spirit." See also the speech on National Radio by the
canon of the cathedral in Salamanca, Aniceto de Castro Albarrán, quoted
in Preston, ibid., pp. 197–198, in which he cries, "Up with the Spirit of
Isabel la Católica!" And the speech by Franco on New Year's Eve, 1939,
in which he praised the Nazi aggressions against Jews, and links their
actions, appreciatively, with Ferdinand and Isabel, Preston, ibid.,
pp. 471–472.

Grand Cross of the Imperial Order of the Yoke and Arrows: For the
awarding of this honor to Himmler, see Preston, ibid., p. 490.

". . . We must be listened to . . .": Levi, *The Drowned and the Saved*,
p. 199.

234 **"the only historic instrument . . .":** in an essay by Rivera, quoted in Payne,
Fascism in Spain, p. 170.

"prepare to revolt . . .": quoted in Payne, ibid., p. 171. José Antonio Primo
de Ribero was one of the principal figures who led Spain into the cataclysm

of Civil War. For his commitment to violence, see Preston, *The Spanish Holocaust*, p. 110. For his active direction of the Falange—the Spanish fascists—as he coordinated its work with the military conspiracy, see Preston, ibid., pp. 117–119. Jose Antonio thought that the Falange would "receive the laurels earned by being first in this holy crusade of violence," Preston, ibid., p. 118.

"We regard Italian Fascism as the most outstanding. . .": quoted in Payne, ibid., p. 162.

A FEW NOTIONS OF GEOMETRY
AND REVELATION

237 **the city's most bizarre stories:** A useful account may be found in Jacobs, *Alhambra*, pp. 51–67. The book is full of artful, well-chosen color photographs by Francisco Fernández. For a finely written examination of the history of the building, see Irwin, *The Alhambra*, pp. 15–67. Irwin's book is a searching and scholarly study of the whole complex, and his reflections are of exceptional value throughout. He suggests, for instance, that the complex around the Patio de los Leones may have been a school, since it so closely resembles schools in Morocco. Another recent, wonderful book is Puerta Vílchez, *Leer la Alhambra*, which gives us, for the first time, a complete translation into Spanish of all the poetry inscribed into the walls of the Alhambra. For those interested in the physical setting and the geological underpinnings of the Alhambra, see Salmerón Escobar, *The Alhambra: Structure and Landscape*, pp. 80–91.

240 **a book to which he gave his life and fortune:** Any of us may go online to the Internet Archive and download this entire world-changing book onto a computer desktop. It gives the savor of the time and a sense of the infinite labors necessary to create such a volume. Fabulous drawings and illustrations of the Alhambra in the 1834–1842 period. The reference is Jones, *Plans, Elevations, Sections, and Details of the Alhambra*.

241 **Pythagoras thought that the world:** For some reflections on the place of Pythagoras in the Islamic prophetic tradition, see Nasr, *Knowledge and the Sacred*, pp. 34–35. For his ideas on the change from qualitative mathematics to purely quantitative mathematics, see pp. 46–47. For Pythagorean harmony in relation to Western science, see pp. 193–194. For a more in-depth discussion of Pythagoras in relation to the great *Ikhwan Al-Safa* (The Brethren of Purity), see Nasr, *Islamic Cosmological Doctrines*, pp. 34–39. Nasr gives crucial context for understanding how Pythagorean ideas, Islamic scientific work, and mystical experience informed the use of mathematics. For a much more full, detailed, and popular treatment of Pythagoras, see Ferguson, *The Music of Pythagoras*, passim.

242 "laboring for some poor portionless man . . .": from Walter Shewring's brilliant translation of the *Odyssey*, p. 139.

243 Its scholars took up the scientific and philosophical heritage: For a comprehensive look at the translating work in Baghdad, see al-Khalili, *The House of Wisdom*, pp. 67–78.

244 "the science of numbers . . .": quoted in Critchlow, *Islamic Patterns: An Analytical and Cosmological Approach*, p. 42.

246 the idea that numbers mean something: The following exposition about the qualitative and associative properties of numbers is taken from a variety of sources. And the historical resonance of each number is far richer than I have portrayed in my condensed version. See, for example, the sections about each of the whole numbers, in Schimmel, *The Mystery of Numbers*. The best way to understand the use and meaning of the whole numbers, conceived as part of a sacred undertaking, is to read straight through Critchlow, ibid., who has unusual and revelatory material on the subject. To look at a modern scientific treatment of numbers in relation to geometry and natural form, see Stevens, *Patterns in Nature*, and Ball, The *Self-Made Tapestry: Pattern Formation in Nature*. These books are current, reverent treatments of universal patterns in nature, and so at least to this reader they bear upon the meaning of pattern as it unfolds in the artful tile work of Al-Andalus. For a more playful and participatory treatment, one might try Schneider, *A Beginner's Guide to Constructing the Universe: The Mathematical Archetypes of Nature, Art, and Science*, for example his chapter on threefold symmetry, pp. 38–59. If a reader wants to sit down and produce the intricate designs of the tile work herself, the indispensable book is Broug, *Islamic Geometric Patterns*. It is an excellent chance to see the way the most complex patterns spring to life, though you will be using nothing more than a compass and straightedge.

249 The golden ratio: For a summary and exposition of this abundantly present and beautiful mathematical relation, see Huntley, *The Divine Proportion*, passim.

257 What if these tiles are meant to teach?: This whole discussion is derived from my own experience of the walls of tiles in the Alhambra and my discussion of the designs with many informed visitors, especially Alexandra Urza. It also takes up the Sufi insistence that beauty does more than enliven the mind and exalt the senses; beauty is instrumental, and may be used to create new capacities of perception.

258 plane crystallographic group theory: For a discussion of the seventeen groups in relation to the geometry and symmetries in the Alhambra, see, for example, Irwin, ibid., pp. 118–120.

Penrose diagram: See Lu, "Decagonal and Quasi-Crystalline Tilings in Medieval Islamic Architecture." For a newspaper summary of the article, see Wilford, "In Medieval Architecture, Signs of Advanced Math." *The New York Times*, 27 February 2007, Section D, page 2.

259 **As Jesus put it in the Nag Hammadi Gospels:** The quotation is from the beautiful translation by Thomas Lambdin of the Gospel of Thomas in the *Nag Hammadi Gospels*, p. 138.

261 **The tambourine is in the hands of a woman named Fatima:** The following material of the work, thought, and life of Ibn El-Arabi is condensed from many sources. For a couple of detailed, accessible accounts of the life of Ibn El-Arabi, see the two introductions of R.W.J. Austin to Ibn El-Arabi's works *Sufis of Andalusia* and *The Bezels of Wisdom*. The material on Fatima is in Austin, *Sufis of Andalusia*, pp. 25–26. Fine and reflective material on the life of the mystic and poet may be found in Nasr, *Three Muslim Sages,* pp. 92–97. Additional information about his life and a valuable contemporary selection of passages from his poetry and philosophy are in Shah, *The Way of the Sufi*, pp. 83–89.

262 **Ibn El-Arabi met Averroes:** The story of this encounter between two of the most influential men in the whole medieval period is told in Austin, Introduction, *Sufis of Andalusia*, pp. 23–24.

263 **"On another occasion . . .":** this quote by Ibn El-Arabi is in Austin, ibid., p. 27.

264 **"a slender child . . .":** quoted in Austin, ibid., p. 36. To read about Ibn El-Arabi's statements that on the contemplation of God in women, see *The Bezels of Wisdom*, p. 275.

265 **"know that when worldly desires . . .":** quoted in Austin, ibid., pp. 44–45.

266 **How did they live?:** All these practical and mystical friends of Ibn El-Arabi, and many more, of the most miscellaneous and fantastical capacities, are found in *Sufis of Andalusia*, passim.

269 **This is just what Sufism claims to possess:** Once again, I must warn that these statements of mine are a few drops of water in the ocean of writing by and about the Sufis. There is simply no way at all to summarize in a chapter or a book, much less in an endnote, the many sources in poetry, stories, and expository writing for my brief summary. Yet one cannot write usefully about Spain and Al-Andalus without taking on the subject. For those who seek an initiatory essay on the Sufis which has its own extensive endnotes, see the introduction by Idries Shah to his collection *The Way of the Sufi*. The works of Idries Shah, in my view, offer an extraordinary portal into the Sufi tradition, and a partial list of his books may be found in the bibliography. Shah's major works are all available in Spanish. For a beautiful sampling of

Sufi poetry, see the work of the twelfth-century Hakim Sanai, *The Walled Garden of Truth*, in the translation by the gifted David Pendlebury. For a source in Spanish on the unity of revelation, see Ibn El-Arabi, *Tratado de la unidad.* A valuable contemporary and anonymous book in Spanish is *Textos Sufis*, published in Argentina. For a more academic exposition of Sufi ideas and many translations of poetry, see Schimmel, *As Through a Veil: Mystical Poetry in Islam.*

270   **"The King sent a private mission . . .":** Shah, *The Exploits of the Incomparable Mulla Nasrudin*, p. 56.

271   **"Call yourself unlucky . . .":** Shah, *The Dermis Probe*, p. 56.

 "If you do not want to be dismissed . . .": 'Ata'Illah, Ibn, *The Book of Wisdom*, p. 103.

 "There is a light deposited in hearts . . .": 'Ata'Illah, Ibn, ibid., p. 152.

272   **"How can the laws of nature be ruptured . . .":** 'Ata'Illah, Ibn, ibid., p. 78.

 "I will not serve God like a labourer . . .": Shah, *The Way of the Sufi*, p. 180.

 "If you do not shave your head . . .": a quotation from the fifteenth-century teacher Hakim Jami, selected and translated in Shah, ibid., p. 103.

273   **"The Blind Ones and the Matter of the Elephant":** Shah, *Tales of the Dervishes*, p. 25.

ON FLAMENCO, POETRY, GENIUS, AND MURDER

281   **Lorca presented a lecture:** Lorca, *Obras completas*, pp. 1067–1079.

282   **"The magical virtue of poetry":** Lorca, ibid., p. 1076.

283   **A bewildering and exultant variety of forms:** For a description in English of the forms of flamenco, with learned commentary by a practitioner of the art, see Pohren, *The Art of Flamenco*, pp. 109–187.

285   **"A cinnamon angel . . .":** For the original Spanish of these and the rest of the cited verses, see Pohren, ibid.. This song is on pp. 149–150.

286   **"The world I live in . . .":** Pohren, ibid., p. 168.

 "I saw her black eyes . . .": Pohren, ibid., p. 171.

 "Misfortune falls upon me . . .": Pohren, ibid., p. 168.

287   **Lorca's talk:** The text of this presentation, called "El Cante Jondo," is in Lorca, *Obras completas*, pp. 973–994.

"... *cante jondo* is like the trill of birds ...": Lorca, ibid., p. 975.

"preserve their Arabic and Moorish affiliation": L.P. Harvey, *Muslims in Spain: 1500 to 1614*, p. 75, notes the Arab elements in flamenco music. For an extended examination and analysis of both Arabic and Jewish sources of flamenco, see Roldan, *El flamenco y la música andalusí*, pp. 15–30.

D.E. Pohren, when he constructed his genealogy: Pohren, ibid., pp. 112–114.

288   "The gypsy *siguiriya* begins with a terrible cry ...": Lorca, ibid., p. 976.

"It is not a matter of coincident sources ...": Lorca, ibid., p. 976.

"The adoption by the Spanish church of liturgical chanting ...": Lorca, ibid., p. 976–977.

"... some Andalusian songs": Lorca, ibid., p. 978.

289   "... we must cry out in defense ...": Lorca, ibid., p. 979.

"It is deep, truly deep ...": Lorca, ibid., p. 982.

"It is the song of night ...": Lorca, ibid., p. 985.

290   "All the poems of *cante jondo* show ...": Lorca, ibid., p. 987.

"Just as the *siguiriya* ...": Lorca, ibid., p. 989.

None other than Hafiz and Omar Khayyam: It is useful, I think, in reading Lorca, to get a sense of this mystical background. For an extended engagement with Omar Khayyam, I do not know of a better text than the translation and extended commentary by Govinda Tirtha, called *The Nectar of Grace*. It is a rare and exceptionally useful book. For a contemporary translation of Hafiz and the poets of his beloved city of Shiraz, see *Faces of Love*, where the verse is translated ably by the fine poet Dick Davis.

291   The *Concurso* on June 13 and 14 of 1922: An extended description of this event is in Gibson, *Federico García Lorca: A Life*, pp. 112–166. Another account, which emphasizes Lorca's close bond with Falla at the time, is in Stainton, *Lorca: A Dream of Life*, pp. 91–101.

292   "When he read the Poem of Deep Song ...": quoted in Stainton, ibid., p. 100.

293   *La Barraca*: This educational initiative coincided with the overall commitment of the Republic to education; thousands of schools were built. Accounts of Lorca in this period on the road doing theater are in Gibson, ibid., pp. 319–324, 330–334, and in Stainton, ibid., pp. 283–304.

295   "... an effervescent child ...": quoted in Stainton, ibid., p. 335.

298 **He told the director, Rivas Cherif:** The most complete account of the context and content of this conversation is in Stainton, ibid., pp. 412–114.

299 **"... a disastrous event":** quoted in Gibson, ibid., p. 439.

300 **"I am totally Spanish ...":** quoted in Gibson, ibid., p. 439.

301 **On July 13, Lorca boarded the train for Granada:** For the complete accounts of the lethal chain of events that led to his murder, see the pioneering work of Gibson, ibid., pp. 446–472. And the later biography of Lorca by Stainton, ibid., pp. 440–461.

304 **At around three in the morning on August 18:** A recent account establishing the date, which had been somewhat in question, is in the short text of Titos Martinez, *Verano de 36 en Granada*. For an understanding of the context and the correspondence discovered and presented in the book, it needs to be read in its entirety.

305 **one of the executioners:** His name was Juan Luis Trascastro Medina. He was a local Falangist leader and had earlier declared that he was ready to "slit the throats of any reds including breast-feeding babies." See Preston, *The Spanish Holocaust*, pp. 173–174.

THE SECRET IN THE LABYRINTH

308 **discovered in a crate:** The poetry of Ismail ibn Neghrela, whose Hebrew name is Shmuel HaNagid. This story is told in the introduction by Peter Cole to his translation of the *Selected Poems of Shmuel HaNagid*, pp. xiv–xv. For an even more extraordinary story about the recovery of four thousand poems of medieval Hebrew poetry, a priceless treasure, just before they were burned in a fire to heat a kitchen pot, see Cole's introduction to the *Selected Poems of Solomon Ibn Gabirol*, pp. 10–11.

311 **"The color of the Angel Gabriel's wings ...":** However unlikely it might seem to anyone, this is an exact transcription of what she said. Her declaration was so sudden, and so detailed, that as soon as she had gone into her ballet class, I sat down and wrote out her words in my notebook, so that I could have them down accurately.

BIBLIOGRAPHY

Abbad of Ronda, Ibn. *Letters on the Sufi Path*. Translated by Jarif Khalidi. New York: Paulist Press, 1986.

Abousenna, Mona, and Mourad Wahba. eds. *Averroes and the Enlightenment*. Amherst, NY: Promethus Books, 1996.

Addas, Claude. "Andalusi Mysticism and the Rise of Ibn 'Arabi." *The Legacy of Islamic Spain*. Leiden, The Netherlands: E.J. Brill, 1992. 909–936.

Agius, Dionisius A., and Richard Hitchcock, eds. *The Arab Influence in Medieval Europe*. Berkshire, UK: Ithaca Press, 1994.

Al-'Alawi, Jamal Al-Din. "The Philosophy of Ibn Rushd." *The Legacy of Islamic Spain*. Leiden, The Netherlands: E.J. Brill, 1992. 804–829.

Al-Azmeh, Aziz. "Mortal Enemies, Invisible Neighbors: Northerners in Andalusi Eyes." *The Legacy of Islamic Spain*. Leiden, The Netherlands: E.J. Brill, 1992. 259–272.

Al-Garnati, Abu Hamid. *Tuhfat Al-albab (el regalo de los espiritus)*. Translated by Ana Ramos. Madrid: C.S.I.C/I.C.M.A, 1990.

Al-Khalili, Jim. *The House of Wisdom*. New York and London: Penguin Press, 2011.

Alvarez, Lourdes María. "Petrus Alfonsi." *The Literature of Al-Andalus*. Edited by María Rosa Menocal, Raymond P. Scheindlin, and Michael Sells. Cambridge: Cambridge University Press, 2000. 282–291.

Ansari, Kwaja Abdullah. *Intimate Conversations*. Translated by Wheeler M. Thackston. New York: Paulist Press, 1978.

Antequerra, Marino. *The Alhambra and the Generalife*. Granada: Ediciones Miguel Sánchez, 1978.

Arbelos, Carlos. *Granada flamenca*. Granada: Caja General de Ahorros de Granada, 2003.

Armistead, Samuel G. "The Sephardim." *The Literature of Al-Andalus*. Edited by María Rosa Menocal, Raymond P. Scheindlin, and Michael Sells. Cambridge: Cambridge University Press, 2000. 455–471.

Armstrong, Karen. *A History of God*. New York: Ballantine Books, 1993.

Ashour, Radwa. *Granada*. Translated by William Ganara. Syracuse, NY: Syracuse University Press, 2003.

'Ata'Illah, Ibn. *The Book of Wisdom*. Translated by Victor Danner. New York: The Paulist Press, 1978.

Austin, R.W.J. Introduction. *The Bezels of Wisdom*. By Ibn El-Arabi. New York, Ramsey, Toronto: The Paulist Press, 1980.

———. Introduction. *The Sufis of Andalusia*. By Ibn El-Arabi. Sherborne, England: Beshara Publications, 1988.

Aznar, Jose Maria. Speech at Georgetown, September 21, 2004. Web. www.youtube.com/watch?v=e7no1WObcRs.

Báez, Fernando. *Historia universal de la destrucción de libros*. Barcelona: Ediciones Destino, 2004.

Barnstone, Willis. *The Poetics of Ecstasy: From Sappho to Borges*. London and New York: Holmes and Meier, 1983.

———. *Six Masters of the Spanish Sonnet*. Carbondale, IL: Southern Illinois University Press, 1993.

Barrios Aguilera, Manuel, ed. "Albaicín Morisco." *El Albaicín: paraíso cerrado, conflicto urbano*. Granada: Diputación de Granada, 2003. 31–41.

———. *Granada morisca, la convivencia negada*. Granada: Serie Granada, Comares, 2002.

———. *Historia del reino de Granada*, 2 vols. Granada: Universidad de Granada, El Legado Andalusí, 2000.

Barrios Rozúa, Juan Manuel, ed. *El Albaicín: paraíso cerrado, conflicto urbano*. Granada, Spain: Diputación de Granada, 2002.

———. "Iconoclastia y resacralización del espacio urbano en el Albaicín." *El Albaicín: paraíso cerrado, conflicto urbano*. 71–92.

Barrucand, Marianne, and Achim Bednorz. *Moorish Architecture in Andalusia*. Hohenzollerernring, Koln: Taschen, 1992.

Bayrak al-Jerrahi al-Halverti, Sheikh Tosun. *The Most Beautiful Names.* Brattleboro, VT: Threshold Books, Amana Books, 1985.

Beevor, Anthony. *The Spanish Civil War.* London: Cassell, 1982.

Bloch, Ariel A., and Chana Bloch, trans. *The Song of Songs: A New Translation with an Introduction and Commentary.* New York: Random House, 1995.

Bloom, Jonathan, and Sheila Blair. *And Diverse Are Their Hues: Color in Islamic Art and Culture.* New Haven and London: Yale University Press, 2009.

Boase, Roger. "Arabic Influences on European Love-Poetry." *The Legacy of Islamic Spain.* Leiden, The Netherlands. E.J. Brill, 1992. 457–482.

Bogin, Meg. *The Women Troubadours.* New York, London: W.W. Norton & Co., 1980.

Bolens, Lucie. "The Use of Plants for Dyeing and Clothing." *The Legacy of Islamic Spain.* Leiden, The Netherlands: E.J. Brill, 1992. 1000–1015.

Bosley, Richard, and Martine Tweedale, eds. *Aristotle and His Medieval Interpreters.* Calgary, Alberta: The University of Calgary Press, 1991.

Bosmajian, Haig A. *Burning Books.* Jefferson, North Carolina: McFarland and Company, Inc. 2006.

Bosque Maurel, Joaquín y Amparo Ferrer Rodríquez. "Geografía de antiguo reino de Granada." *Historia del reino de Granada.* Granada: Universidad de Granada y El Legado Andalusí, 2000. 17–53.

Bourgoin, J. *Arabic Geometrical Pattern and Design.* New York: Dover Publications, Inc., 1973.

Brann, Ross. "The Arabized Jews." *The Literature of Al-Andalus.* Cambridge: Cambridge University Press, 2000. 435–454.

———. "Judah Halevi." *The Literature of Al-Andalus.* Cambridge: Cambridge University Press, 2000. 265–281.

Brenan, Gerald. *The Face of Spain.* New York: Penguin Books, 1950.

———. *South From Granada.* New York, Tokyo, London: Kodansha International, 1957.

Brogden, John, trans. "The Calendar of Cordoba." *Sonnenstand. Medieval Hermitages Along the Route to Santiago de Compostela.* Dusseldorf, Germany; Washington, DC; and Chicago: Corcoran Gallery of Art, Art Institute of Chicago, Gallery Wittrock, 1996.

Broug, Eric. *Islamic Geometric Patterns.* London and New York: Thames and Hudson, 2008.

Bueno, Francisco. *Los Júdios de Sefarad*. Granada: Ediciones Miguel Sánchez, 2005.

Burckhardt, Titus. *Moorish Cultures in Spain*. Translated by Alisa Jaffa and William Stoddart. Louisville, KY: Fons Vitae, 1999.

Burgel, J. C. "Ecstasy and Control in Andalusi Art: Steps Towards a New Approach." *The Legacy of Islamic Spain*. Leiden, The Netherlands: E.J. Brill, 1992. 626–638.

———. "Ibn Tufayl and His *Hayy Ibn Yaqzan*: A Turning Point in Arabic Philosophical Writing." *The Legacy of Islamic Spain*. Leiden, The Netherlands: E.J. Brill, 1992. 830–848.

Burman, Thomas E. "Michael Scot and the Translators." *The Literature of Al-Andalus*. Cambridge: Cambridge University Press, 2000. 404–412.

Burnett, Charles. "The Translating Activity in Medieval Spain." *The Legacy of Islamic Spain*. Leiden, The Netherlands: E.J. Brill, 1992. 1036–1058.

Butler, Reverend Alban. Revised by Teresa Rodrigues. *Butler's Lives of the Saints: March*. Collegeville, MN: Liturgical Press, 1999.

Buturovic, Amila. "Ibn Quzman." *The Literature of Al-Andalus*. Cambridge, England: Cambridge University Press, 2000. 292–305.

Cabrera, Emilio. *Abdarrahman III y su época*. Córdoba: Coleccion Viana, Caja Provincial de Ahorros de Granada, 1991.

———. "La pacificación de Al-Andalus." *Abdarrahman III y su época*. Cordoba: Coleccion Viana, Caja Provincial de Ahorros de Granada, 1991. 11–32.

Cachia, Pierre. "Andalusi Belles Lettres." *The Legacy of Islamic Spain*. Leiden, The Netherlands: E.J. Brill, 1992. 307–316.

Cachia, Pierre, and W. Montgomery Watt. *A History of Islamic Spain*. Edinburgh: Edinburgh University Press, 1965.

Calatrava, Juan, and Mario Ruíz Morales. *Los planos de Granada*. Granada: Diputación de Granada, 2005.

Cano Piedra, Carlos, and Jose Luis Garzón Cardenete. *La cerámica en Granada*. Granada: Publicaciones Diputación de Granada, 2004.

Carrascosa Salas, Miguel J. *El Albayzín en la historia*. Granada: Proyecto Sur de Ediciones, S.L., 2001.

———. *El Albayzín en la leyenda, las tradicciones, y la literatura*. Granada: Proyecto Sur de Ediciones, S.L., 2003.

————. *El Albayzín y su patrimonio*. Granada: Proyecto Sur de Ediciones, S. L., 2007.

Castello Nicás, Montserrat. *La renovación urbana en el Albaicín*. Granada: Editorial Comares, 2003.

Castilla Brazalez, Juan, and Antonio Orihuela Uzal. *En busca de la Granada andalusí*. Granada: Comares, 2002.

Castro, Americo. *The Spaniards*. Berkeley, Los Angeles, and London: University of California Press, 1971.

Chalmeta, Pedro. "An Approximate Picture of the Economy of al-Andalus." *The Legacy of Islamic Spain*. Leiden, The Netherlands: E.J. Brill, 1992. 741–758.

Clark, Gillian, et.al. *Conquerors and Chroniclers of Early Medieval Spain*. Translated by Kenneth Baxter Wolf. Liverpool: Liverpool University Press, 1990.

Cole, Peter, ed., trans. Introduction. *The Dream of the Poem*. Princeton, NJ: Princeton University Press, 2007.

Cole, Peter, trans., and Aminadav Dykman, co-ed. *The Poetry of Kabbalah*. New Haven and London: Yale University Press, 2012.

Colish, Marcia L. *Medieval Foundations of the Western Intellectual Tradition 400–1400*. New Haven and London: Yale University Press, 1997.

Constable, Olivia Remie, ed. *Medieval Iberia*. Philadelphia, PA: University of Pennsylvania Press, 1997.

————. "Muslim Merchants in Aldalusi International Trade." *The Legacy of Islamic Spain*. Leiden, The Netherlands: E.J. Brill, 1992. 759–776.

Corriente, F. "Linguistic Interference Between Arabic and the Romance Language of the Iberian Peninsula." *The Legacy of Islamic Spain*. Leiden, The Netherlands: E.J. Brill, 1992. 443–451.

Cortés, Inmaculada, ed. *El esplendor de los omeyas cordobeses*. Granada: Fundación el Legado Andalusí, 2001.

Council of Elvira, ca. 306. Catholic University of America. Web. n.d. http://faculty.cua.edu/pennington/Canon%20Law/ElviraCanons.htm.

Cowans, Jon, ed. *Early Modern Spain*. Philadelphia, PA: University of Pennsylvania Press, 2003.

Cowley, Robert, ed. *What If: Eminent Historians Imagine What Might Have Been*. New York: G. P. Putnam's Sons, 1999 and 2001.

Critchlow, Keith. *Islamic Patterns*. New York: Schocken Books, 1976.

Crow, John A. *Spain, the Root and the Flower*. Berkeley and Los Angeles: University of California Press, 1963.

Cruces Blanco, Esther. ed. *Tejidos y alfombras del museo de la Alhambra*. Granada: Archivos y Publicaciones Scriptorium, S.L., 1997.

Cruces Roldán, Cristina. *El flamenco y la música andalusí*. Barcelona: Ediciones Carena, 2003.

Cruz Hernandez, Miguel. "Islamic Thought in the Iberian Peninsula." *The Legacy of Islamic Spain*. Leiden, The Netherlands: E.J. Brill, 1992. 777–803.

Dale, Alfred William Winterslow. *The Synod of Elvira and Christian Life in the Fourth Century*. London: Macmillan and Co., 1882.

Danby, Miles. *The Fire of Excellence*. Reading, England: Garnet Publishing, 1997.

Dante Studies, with the Annual Report of the Dante Society. Edited by Richard Lansing, Dante Society of America. New York: Fordham University Press, 2007.

Dickie, James. "Granada: A Case Study of Arab Urbanism in Muslim Spain." *The Legacy of Islamic Spain*. Leiden, The Netherlands: E.J. Brill, 1992. 88–111.

———. "The Hispano-Arab Garden: Notes Towards a Typology." *The Legacy of Islamic Spain*. Leiden, The Netherlands: E.J. Brill, 1992. 1016–1035.

———. "Space and Volume in Nasrid Architecture." *The Legacy of Islamic Spain*. Leiden, The Netherlands: E.J. Brill, 1992. 621–625.

Dodds, Jerrilynn, ed. *Al-Andalus: The Art of Islamic Spain*. New York: The Metropolitan Museum of Art, 1992.

———. "The Arts of Al-Andalus." *The Legacy of Islamic Spain*. Leiden, The Netherlands: E.J. Brill, 1992. 599–621.

———. "The Mudejar Tradition in Architecture." *The Legacy of Islamic Spain*. Leiden, The Netherlands: E.J. Brill, 1992. 592–598.

———. "Space." *The Literature of Al-Andalus*. Cambridge: Cambridge University Press, 2000. 83–95.

Drory, Rina. "The Maqama." *The Literature of Al-Andalus*. Cambridge: Cambridge University Press, 2000. 190–210.

Dunn, Ross E. *The Adventures of Ibn Battuta*. Los Angeles, Berkeley, London: University of California Press, 1989.

Eatwell, John, Murray Milgate, and Peter Newman, eds. *Economic Development*. New York and London: Macmillan Press Limited. 1987.

Ecker, Heather. *Caliphs and Kings*. Washington, DC: Arthur M. Sackler Gallery, Smithsonian Institution, 2004.

Edict of Expulsion. Translated by Edward Peters. Foundation for the Advancement of Sephardic Studies. Web. n.d. www.sephardicstudies.org/decree.html.

Ehrenkreutz, Andrew S. *Monetary Change and Economic History in the Medieval Muslim Spain*. Hampshire, England: Variorum, 1992.

El 'Arabi, Ibn. *The Bezels of Wisdom*. Translated by R.W.J. Austin. New York, Ramsey, Toronto: Paulist Press, 1980.

———. *Divine Governance of the Human Kingdom*. Translated by Shaykh Tosun Bayrak. Louisville, KY: Fons Vitae, 1997.

———. *Las contemplaciones de los misterios*. Suad Hakim and Pablo Beneito, eds. Murcia: Consejería de Cultura y Educación, 1994.

———. *Sufis of Andalusia*. Translated by R.W.J. Austin. Sherborne, England: Beshara Publications, 1988.

———. *Tratado de la unidad*. Translated by Roberto Pla. Málaga: Editorial Sirio, S.A., 2002.

Elexpury, Inés, and Margarita Serrano. *Al-Andalus, magia y seducción culinarias*. Madrid: Ediciones Al–Fadila, 1991.

El-Naggar, Zaghlul. *Treasures in the Sunnah: A Scientific Approach*. Translated by Nancy Ewiss. Cairo: Al-Falah Foundation, 2005.

Encinas Moral, Ángel Luis. *Cronología histórica de Al-Andalus*. Madrid: Miraguano Ediciones, 2005.

Enrique, Antonio. *Tratado de la Alhambra hermética*. Granada: Port Royal, 2005.

Epalza, Míkel de. *Jesús entre judíos, cristianos y musulmanes hispanos*. Granada: Universidad de Granada, 1999.

———. "Mozarabs: Worthy Bearers of Islamic Culture." *The Legacy of Islamic Spain*. Leiden, The Netherlands: E.J. Brill, 1992. 171–174.

Farrar, Linda. *Ancient Roman Gardens*. Gloucestershire, England: Sutton Publishing Limited, 2000.

Ferguson, Kitty. *The Music of Pythagoras*. New York: Walker and Company, 2008.

Fernández Bustos, Jorge, and José Luis Vázquez Gonzalez. *Herencia de la cocina andalusí*. Granada: Fundación Al Andalus, 1996.

Fernández, Gloria. *Nueva Granada*. Granada: Caja General de Ahorros de
Granada, 1999.

Fernández Gómez, Fernando, and Carmen Martín Gómez. *Museo arqueológico
de Sevilla*. Sevilla: Junta de Andalucía, 2005.

Fernandez-Puertas, A. "Calligraphy in Al-Andalus." *The Legacy of Islamic Spain*.
Leiden, The Netherlands: E.J. Brill, 1992. 639–678.

Fitzgerald, E.V.K. "Latifundia." *Economic Development*. 204–206.

Fletcher, Madeline. "Al-Andalus and North Africa in the Almohad Ideology."
The Legacy of Islamic Spain. Leiden, The Netherlands: E.J. Brill, 1992.
235–258.

Fletcher, Richard. *Moorish Spain*. Berkeley and Los Angeles: University of
California Press, 1992.

Ford, Richard. *Gatherings from Spain*. Ian Robertson, ed. London: Pallas Athene,
2000.

Gabirol, Solomon Ibn. *A Crown for the King*. Translated by David R. Slavitt.
Oxford: Oxford University Press, 1998.

Gambel, Benjamin R. "Jews, Christians, and Muslims in Medieval Iberia:
Convivencia through the Eyes of Sephardic Jews." *Convivencia*. New York:
George Braziller, Inc., 1992. 11–35.

García Lorca, Federico. *Collected Poems*. Edited by Christopher Maurer. New
York: Farrar Straus Giroux, 1991.

———. *Granada, paraíso cerrado y otras páginas granadinas*. Granada: Ediciones
Miguel Sánchez, 1989.

———. *Obras completas*. Madrid: Aguilar, 1954.

———. *Selected Verse*. Edited by Christopher Maurer. New York: Farrar Straus
Giroux, 1995.

Garcia Sanchez, Expiración. "Agriculture in Muslim Spain." *The Legacy
of Islamic Spain*. Leiden, The Netherlands: E.J. Brill, 1992. 987–999.

Garrido Atienza, Miguel. *Las aguas del Albaícin y Alcazaba*. Granada: University
of Granada, 2002.

Gibson, Ian. *En Granada, su Granada*. Granada: Diputación Provincial de
Granada, 1997.

———. *Federico García Lorca—a Life*. New York: Pantheon, 1989.

Giffen, Lois A. "Ibn Hazm and the *Tawq al-Hamama*." *The Legacy of Islamic
Spain*. Leiden, The Netherlands: E.J. Brill, 1992. 420–442.

Girón López, César. *En torno al Darro.* Granada: Caja General de Ahorros de Granada, 2000.

Glick, Thomas F. "Hydraulic Technology in al-Andalus." *The Legacy of Islamic Spain.* Leiden, The Netherlands: E.J. Brill, 1992. 974–986.

———. *Islamic and Christian Spain in the Early Middle Ages.* Leiden, The Netherlands: E.J. Brill, 2005.

Gonzalez Román, Cristóbal. "La Antiguedad." *Historia del reino de Granada.* 3 vols. Granada: Universidad de Granada y El Legado Andalusí, 2000. 58–112.

Goodman, Lenn. "Ibn Tufayl." *The Literature of Al-Andalus.* Cambridge: Cambridge University Press, 2000. 318–330.

Grabar, Oleg. *La formación del arte islamico.* Madrid: Edicíones Cátedra, 2000.

———. "Two Paradoxes in Islamic Art of the Spanish Peninsula." *The Legacy of Islamic Spain.* Leiden, The Netherlands: E.J. Brill, 1992. 583–591.

Granara, William. "Ibn Hamdis and the Poetry of Nostalgia." *The Literature of Al-Andalus.* Cambridge: Cambridge University Press, 2000. 388–403.

Gruendler, Beatrice. "The Quasida." *The Literature of Al-Andalus.* Cambridge: Cambridge University Press, 2000. 211–232.

Guardiola-Griffiths, Cristina. *Legitimizing the Queen: Propaganda and Ideology in the Reign of Isabel I of Castile.* Plymouth, England: Bucknell University Press, 2011.

Guichard, Pierre. "The Social History of Muslim Spain." *The Legacy of Islamic Spain.* Leiden, The Netherlands: E.J. Brill, 1992. 679–708.

Hafez. *Faces of Love: Hafez and the Poets of Shiraz.* Translated by Dick Davis. Washington, DC: Mage Publishers, 2012.

Halkin, Hillel. *Grand Things.* Jerusalem, Israel: Gefen Publishing House, 2000.

Hamdani, Abbas. "An Islamic Background to the Voyages of Discovery." *The Legacy of Islamic Spain.* Leiden, The Netherlands: E.J. Brill, 1992. 273–306.

HaNagid, Shmuel. *Selected Poems of Shmuel HaNagid.* Translated by Peter Cole. Princeton, NJ: Princeton University Press. 1996

Harris, A. Katie. *From Muslim to Christian Granada.* Baltimore: John Hopkins University Press, 2007.

Harrison, Robert Pogue. *Gardens, an Essay on the Human Condition.* Chicago and London: University of Chicago Press, 2008.

Harvey, L.P. *Islamic Spain*. Chicago and London: University of Chicago Press, 1990.

―――. "The Mudejars." *The Legacy of Islamic Spain*. Leiden, The Netherlands: E.J. Brill, 1992. 176–187.

―――. *Muslims in Spain*. Chicago: University of Chicago Press, 2005.

―――. "The Political, Social, and Cultural History of the Moriscos." *The Legacy of Islamic Spain*. Leiden, The Netherlands: E.J. Brill, 1992. 201–234.

Heath, Peter. "Knowledge." *The Literature of Al-Andalus*. Cambridge: Cambridge University Press, 2000. 96–125.

Henares Cuéllar, Ignacio, and Rafael López Guzman. *Guía del Albayzín*. Granada: Editorial Comares, 2001.

Hess, Hamilton. *The Early Development of Canon Law and the Council of Serdica*. Oxford: Oxford University Press, 2002.

Hillenbrand, Robert. "The Ornament of the World: Medieval Córdoba as a Cultural Center." *The Legacy of Islamic Spain*. Leiden, The Netherlands: E.J. Brill, 1992. 112–135.

Hobhouse, Penelope. *Gardens of Persia*. Carlsbad, CA: Kales Press, 2004.

Hodgson, Marshall G.S. *The Venture of Islam*. 3 vols. Chicago: University of Chicago Press, 1974.

The Holy Quran. Edited by Abdullah Yusuf Ali. Lahore, Pakistan: SH. Muhammad Ashraf, 1988.

Homer. *The Odyssey*. Translated by Walter Shewring. Oxford and New York: Oxford University Press, 1980.

Ibn Hazm. *The Ring of the Dove*. Translated by A. J. Arberry. London: Luzac Oriental, 1994.

Intercentres. *Historia/franquismohistoricos*. Web. n.d. http://intercentres.edu.gva. es/intercentres/03007406/historia/franquismohistoricos.htm.

Irving, Washington. *Tales of the Alhambra*. Madrid: Editorial Escudo de Oro, S.A., 2001.

Irwin, Robert. *The Alhambra*. Cambridge, MA: Harvard University Press, 2004.

Isabel Fierro, Maria. "Heresy in Al-Andalus." *The Legacy of Islamic Spain*. Leiden, The Netherlands: E.J. Brill, 1992. 895–908.

Jackson, Gabriel. *The Making of Medieval Spain*. Edited by Geoffrey Barraclough. New York: Harcourt Brace Jovanovich, Inc., 1972.

Jashemski, Wilhemina F. *The Gardens of Pompeii: Herculaneum and the Villas Destroyed by Vesuvius.* New Rochelle, NY: Caratazas Brothers Publishers, 1979.

Jayyusi, Salma Khadra, ed. *The Legacy of Islamic Spain.* Leiden, The Netherlands: E.J. Brill, 1992.

———. "Andalusi Poetry: The Golden Period." *The Legacy of Islamic Spain.* Leiden, The Netherlands: E.J. Brill, 1992. 317–366.

———. "Nature Poetry in Al-Andalus and the Rise of Ibn Khafaja." *The Legacy of Islamic Spain.* Leiden, The Netherlands: E.J. Brill, 1992. 367–397.

Jiménez Bolìvar, Mercedes. *Granada in Memoriam.* Málaga: Arguval, 1996.

Jiménez, Juan Ramón. *Olvidos de Granada.* Granada: Diputación de Granada, 2002.

Kamen, Henry. *The Spanish Inquisition: A Historical Revision.* New Haven and London: Yale University Press, 1998.

Jiménez Rodríguez, Francisco, ed. *El Albayzín.* Granada: COPARTGRAF, 2004.

Jones, Owen. Drawings by Owen Jones and Jules Goury. Internet Archive. Web. n.d. www.archive.org/details/Planselevations1Gour.

Kaplan, Robert. *The Nothing That Is: A Natural History of Zero.* Oxford: Oxford University Press, 2000.

Kennedy, Hugh. *When Baghdad Ruled the Muslim World.* Cambridge, MA: De Capo Press, 2004.

Khalidi, Jarif, ed., trans. *The Muslim Jesus.* Cambridge, MA and London: Harvard University Press, 2001.

Khalili, Khaliliullah. *Quatrains of Khalilullah Khalili.* London: Octagon Press, 1981.

Khayyam, Omar. *The Nectar of Grace: Omar Khayyam's Life and Works.* Translated by Swami Govinda Tirtha. Hyderabad, India: Government Central Press, 1941. Reprint, Oxford City Press, 2010.

Knysh, Alexander. "Ibn al-Khatib." *The Literature of Al-Andalus.* Cambridge: Cambridge University Press, 2000. 358–372.

———. "Ibn 'Arabi." *The Literature of Al-Andalus.* Cambridge: Cambridge University Press, 2000. 331–344.

Koyman-Appel, Katrin. *Jewish Book Art Between Islam and Christianity.* Leiden, The Netherlands and Boston: E.J. Brill, 2004.

La Associación de Vecinos y Vecinas del Bajo Albayzín. *El Albayzín, inspiración de pintores.* Granada: 2004.

Ladero Quesada, Miguel Á. *La España de los Reyes Católicos.* Madrid: Alianza Editorial, S.A., 2014.

Lambdin, Thomas O. "The Gospel of Thomas." The Nag Hammadi Gospels. San Francisco: Harper and Row, 1998. 124–138.

Landa, Diego. *Yucatan Before and After the Conquest.* New York: Dover, 1978.

Lane-Poole, Stanley. *The Muslims in Spain.* New Delhi: Goodword Books, 2001.

Lapidus, Ira M. *A History of Islamic Societies.* Cambridge: Cambridge University Press, 1988.

Larios, Juan. *El hospital y la basílica de San Juan de Dios.* Granada: Publicaciones Diputación de Granada, 2004.

Leaman, Oliver. *Averroes and His Philosophy.* Oxford: Clarendon Press, 1988.

Lehrman, Jonas. *Earthly Paradise.* Berkeley and Los Angeles: University of California Press, 1980.

Les Jardins de l'Islam. Conseil International des Monuments et des Sites, Centre de Documentation UNESCO/ICOMOS. Granada: Graficas LUCAMO, 1976.

Lewis, Bernard. *The Jews of Islam.* Princeton, NJ: Princeton University Press, 1987.

———. *The Muslim Discovery of Europe.* New York and London: W.W. Norton & Company, 1982.

Lewis, Daniel Levering. *God's Crucible: Islam and the Making of Europe, 570–1215.* New York: W.W. Norton & Company. 2008.

Liddell, Henry George, and Robert Scott. *A Greek-English Lexicon.* Revised and augmented throughout by Sir Henry Stuart Jones with the assistance of Robert McKenzie. Oxford: Clarendon Press, 1940.

Liss, Peggy K. *Isabel the Queen.* Philadelphia, PA: University of Pennsylvania Press, 2004.

Llull, Ramon. *Selected Works of Ramon Llull (1232–1316),* 2 vols. Edited and translated by Anthony Bonner. Princeton, NJ: Princeton University Press, 1985.

Lopez-Baralt, Luce. "The Legacy of Islam in Spanish Literature." *The Legacy of Islamic Spain.* Leiden, The Netherlands: E.J. Brill, 1992. 483–504.

———. "The Moriscos." *The Literature of Al-Andalus.* Cambridge: Cambridge University Press, 2000. 472–490.

———. *Un Kama Sutra español.* Madrid: Ediciones Siruela, 1992.

Lopez Gomez, Margarita. "Islamic Civilization in Al-Andalus: A Final Assessment." *The Legacy of Islamic Spain.* Leiden, The Netherlands: E.J. Brill, 1992. 1059–1062.

Lopez Guzman, D. Rafael, ed. *Al-Andalus: The Scientific Legacy.* Ronda, Spain: Proyecto Sur de Ediciones s.a., 1995.

———. *Al-Andalus y el Mediterraneo.* Cadíz: El Legado Andalusí, 1995.

———. *Casas y palacios de Al-Andalus.* Murcia: El Legado Andalusí, 1995.

———. *El mudejar iberoamericana: del Islam al nuevo mundo.* Málaga: El Legado Andalusí, 1995.

———. *El zoco: vida economica y artes tradicionales en Al-Andalus y marruecos.* Jaén: El Legado Andalusí, 1995.

———. *Musica y poesia al sur de Al-Andalus.* Seville: El Legado Andalusí, 1995.

López Burgos, Maria Antonia. *Traveling Through a Land of Bandits.* Málaga: Airon Sesenta, S.L., 2003.

López, Miguel L., and Guadalupe Muñoz. *La semana santa de Granada.* Málaga: Editorial Sarría, 2003.

López-Morillas, Consuelo. "Language." *The Literature of Al-Andalus.* Edited by María Rosa Menocal, Raymond P. Scheindlin, and Michael Sells. Cambridge: Cambridge University Press, 2000. 33–59.

Lowney, Chris. *A Vanished World.* New York: Oxford University Press, 2005.

Lu, Peter J., and Paul J. Steinhardt. "Decagonal and Quasi-Crystalline Tilings in Medieval Islamic Architecture." *Science* 315 (2007): 1106–1110.

Maalouf, Amin. *Leo the African.* London: Abacus, 1986.

Macnab, Angus. *Spain Under the Crescent Moon.* Louisville, KY: Fons Vitae, 1999.

Mahdi, Muhsin. *The Arabian Nights.* Translated by Husain Haddawy. London and NY: W.W. Norton & Company, 1990.

Maimonides. *The Guide of the Perplexed.* Indianapolis and Cambridge: Hackett Publishing Company, Inc., 1952.

Makki, Mahmoud. "The Political History of Al-Andalus." *The Legacy of Islamic Spain.* Leiden, The Netherlands: E.J. Brill, 1992. 3–87.

Mallette, Karla. "Poetries of the Norman courts." *The Literature of Al-Andalus.* Edited by María Rosa Menocal, Raymond P. Scheindlin, and Michael Sells. Cambridge: Cambridge University Press, 2000. 377–387.

Mann, Vivian, Thomas Glick, and Jerrilynn D. Dodds, eds. *Convivencia.* New York: George Braziller, Inc., 1992.

Marín, Manuela. "Muslim Religious Practices in Al-Andalus." *The Legacy of Islamic Spain.* Leiden, The Netherlands: E.J. Brill, 1992. 878–894.

Mármol Carvajal, Luis de. *Historia de la rebelion y castigo de los moriscos del reino de Granada.* Málaga: Editorial Arguval. 2004.

Martín Martín, Eduardo, and Nicolás Abarca Torices. *Guía de arquitectura de Granada.* Granada: Junta de Andalucía, 1998.

Martínez, Carmen, and Rafael Villanueva. *Isabela la Católica en Granada.* Granada: Editorial Atrio, 2004.

Martínez Gásquez, Jose. "Translations of the Qur'an and Other Islamic Texts Before Dante (Twelfth and Thirteenth Centuries)." *Dante Studies, with the Annual Report of the Dante Society.* New York: Fordham University Press, 2007. 79–92.

Martínez, Manuel Titos. *Verano del 36 en Granada.* Granada: Atrio Ensayo, 2006.

Matt, Daniel C., trans. *The Zohar.* Pritzker Edition. 4 vols. Stanford, CA: Stanford University Press. 2003–2007.

———. *Zohar: The Book of Enlightenment.* Mahwah, NJ: Paulist Press, 1983.

Menendez Amor, Josefa. "Aplicación de modernas tecnicas de la ciencia paleobotanica a la restauración de los antiguos jardines, mediante la recogida de muestras de tierra." *Les jardins de l'Islam.* Conseil International des Monuments et des Sites, Centre de Documentation UNESCO/ICOMOS. Granada: Graficas LUCAMO, 1976. 211–219.

Menocal, María Rosa. "Al-Andalus and 1492: The Ways of Remembering." *The Legacy of Islamic Spain.* Leiden, The Netherlands: E.J. Brill, 1992. 483–504.

———. *The Arabic Role in Medieval Literary History.* Philadelphia, PA: University of Pennsylvania Press, 1987.

———. *The Ornament of the World.* Boston, New York, and London: Little, Brown and Company, 2002.

———. "Visions of Al-Andalus." *The Literature of Al-Andalus.* Cambridge, England: Cambridge University Press, 2000. 1–20.

Menocal, María Rosa, Jerrilynn Dodds, and Abigail Krasner Balbale. *The Arts of Intimacy*. New Haven and London: Yale University Press. 2008.

Menocal, María Rosa, Raymond P. Schneidlin, and Michael Sells, eds. *The Literature of Al-Andalus*. Cambridge: Cambridge University Press, 2000.

Messner, Dieter. "Further Listings and Categorizations of Arabic Words in Ibero-Romance Languages." *The Legacy of Islamic Spain*. Leiden, The Netherlands: E.J. Brill, 1992. 452–456.

Miller, H. D., and Hanna E. Kassis. "The Mozarabs." *The Literature of Al-Andalus*. Cambridge, England: Cambridge University Press, 2000. 417–434.

Monroe, James T. "Zajal and Muwashaha: Hispano-Arab Poetry and the Romance Tradition." *The Legacy of Islamic Spain*. Leiden, The Netherlands: E.J. Brill, 1992. 398–421.

Morgan, Michael Hamilton. *Lost History: The Enduring Legacy of Muslim Scientists, Thinkers, and Artists*. Washington, DC: National Geographic, 2007.

Morris, Jan. *Spain*. London: Penguin Books, 1982.

Moynihan, Elizabeth B. *Paradise as a Garden in Persia and Mughal India*. London: Scholar Press, 1979.

Munzer, Hieronymous. *Viaje por España y Portugal*. Granada: Granada Tat, 1987.

Murphy, Cullen. *God's Jury: The Inquisition and the Making of the Modern World*. New York: Houghton Mifflin Harcourt, 2012.

Musica y poesia al sur de Al-Andalus. Sevilla: El Legado Andalusí, 1995.

Nasr, Seyyed Hossein. *An Introduction to Islamic Cosmological Doctrines*. Albany, NY: State University of New York Press, 1993.

———. *Knowledge of the Sacred*. New York: State University of New York Press, 1989.

———. *Religion and the Order of Nature*. New York and Oxford: Oxford University Press, 1996.

———. *Three Muslim Sages*. Delmar, NY: Caravan Books, 1964.

Nasr, Seyyed Hossein, and Oliver Leaman. *History of Islamic Philosophy*. 2 vols. London: Routledge, 1996.

Nuñez Guarde, J. Augustín, ed. *The Alhambra and Generalife in Focus*. Translated by Jon Trout. Granada: Edilux, 2006.

Nuñez Muley, Francisco. *A Memorandum for the President of the Royal Audiencia and Chancery Court of the City and Kingdom of Granada.* Translated by Vincent Barletta. Chicago and London: University of Chicago Press, 2007.

Olague, Ignacio. *La revolución islámica en occidente.* Huesca, Spain: Plurabelle, 2004.

Ormsby, Eric. "Ibn Hazm." *The Literature of Al-Andalus.* Cambridge: Cambridge University Press, 2000. 237–251.

Ortega, José, and Celia Del Moral. *Diccionarios de escritores granadinos.* Granada: Universidad de Granada, 1991.

Oxford University. *Cantigas de Santa Maria* database. Web. http://csm.mml. ox.ac.uk/index.php?p=poem. April 2010.

Pancaroglu, Oya. *Perpetual Glory.* Translated by Manijeh Bayani. Chicago: The Art Institute of Chicago, 2007.

Paniagua, Eduardo. *La llamada de Al-Andalus.* 2001. CD.

———. *La música de pneuma: las tres culturas de la música medieval española.* 2001. CD.

———. *Latidos de Al-Andalus.* 2004. CD.

Patai, Raphael. *The Arab Mind.* New York: Charles Scribner's Sons, 1973.

Payne, Stanley G. *Fascism in Spain.* Madison, WI: University of Wisconsin Press, 1999.

Peinado Santaella, ed. *Historia del reino de Granada.* 3 vols. Granada: Universidad de Granada y El Legado Andalusí, 2000.

Perez de Colosia, María Isabel. "La inquisición: estructura y actuación." *Historia del reino de Granada,* 2 vols. Granada: Universidad de Granada, El Legado Andalusí, 2000. 309–355

Peréz, Joseph. *The Spanish Inquisition.* New Haven and London: Yale University Press, 2004.

Perry, Mary Elizabeth. *The Handless Maiden.* Princeton, NJ: Princeton University Press, 2005.

Pinar Savos, Javier. *Antiguos carmenes de Granada.* Granada: Editorial Universidad de Granada, 2004.

Pinilla, Rafael. "Figuras relevantes de la Corte." *Abdarrahman III y su época.* Cordoba: Coleccion Viana, Caja Provincial de Ahorros de Granada, 1991. 57–67.

Pohren, D.E. *The Art of Flamenco*. Madrid: Society of Spanish Studies, 1967.

———. *Lives and Legends of Flamenco*. Madrid: Society of Spanish Studies, 1988.

———. *A Way of Life*: Madrid: Society of Spanish Studies, 1980.

Pozo Felguera, Gabriel. *Albayzín solar de reyes*. Granada: Caja General De Ahorros de Granada, 1999.

Preston, Paul. *The Spanish Holocaust: Inquisition and Extermination in Twentieth-Century Spain*. New York: W.W. Norton & Company, 2012.

Puerte Vilchez, José Miguel. *Leer la Alhambra: guia visual del monumento a través de sus inscripciones*. Granada: Edilux, s.l., 2010.

Read, Piers Paul. *The Templars*. New York: St. Martin's Press, 1999.

Reina, Ramón Barragán. *Abu Maydan, el amigo de Dios: un maestro de maestros*. Madrid: Bubok Publishing S.L., 2009.

Reinhart, Carmen M., and Kenneth S. Rogoff. *This Time Is Different*. Princeton and London: Princeton University Press, 2009.

Reston, James, Jr. *Dogs of God*. New York: Anchor Books, 2006.

Reynolds, Dwight. "Music." *The Literature of Al-Andalus*. Cambridge: Cambridge University Press, 2000. 60–82.

Ríos Ruíz, Manuel. *Ayer y hoy del cante flamenca*. Madrid: Ediciones ISTMO, 1997.

Robinson, Cynthia. "The Aljafería in Saragoza and Taifa Spaces." *The Literature of Al-Andalus*. Cambridge: Cambridge University Press, 2000. 233–236.

Robinson, James M., ed. *The Nag Hammadi Gospels*. San Francisco: Harper and Row, 1988.

Romero, Felipe. *El segundo hijo del mercador de sedas*. Granada: Comares Narrativa, 1995.

Rosen, Tova. "The Muwashshah." *The Literature of Al-Andalus*. Cambridge: Cambridge University Press, 2000. 165–189.

Rosenthal, Franz. *The Classical Heritage in Islam*. London and New York: Routledge, 1975.

———. *Greek Philosophy in the Arab World*. Hampshire, England: Variorum, 1990.

Rubens, Margaret, ed. *Islamic Gardens*. Granada: ICOMOS, 1978.

Rueda Córdoba, Javier, Miriam Sicre Márquez et al. *Certamen Andaluz de escritores noveles*. Granada: Asociación de editores de Andalucia, 2004.

Ruggles, D. Fairchild. "The Dual Heritage in Sicilian Monuments." *The Literature of Al-Andalus*. Cambridge: Cambridge University Press, 2000. 373–376.

——. *Gardens, Landscape, & Vision*. University Park, PA: Penn State Press, 2003.

——. "The Great Mosque of Córdoba." *The Literature of Al-Andalus*. Cambridge: Cambridge University Press, 2000. 159–164.

——. "Madinat al-Zahra' and the Umayyad Palace." *The Literature of Al-Andalus*. Cambridge: Cambridge University Press, 2000. 25–34.

——. "Mudejar Teruel and Spanish identity." *The Literature of Al-Andalus*. Cambridge: Cambridge University Press, 2000. 413–416.

Ruidor Carol, Luis. "Plantes employées dans les jardins historique de Islam." *Les jardins de l'Islam*. Conseil International des Monuments et des Sites, Centre de Documentation UNESCO/ICOMOS. Granada: Graficas LUCAMO, 1976. 221–233.

Ruiz, Juan. *The Book of Good Love*. Translated by Elizabeth Drayson MacDonald. London: J.M. Dent Orion Publishing Group, 1999.

Rumi, Jalal ad-Din Muhammad Mohammad b. Mohammad Jalaloddin Rumi, and Galal al-Din Rumi. *The Mathnawí of Jaláluddín Rúmí*. Edited by Reynold Alleyne Nicholson. Cambridge: EJW Gibb Memorial Trustees, 1990.

Ruthven, Malise, and Azim Nanji. *Historical Atlas of Islam*. Cambridge, MA: Harvard University Press, 2004.

Ruy-Sanchéz, Alberto, Ignacio Henares Cuéllar, et al. *Sintesis de culturas mudéjar*. Granada: Consejería de Cultura, Junta de Andalucía, 2002.

Saiz-Pardo de Benito, Julia. *De la medina al renacimiento*. Granada: Caja General de Ahorros de Granada, 2001.

Saliba, George. *Islamic Science and the Making of the European Renaissance*. Cambridge, MA and London: MIT Press, 2007.

Salmerón Escobar, Pedro. *The Alhambra: Structure and Landscape*. Granada: Caja General de Ahorros de Granada, 1999.

Samso, Julio. "The Exact Sciences in Al–Andalus." *The Legacy of Islamic Spain*. Leiden, The Netherlands: E.J. Brill, 1992. 952–973.

Sanai, Hakim. *The Walled Garden of Truth*. Translated by David Pendlebury. London: Octagon Press, 1974.

Scheindlin, Raymond P. "Hebrew Poetry in Medieval Iberia." *Convivencia*. New York: George Braziller. 1992. 39–60.

———. "The Jews in Muslim Spain." *The Legacy of Islamic Spain*. Leiden, The Netherlands: E.J. Brill, 1992. 188–200.

———. "Moses Ibn Ezra." *The Literature of Al-Andalus*. Cambridge: Cambridge University Press, 2000. 252–264.

Schimmel, Annemarie. *As Through a Veil*. New York: Columbia University Press, 1982.

———. *The Mystery of Numbers*. Oxford and New York: Oxford University Press, 1993.

———. *Mystical Dimensions of Islam*. Chapel Hill, NC: University of North Carolina Press, 1975.

Schneider, Michael S. *A Beginner's Guide to Constructing the Universe: The Mathematical Archetypes of Nature, Art, and Science*. New York: Harper Collins Publishers, 1994.

Schultz-Dornburg, Ursula. *Sonnenstand: Medieval Hermitages Along the Route to Santiago de Compostela*. Translated by John Brogdan. Berlin: Buchbinderei Stein, 1996.

Seguro Bueno, Juan Manual. *Granada au natural*. Granada: Copartgraf, 2000.

Seife, Clark. *Zero: The Biography of a Dangerous Idea*. New York: Viking Penguin, 2000.

Sells, Michael. "Love." *The Literature of Al-Andalus*. Cambridge: Cambridge University Press, 2000. 126–158.

Shabistari, Mahmud. *Garden of Mystery*. Translated by Robert Abdul Hayy Darr. Cambridge: St. Edmundsbury Press, 2007.

Shah, Idries. *Caravan of Dreams*. London: Octagon Press, 1968.

———. *The Dermis Probe*. London: Octagon Press, 1970.

———. *The Exploits of the Incomparable Mulla Nasrudin*. London: Octagon Press, 1983.

———. *Learning How to Learn*. London: Octagon Press, 1978.

———. *The Magic Monastery*. London: Octagon Press, 1972.

———. *Neglected Aspects of Sufi Study*. London: Octagon Press, 2002.

———. *A Perfumed Scorpion*. London: Octagon Press, 1978.

———. *Reflections*. London: Octagon Press, 1968.

———. *Seeker After Truth*. London: Octagon Press, 1982.

———. *Special Illumination*. London: Octagon Press, 1977.

———. *The Sufis*. New York: Anchor Books, 1964.

———. *Tales of the Dervishes*. London: Octagon Press, 1967.

———. *Thinkers of the East*. London: Octagon Press, 2002.

———. *A Veiled Gazelle*. London: Octagon Press, 1978.

———. *The Way of the Sufi*. London and New York: Penguin Group, 1974.

———. *Wisdom of the Idiots*. London: Octagon Press, 1970.

Shah, Tahir, ed. *The Middle East Bedside Book*. London: Octagon Press, 1991.

Smithsonian Timeline of Science. New York: DK Publishing, 2013.

Song of Roland. Translated by Dorothy L. Sayers. London and Tonbridge: Penguin Classics, 1957.

Sougez, Marie-Loup, Gerardo Kurtz, et al. *Images in Time*. Granada: Tf. Editores, 2003.

Stainton, Leslie. *Lorca: A Dream of Life*. New York: Farrar Straus Giroux, 1999.

Stein, Barbara H., and Stanley J. Stein. *Apogee of Empire*, Baltimore: John Hopkins University Press, 2003.

———. *Edge of Crisis*, Baltimore: John Hopkins University Press, 2009.

———. *Silver, Trade and War*. Baltimore: John Hopkins University Press, 2000.

Steward, Devin J. "Ibn Zaydun." *The Literature of Al-Andalus*. Cambridge: Cambridge University Press, 2000. 306–317.

Stone, Gregory B. "Ramon Llull." *The Literature of Al-Andalus*. Cambridge: Cambridge University Press, 2000. 345–357.

Tanenbaum, Adena. *The Contemplative Soul*. Leiden, Boston, and Köln: E.J. Brill, 2002.

Tenison, Louisa. *Castile and Andalucia*. London: R. Bentley, 1853.

Teresa of Avila. *The Life of St. Teresa of Jesus*. Boston: Indy Publish, 2008.

Textos sufis. Argentina: Dervish International, 1982.

Thomas, Hugh. *Rivers of Gold*. New York: Random House, 2003.

———. *The Spanish Civil War*. London: Penguin Books, 1989.

Tito Rojo, José. "Los cármenes del Albaicín, entre la tradición y el invento." *El Albaicín: paraíso cerrado, conflicto urbano*. Granada, Spain: Diputación de Granada, 2002. 57–70.

Tito Rojo, José, Javier Piñar Samos, and Juan Manuel Segura Bueno. *Antiguos cármenes de Granada*. Granada: Editorial Universidad de Granada, 2004.

Titos Martinez, Manuel. *Verano de 36 en Granada*. Granada: Editorial Atrio, 2005.

———. *Agua y paisaje en Granada*. Granada: Diputación de Granada, 2003.

Trillo San José, Carmen. *Agua, tierra y hombres en Al-Andalus*. Granada. Universidad de Granada, 2004.

Tufail, Ibn. *The Journey of the Soul*. Translated by Dr. Riad Kocache. London: Octagon Press, 1982.

Underhill, Evelyn. *Mysticism*. New York: Meridian, 1974.

———. "The *Ulama'* of Al-Andalus." *The Legacy of Islamic Spain*. Leiden, The Netherlands: E.J. Brill, 1992. 849–877.

Urvoy, Dominique. "Ibn Rushd." *History of Islamic Philosophy*. 2 vols. London: Routledge, 1996. 330–343.

Valencia, Rafael. "Islamic Seville: Its Political, Social, and Cultural History." *The Legacy of Islamic Spain*. Leiden, The Netherlands: E.J. Brill, 1992. 136–148.

Vallejo Triano, Antonio. "Madinat az-Zahra." *Abdarrahman III y su época*. Cordoba: Coleccion Viana, Caja Provincial de Ahorros de Granada, 1991. 233–244.

———. *Madinat al-Zahra: guia oficial del conjunto arqueológico*. Cordoba: Junta de Andalucia, Consejería de Cultura. 2004.

Vernet, Juan. "The Legacy of Islam in Spain." *Al-Andalus: The Art of Islamic Spain*. Edited by Jerrilynn Dodds. New York: The Metropolitan Museum of Art, 2013. 173–187.

———. *Lo que Europa debe al Islam de España*. Barcelona: Acantilado, 2006.

———. "Natural and Technical Sciences in al-Andalus." *The Legacy of Islamic Spain*. Leiden, The Netherlands: E.J. Brill, 1992. 937–951.

Viguera, Maria J. "Asluhu li' l-ma'ali: On the Social Status of Andalusi Women." *The Legacy of Islamic Spain*. Leiden, The Netherlands: E.J. Brill, 1992. 709–724.

Villa-Real, Ricardo. *Historia de Granada: acontecimientos y personajes.* Granada: Ediciones Miguel Sánchez, 2003.

———. *Homenaje a Granada.* Edited by Miguel Sanchez. Granada: Ediciones Miguel Sánchez, 1990.

Viñes, Cristina. *Granada en los libros de viaje.* Granada: Ediciones Miguel Sánchez, 1999.

Von Hantelmann, Christa, ed. *Gardens of Delight.* London: DuMont Monte UK, 2001.

Waines, David. "The Culinary Culture of al-Andalus." *The Legacy of Islamic Spain.* Leiden, The Netherlands: E.J. Brill, 1992. 725–740.

Watt, W.M. *The Influence of Islam on Medieval Europe.* Edinburgh: Edinburgh University Press, 1972.

Webster, Jason. *Duende: A Journey Into the Heart of Flamenco.* New York: Broadway Books, 2002.

Wilford, John Noble. "In Medieval Architecture, Signs of Advanced Math." *New York Times,* February 27, 2007, D2.

Wright, Owen. "Music in Islamic Spain." *The Legacy of Islamic Spain.* Leiden, The Netherlands: E.J. Brill, 1992. 555–582.

INDEX

10/17/15 (2) 12/16/15